ROUTLEDGE LIBRARY EDITIONS:
COLD WAR SECURITY STUDIES

Volume 43

SECURITY AND INTELLIGENCE IN A CHANGING WORLD

T0134093

SECURITY AND INTELLIGENCE IN A CHANGING WORLD

New Perspectives for the 1990s

Edited by
A. STUART FARSON, DAVID STAFFORD
AND WESLEY K. WARK

Routledge
Taylor & Francis Group

LONDON AND NEW YORK

First published in 1991 by Frank Cass and Co. Ltd

This edition first published in 2021
by Routledge
2 Park Square, Milton Park, Abingdon, Oxon OX14 4RN

and by Routledge
52 Vanderbilt Avenue, New York, NY 10017

Routledge is an imprint of the Taylor & Francis Group, an informa business

© 1991 Frank Cass & Co. Ltd

British Library Cataloguing in Publication Data
A catalogue record for this book is available from the British Library

ISBN: 978-0-367-56630-2 (Set)
ISBN: 978-1-00-312438-2 (Set) (ebk)
ISBN: 978-0-367-60756-2 (Volume 43) (hbk)
ISBN: 978-1-00-310035-5 (Volume 43) (ebk)

Publisher's Note
The publisher has gone to great lengths to ensure the quality of this reprint but points out that some imperfections in the original copies may be apparent.

Disclaimer
The publisher has made every effort to trace copyright holders and would welcome correspondence from those they have been unable to trace.

SECURITY
AND INTELLIGENCE
IN A CHANGING WORLD
New Perspectives for the
1990s

Edited by

A. STUART FARSON, DAVID STAFFORD
and WESLEY K. WARK

FRANK CASS

First published 1991 in Great Britain by
FRANK CASS AND CO. LTD
Gainsborough House, Gainsborough Road,
London E11 1RS, England

and in the United States of America by
FRANK CASS
c/o International Specialized Book Services, Inc.,
5602 N.E. Hassalo Street, Portland, Oregon 97213

British Library Cataloguing in Publication Data

Security and intelligence in a changing world: new
  perspectives for the 1990s. – (Cass series: studies in
  intelligence).
  1. Intelligence services
  I. Farson, A. Stuart   II. Stafford, David   III. Wark,
  Wesley K.
  327.12

ISBN 0-7146-3395-X

Library of Congress Cataloging-in-Publication Data

Conference on Canadian Security and Intelligence Needs for the 1990s
  (1989 : Ottawa, Ont.)
    Security and intelligence in a changing world : new perspectives
  for the 1990s / edited by A. Stuart Farson, David Stafford, and
  Wesley K. Wark.
      p.   cm.— (Cass series—studies in intelligence)
    "First presented at a Conference on Canadian Security and
  Intelligence Needs for the 1990s, organized by the Canadian
  Association for Security and Intelligence Studies and held at
  Ottawa, Ontario, on 28–30 September 1989"—T.p. verso
      ISBN 0/7146/3395-X
    1. Intelligence service—Congresses. 2. Military Intelligence—
  —Congresses. I. Farson, Anthony Stuart, 1944– . II. Stafford,
  David. III. Wark, Wesley K., 1952– . IV. Canadian Association for
  Security and Intelligence Studies. V. Title, VI. Series.
  UB250.C69 1989   91-2581
  327.1'2—dc20   CIP

This group of studies was first presented at a Conference on Canadian Security
and Intelligence Needs for the 1990s, organized by the Canadian Association
for Security and Intelligence Studies and held at Ottawa, Ontario, on 28–30
September 1989. The views expressed are those of the authors and do not represent
those of any official body.

Printed and bound in Great Britain by
Antony Rowe Ltd, Chippenham

Contents

Editors' Preface

Canada might be regarded as an unusual birthplace for a volume of essays on security and intelligence. The country employs no foreign intelligence service, unlike for example its Australian Commonwealth partner, and its internal security service is little in the news beyond Canadian shores. On the map of international intelligence, Canada appears as a blank, as *terra incognita*. Jeffrey Richelson and Desmond Ball encapsulated this vision in their survey of modern-day intelligence alliances, *The Ties that Bind*. Canada, they wrote, 'is generally perceived to be a nation which does not devote a significant amount of resources to security and intelligence activity ... The very concept of a Canadian security and intelligence community may thus seem somewhat peculiar'.[1] Given that much of the literature on intelligence is inevitably driven by distinct national debates about the historical impact of clandestine information on decision-making, about intelligence services and political scandal, and about the uses and abuses of secret services in forging a security shield for the state, it may also seem 'peculiar' that such a volume as this has a Canadian dateline. But, of course, a wide gap exists between perception and reality. In reality, Canada does devote significant resources to intelligence and security and has done so historically, at least in times of national crisis and war, for a considerable time.[2] Canada has a signals intelligence agency, itself a symbol of investment in the leading and very high-tech edge of intelligence gathering. No spy satellites yet sport a Canadian decal, but there has long been talk of a Canadian entry into what John Gaddis calls the 'reconnaissance satellite regime', either for purposes of defending Canadian sovereignty, particularly in the north, or for international arms control.[3] Need it be added that Canada has had its share of security intelligence scandals, and suffered its portion of intelligence failures?[4] It follows that, in reality, a genuine debate exists in Canada over the purposes and future of a security and intelligence community that, most decidedly, exists. It is symptomatic, perhaps, of the alliance-orientated drive of much Canadian national security policy that the Canadian debate incorporates an international perspective.

The purpose of this volume, however, is not principally to construct an account of Canadian security intelligence, although Canadian problems are addressed in these essays. The issue of Canada is raised here in order to provide some explanation of the genesis of this volume and to make some modest claims for its uniqueness.

The essays in this volume had their origin in a public conference on 'Security and Intelligence Requirements for the 1990s', organized by the Canadian Association for Security and Intelligence Studies (CASIS), which took place in Ottawa in September 1989. The conference, which was held in the main auditorium of the Department of External Affairs, was testimony to the seriousness with which intelligence issues are now treated in official Ottawa, to a growing public and academic interest in intelligence matters, and to a new climate of openness and candour – Canadian-style *glasnost* – that allowed such matters to be aired in public with the full participation of currently serving and former members of the Canadian intelligence community. The conference was also decidedly international, not only in its body of participants but also in the issues addressed. These incorporated Canadian themes, but ranged far beyond national horizons.

The key to this mixture of national and international themes was to be found in the nature of the questions asked. For the purpose of the conference was to explore the likely environment in which security and intelligence agencies would have to operate in the 1990s. The timeliness of this conference agenda proved to be far greater than the editors of this volume imagined when they first set about making plans for the Ottawa conference. In the end a happy conjunction of design and accident energized the conference and, we hope, this volume. The element of design featured in the decision to stage the conference as a public contribution to the parliamentary review of the functions and legislation of the Canadian Security Intelligence Service at the end of its first five years of existence. The essays by Peter Gill, John Starnes and Jean-Paul Brodeur lay out some of the background and issues of this Canadian debate.

The element of accident – or chance – intervened in the shape of rapid change in Eastern Europe and the emergence of signs that this change would affect in radical ways the functioning and status of intelligence and security agencies. John Dziak's essay focuses on the fundamentally difficult problem of predicting the future of the Soviet intelligence community in this new age; he approaches this question in the only manner possible, namely by considering the historical roots of Soviet intelligence and arguing a case for the tenacity of the 'counter-intelligence state'. But change is not a prerogative of Central and Eastern Europe. This volume appears at a moment when fundamental questions are being asked in the West about the scope and operations of intelligence agencies in a new landscape of threats that have as much to do with international crime and environmental degradation as with ideological confrontations between nation-states and alliance blocs. Both Franklyn Griffiths and Reg Whitaker take up these questions in their essays – in the context of reforms and changes of approach necessary for the Canadian Security Intelligence Service, and by implication its allies, to adapt to this environment. Pressures for change are also having a profound effect on the ways in which security intelligence agencies are integrated into democratic societies in countries such as the United Kingdom and Australia. The essays by Christopher Andrew and Frank Cain discuss, respectively, the problems of secrecy and accountability in the UK and Australia. In both countries, to use Christopher Andrew's telling phrase, 'old taboos' are threatened with extinction.

Coherence is lent to all of these discussions on change in the operating environment of intelligence agencies by the fact that scholarship on intelligence matters is beginning to reach a significant level of maturity. Robert Jervis's essay is a potent reminder of the limitations that affect the impact of intelligence on policy. Loch Johnson provides an account of the comparative features of strategic intelligence agencies and makes a case for the uniqueness of the American experience. During the conference, Adda Bozeman, whose paper unfortunately could not be reproduced here, added a warning that for all that a global agenda of problems may emerge to challenge intelligence agencies in the future, the very nature of political intelligence is culture-bound. East and West, in her view, may never meet.[5]

In the end, this volume represents an effort to predict what lies ahead for security and intelligence agencies as the twentieth century draws to a close. A spirit of *fin-de-siècle* excitement and anxiety permeates the volume. The common assumption here is that intelligence and security agencies are unlikely to wither away. The problems that they will face in the 1990s and beyond are massive, and will certainly require radical changes of approach to the very definition of what constitutes good intelligence. Talk of change is everywhere; it is only natural that it should infiltrate the intelligence world. What is perhaps surprising is that the expectations of change reflected in these essays reveal a considerable spirit of optimism. As John Dziak says, stay tuned.

STUART FARSON
DAVID STAFFORD
WESLEY K. WARK
June 1990

NOTES

1. Jeffrey Richelson and Desmond Ball, *The Ties that Bind: Intelligence Co-operation between the UKUSA* (London: Allen & Unwin, 1985), p. 82.
2. Surveys of aspects of the history of Canadian intelligence can be found in Richard Cleroux, *Official Secrets* (Toronto: McGraw-Hill Ryerson, 1990); S.W. Horrall, 'Canada's Security Service: A Brief History', *RCMP Quarterly* (Summer 1985), pp.38–49; John Sawatsky, *Men in the Shadows: The RCMP Security Service* (Toronto: Doubleday, 1980); J.L. Granatstein and David Stafford, *Spy Wars: Espionage and Canada from Gouzenko to Glasnost* (Toronto: Key Porter, 1990); and Wesley K. Wark, 'The Evolution of Military Intelligence in Canada', *Armed Forces and Society*, Vol. 16, No. 1 (Fall 1989), pp.77–98.
3. John Lewis Gaddis, *The Long Peace: Inquiries into the History of the Cold War* (New York: Oxford University Press, 1987), Ch. 7.
4. A potential scandal concerns the effectiveness of the Canadian authorities in handling the investigation (still in progress) into the downing of an Air India flight over the Atlantic in 1985 which killed 329 people, many of them Canadian. On this episode, see the claims of Zuhair Kashmeri and Brian McAndrew, *Soft Target* (Toronto: James Lorimer, 1989). Arguably the greatest intelligence failure of recent years involved the RCMP security service's hapless efforts to investigate political radicalism in Quebec before and after the October crisis of 1970. For a qualitative analysis of the alleged failure see Richard French and André Beliveau, *The RCMP and the Management of National Security* (Montreal: Institute for Research on Public Policy, 1979).
5. See Adda Bozeman, *Strategic Intelligence and Statecraft* (Pergamon-Brassey's, forthcoming).

Acknowledgements

The editors wish to thank the following institutions for their support, without which neither the conference nor this volume would have been possible: The Department of the Solicitor General of Canada, the Security Intelligence Review Committee, the Department of External Affairs, the Department of the Secretary of State, the Government of Quebec and the staff of the Canadian Institute of International Affairs.

PART ONE

International Perspectives on Intelligence

1

Introduction: The *Fin-de-siècle* Phenomenon

WESLEY K. WARK

To anticipate great societal ferment and change, often stemming from a sense of boredom, frustration and anger with orthodoxy, seems a prominent characteristic of *fin-de-siècle*. Certainly it seems to have pervaded the climate of European thought at the dawn of the nineteenth and twentieth centuries. Cataclysms – revolutions and wars – soon ensued to translate glorious visions into what often proved to be dark realities. While no rational person would welcome the onset of yet another cataclysm, the Western world as it watches the twentieth century draw to a close seems nevertheless to be repeating this human pattern of anticipation. Expectations of major changes affect virtually every sphere of life, from the intimacy of gender relations, to widespread national revolutions in economic behaviour (the coming of market economies to the Soviet Empire and the arrival of the philosophy of 'sustainable development' in the West), to global environmental shifts and radical alterations in patterns of the weather.

It is perhaps inevitable that within this context of prophecies of change there should emerge a debate about the adaptability and reform of intelligence systems in a variety of countries. Two features are remarkable about these *fin-de-siècle* reflections on intelligence. One is that they often feature pronounced expectations of change, despite the fact that intelligence services are commonly regarded as highly conservative institutions, especially within authoritarian regimes. Moreover, these expectations are invested in a political institution which is itself a stripling product of the twentieth century and has already undergone massive evolution since 1900. The second noteworthy feature of these futuristic thoughts is that they are frequently quite optimistic, in marked contrast to some of the doomsday pronouncements that have emerged from debate over the war between the sexes, economic degradation and ecological collapse. To an extent, imagining

3

a future for the international community of intelligence services has become an exercise in tracing the avenues and limits of political change itself. Change in the *modus operandi* of intelligence services is looked to, by many, as a vital sign of health in the new, post-Cold War system of international relations. The ability of intelligence services to make radical alterations to their traditional habits of secrecy, ways of thinking about national security threats, and of making decisions about targets of priority for intelligence collection and analysis is also taken as a visible symbol of the willingness of their government masters to adapt to the new realities and dangers of international politics in the twenty-first century. That intelligence agencies will have to confront such issues as international drug-trafficking, ecological pollution, terrorism, illegal technology transfers, rapid environmental change and population movements is now accepted by both intelligence professionals and public commentators.[1] The classical age of order-of-battle intelligence and of unmasking foreign spies and saboteurs, which reached its climax in the 1930s and 1940s, is now clearly over.

But how to assess the likely degree of change that will come over the practice of intelligence as one century gives way to the next? Three tools may be helpful: a knowledge of the historical evolution of intelligence services during the twentieth century; a national perspective on the culture-bound determinants of intelligence agencies; and, perhaps most important, an international perspective on what Professor Loch Johnson calls the 'commonalities' of intelligence. Such an international perspective can also serve to indicate the degree of convergence or divergence that affects national intelligence communities in a global system and can serve as a way of synthesizing the evidence drawn from historical enquiry and national or comparative history.

At the dawn of the twentieth century, centrally organized and professional intelligence agencies were the preserve of a few European great powers. Even then, in most instances, these intelligence services were bureaucratic newcomers; they operated on the fringes of power in governmental decision-making, were physically minuscule and fiscally puny. They were sometimes able to collect important intelligence, particularly in the military field, but rarely able to influence decisions.[2] The British intelligence community before the First World War, now ably and thoroughly documented by the work of Christopher Andrew and Bernard Porter, provides an excellent example.[3] The exception to the rule was, arguably, the Russian secret police system. The Tsarist Okhrana had developed a massive network of political information-gathering and repression and a catalogue of sophisticated counter-subversion techniques.[4] But the Okhrana was, in the end, ineffective in its main task of suppressing revolutionary change and was largely a domestic intelligence-gathering agency with little in the way of foreign intelligence capabilities or concerns. It was, simply, unique in the limited, pre-1914 world of intelligence.

Since the onset of the First World War, the practice of intelligence has changed almost beyond recognition. It has ceased to be the preserve of the European state system, a process itself generated in part by the emergence of new non-European powers, such as Japan and the United States, and by the decline of European hegemony in the course of two world wars. Intelligence is now a global phenomenon, practised by great, medium and small powers alike, though of course with differing degrees of scope and success. Intelligence has also ceased to be a politically marginal task. The proof is to be found in the vastly increased size and budgets of modern intelligence agencies, in comparison with their pre-1914 predecessors. The reasons for this change are perhaps a little more elusive. They have to do with the arrival of a permanent condition of fear and insecurity in twentieth-century international politics, coupled with a slow process of recognition by governments and societies that good intelligence is a vital prerequisite of security and a means of reducing the uncertainties of life and cohabitation in a complex system of international anarchy. This process of recognition was largely stimulated by the experiences of two world wars, which taught the hard and necessary lessons about the need for accurate intelligence in the wake of repeated 'Pearl Harbors'.[5] The technology of intelligence has also been revolutionized. The age of the spy has been replaced by the age of the spy satellite, by computer processing, Sigint (signals intelligence) and sophisticated political, military and economic analysis which requires massive application of research expertise.[6]

Perhaps only two areas of intelligence practice have not been profoundly altered by change thus far in the course of the twentieth century. Intelligence agencies remain, for the most part, adversarial in their relations to their foreign counterparts and sometimes even within their own polities. Even within intelligence alliances, friction persists along-side co-operation, as was evident, for example, in the great Anglo-American intelligence condominium of the Second World War. Nor has the traditional secrecy which surrounds intelligence services been much eroded, despite the advent of systems of political and public accountability in a number of states, including Australia, Canada and the United States.

On the basis of a reading of the lessons of the past, we might

5

anticipate that the process and pace of historical change in intelligence practice will be, at the very least, sustained in the domains of global expansion, political importance and technological sophistication. This anticipation is founded on assumptions about the continuing attraction that good-quality intelligence, or the hope of acquiring such know-ledge, will continue to have for states operating in a troubled, and con-flictual international system. The targets for intelligence, the identified and feared threats to security will undoubtedly change, as they are at the moment doing with respect to the process of liberalization in the Soviet Empire, but the profession of intelligence will remain and may even enjoy considerable growth. Undoubtedly, as Professor Loch Johnson notes, states will continue to be tempted and attracted by the 'quiet option' – the use of covert operations as an alternative to public diplomacy or the exercise of war. Yet it is relatively easy and safe to predict continuities.

The spirit of *fin de siècle* seems to call for predictions of change which break the patterns of the past. In the case of intelligence this would mean explorations of the likelihood of a diminution of intelligence wars between states and rival services, possibly even movement towards international co-operation in espionage against new kinds of threats understood as dangers to the commonweal, and a radical alteration in the pattern of relations between intelligence agencies and the societies that employ them.

In both areas of this anticipated and happy revolution in intelligence, prospective change clearly depends on the rigidity of the historical patterns that have thus far determined the evolution of intelligence services and on the degree of uniqueness impressed on espionage services by their respective national or regional cultures. The essays in this part of the volume send mixed signals regarding the likely future of a variety of national intelligence services. Yet in sum they suggest an interesting convergence. In two of the national intelligence agencies surveyed here – those of Great Britain and the Soviet Union – *glasnost* is under way. Christopher Andrew calls 1989 the 'year of intelligence' in the UK, largely owing to the passage of new legislation that revised the hoary Official Secrets Act and regularized the position of the security service, MI5, in the affairs of state. Andrew also sees a critical evolution at work: one that is serving to break down the traditional habits of government secrecy with respect to the operations of the security and intelligence services (what he calls the 'storks and goose-berry bushes' fairy-tale of intelligence for public consumption) and leading towards what he believes to be the eventual outcome of a system of public accountability, probably on the Canadian and

Australian (parliamentary) model. In so far as the security services in Britain may reluctantly share this sense of the inevitability of a new age of accountability, conviction may have been lent by the damaging impact of the conspiracy theories that have circulated freely and fiercely over the years in Britain, especially concerning moles and secret plots. As the romance of secret service gradually wears off, a romance aided and abetted by decades of spy fiction and film, intelligence services are learning that they need public respectability to operate effectively. One route to achieving such respectability is some system of accountability; another, Andrew suggests, will especially excite historians and journalists. It is the opening of the British intelligence archive, for the most part firmly shut since the pre-1914 days of the secret service.[7] Only then will the wilder tales of conspiracy and plot find any competition for attention.

Glasnost is, of course, a Soviet phenomenon. Dr John Dziak addresses in his essay the issue of just how far *glasnost* may have penetrated Soviet intelligence, and the nature of the KGB's response. Dziak sees Soviet intelligence as functioning within the historic traditions of the 'counter-intelligence state'. The primary task of Soviet intelligence has been, and continues to be, the defence of the party against enemies within, with all this role implies for perceptions of threat, and loyalty to the existing political order. *Glasnost* by no means alters this function of intelligence, especially given the challenges that have followed in its wake to Soviet imperial sway in non-Russian territories, and increasing popular disgruntlement with the progress of economic and political reform. Yet one aspect of the KGB's role in society has been revolutionized by *glasnost*. This is its image as a praetorian guard. Once untouchable, the KGB now finds itself under public assault, in the Congress of People's Deputies, in the media, and in the streets. The force of this assault, Dziak argues, has made the KGB engage in a campaign to alter its public image and to re-create respect for itself as an institution. Interestingly, it has done so in part by arguing that it is just another intelligence service in a world of intelligence services; that there is nothing unique, and by implication, nothing dangerous, in the existence of the KGB. The KGB's public-relations campaign may not reflect its genuine self-image, but once started down the path of arguing a moral symmetry between Soviet and Western intelligence practices, the road to convergence may hold surprises for everyone.[8] Dziak argues, on the other hand, that the 'counter-intelligence state doesn't wither easily'. The language is fitting, although the implications may not be. Three forces are at work: government requirements for intelligence under *glasnost* (what mixture of the new and old will emerge?); the KGB's own momentum towards reform; and public pressure for change. As Dziak himself argues, it is difficult to see how the KGB can avoid change, now that the foundations for its service as praetorian guard have been undermined by a flood of historical revelations. What direction events take will depend on whose demands for change ultimately dominate. No doubt the minimal future is one shaped by the KGB's own process of PR reform, but even that stimulus might take events in surprising directions. Intelligence *glasnost*, the senior version in the USSR, like the junior version in the UK, seems to have a certain inevitability.

To argue that the older intelligence services in Europe are beginning to move towards recognizably similar modes of behaviour, under similar pressures for a diminution of secrecy and an increase in accountability, might suggest the triumph of an American model. The United States intelligence community, as Loch Johnson reminds us, was forced to undergo its own 'year of intelligence' in 1975, when it found itself under intense public and Congressional scrutiny and criticism, focused primarily on the conduct of covert operations. The result was the creation of a tight (although as the Iran–Contra affair would demonstrate, clearly not foolproof) system of Congressional oversight; further by-products involved the rise of a formidable apparatus of investigative journalism targeted on the intelligence community, centred largely on the newspaper staffs of the *New York Times* and the *Washington Post*, and the creation of a public mood of profound unease or distrust of the intelligence services. Surely this was the forerunner of intelligence '*glasnost*'?

Yet Loch Johnson argues that the 'commonalities' that link intelligence agencies today are not a product of slowly converging methods of operation and approaches to the problem of public respectability, but rather of a shared understanding of the uses of intelligence. All countries feel anxious about their security, about the limits on their knowledge of threats to that security; all countries are attracted to intelligence gathering as a means to solve the national security dilemma; some countries, with the necessary means and the necessary problems, look to a special brand of intelligence, covert operations, to provide an alternative form of action to the polarities of diplomacy and war. This nexus of ideas about intelligence is itself a product of recent history and represents a revolutionary change from *laissez-faire* approaches to information gathering that dominated in most great powers until the onset of the Second World War. If the intelligence revolution has been near-universal, Johnson argues that its impact on the United States has been unique, and has led to the creation of a

uniquely structured intelligence community. Johnson sees this uniqueness at work in all four of the comparative features that he identifies in
his discussion of strategic intelligence: scope, pluralism, accountability
and ethics. His argument is compelling, even if one is tempted to
question the degree of American uniqueness in such dimensions as
accountability and ethics. But the implication is that national characteristics will continue to determine the shape of intelligence services
into the foreseeable future. Every state gets the intelligence service it
deserves.

Mixed signals, then, about the future of intelligence in its international setting. The democratization of intelligence services seems
under way in countries traditionally and sometimes even fiercely
resistant to such methods in the past. Yet national characteristics
continue to shape both the structures and methods of intelligence
services, providing a potential obstacle to future requirements for
international co-operation and suggesting the strong possibility of
a continuance of adversarial relations and more intelligence wars,
whether in the shape of the vigorous collection of clandestine intelligence, the vacuuming of economic secrets or the prosecution of covert
operations. *Fin de siècle* makes us want to believe that change will
triumph over continuity. It is probably in our best interest if it did.

NOTES

1. Jessica Tuchman Mathews, 'Redefining Security', *Foreign Affairs*, Vol. 68, No. 2
   (Spring 1989), pp.162–7; Norman Myers, 'Environment and Security', *Foreign
   Policy*, Vol. 74 (Spring 1989), pp.23–41; John Newhouse, 'Annals of Intelligence:
   Changing Targets', *The New Yorker*, 10 July 1989.
2. The collection of essays edited by Ernest May, *Knowing One's Enemies: Intelligence
   Assessment before the Two World Wars* (Princeton: Princeton University Press,
   1984) provides the best available survey of pre-1914 intelligence systems.
3. Christopher Andrew, *Secret Service: The Making of the British Intelligence Community* (London: Heinemann, 1985); Bernard Porter, *Plots and Paranoia: A History
   of Political Espionage in Britain 1790–1988* (London: Unwin Hyman, 1989).
4. See Ronald Hingley, *The Russian Secret Police: Muscovite, Imperial Russian and
   Soviet Political Security Operations* (New York: Simon & Schuster, 1970).
5. The classic account of intelligence failure in the Second World War is Roberta
   Wohlsetter, *Pearl Harbor: Warning and Decision* (Stanford: Stanford University
   Press, 1960).
6. For a survey of some of the recent developments in intelligence see Walter Laqueur,
   A World of Secrets: The Uses and Limits of Intelligence (New York: Basic Books,
   1985).
7. For two different views, see D. Cameron Watt, 'Intelligence and the Historian',
   Diplomatic History, Vol. 14, No. 2 (Spring 1990), pp.199–204 and Wesley K. Wark,
   'In Never-Never Land: The British Archives on Intelligence', *Historical Journal*,
   forthcoming 1991.
8. See also the chapter by Franklyn Griffiths in this volume.

2

The British View of Security and Intelligence

CHRISTOPHER ANDREW

Her Majesty's Governments in both Ottawa and London refuse to acknowledge that they have foreign espionage agencies. There, however, the similarity ends. Canada does not possess a foreign intelligence service. Britain does but refuses to admit it. This curious contrast between Ottawa and London encapsulates the three major differences between the British and Canadian intelligence communities: differences in their structure, in their accountability, and in the extent of the secrecy which surrounds them.

The most basic difference is one of structure. Foreign intelligence in the British view requires human espionage by the Secret Intelligence Service (SIS or MI6) as well as technical collection, especially by the signals intelligence (Sigint) agency, the Government Communications Headquarters (GCHQ). The official view in Ottawa is that Canada's foreign intelligence needs require its direct involvement in Sigint but not in human intelligence (Humint). It is not, if I have understood the Ottawa view correctly, that Canada has no interest in Humint – simply that Canada believes it can get all the Humint it requires from its intelligence allies, in particular Britain and the United States. Though Whitehall would never say so in public, Ottawa's attitude to espionage seems as eccentric in London as London's attitude to intelligence accountability seems in Ottawa. Canada long ago decided to stop subcontracting its diplomacy to Britain and set up its own embassies abroad. It seems curious in Britain that Canada is still willing to subcontract its Humint, though not its Sigint, to its allies.

Beyond the belief that major powers require Humint as well as Sigint, it is difficult any longer to talk about 'the British view of security and intelligence'. Nowadays there is a variety of British views about intelligence but no single predominant view. Things used to be different. At the beginning of the Thatcher decade, there was still a broadly based bipartisan consensus which went back almost to the origins of the modern British intelligence community. That consensus was based on two highly dubious constitutional doctrines: first, that intelligence is undiscussable in public; second, that Parliament surrenders all its powers in intelligence matters to the executive. The classic formulation of the first principle is that by Austen Chamberlain, speaking to the Commons as Foreign Secretary in November 1924:

> It is of the essence of a Secret Service that it must be secret, and if you once begin disclosure it is perfectly obvious to me as to hon. members opposite that there is no longer any Secret Service and that you must do without it.[1]

This absurd inflation of the common-sense doctrine that all intelligence operations require secrecy originated not as carefully-considered government policy but as an inherited taboo, akin to the Victorian belief that civilization would collapse if sex were mentioned in public. Professor Sir Michael Howard, one of the official historians of British wartime intelligence, explains the traditional British view of intelligence thus:

> In Britain the activities of the intelligence and security services have always been regarded in much the same light as intra-marital sex. Everyone knows that it goes on and is quite content that it should, but to speak, write or ask questions about it is regarded as exceedingly bad form. So far as official government policy is concerned, the British security and intelligence services, MI5 and MI6, do not exist. Enemy agents are found under gooseberry bushes, and our intelligence is brought by the storks. Government records bearing on intelligence activities are either industriously 'weeded', or kept indefinitely closed.[2]

It follows from the storks-and-gooseberry-bush tradition in Whitehall that the mysteries of intelligence must be left entirely to the grown-ups (the government), and that the children (Parliament and the public) must not meddle with them. The second constitutional doctrine which underpins the traditional British view of intelligence is thus that Parliament must abdicate its powers in this area to the executive.

The most astonishing thing about these two extraordinary doctrines is that until a decade ago they represented an almost unchallenged bipartisan consensus. Indeed they were stoutly defended by both the Labour governments of the 1970s. In 1977, a year after resigning as Prime Minister, Harold Wilson (now Lord Wilson of Rievaulx) published his distillation of the constitutional wisdom of the ages in a volume grandly entitled *The Governance of Britain*. The chapter on 'The Prime Minister and National Security' may be the shortest ever written by a British politician. It is barely a page long and begins by quoting approvingly Harold Macmillan's warning to the Commons after Philby's defection in 1963: 'It is dangerous and bad for our general national interest to discuss these matters.' (What Macmillan really meant, of course, is that such discussion would be politically embarrassing.) Lord Wilson concludes his mini-chapter thus:

> The prime minister is occasionally questioned on [security] matters arising out of his responsibility. His answers may be regarded as uniformly uninformative.
> There is no further information that can usefully or properly be added before bringing this Chapter to an end.[3]

Wilson's successor, Jim Callaghan (now also ennobled), was an equally stout defender of intelligence storks and gooseberry bushes. The Callaghan government, like its predecessors, insisted on the omnipotence of the executive in the management of the intelligence community. 'Parliament', it declared, 'accepts that accountability must be to Ministers rather than to Parliament, and trusts Ministers to discharge that responsibility faithfully.'[4]

But though Labour governments have always publicly defended the traditional taboos, there is also a recurrent strain of Labour distrust for the intelligence services in general and in particular for the Security Service (MI5), which has regularly been accused of plotting the downfall of Labour governments. These suspicions go back to the Zinoviev Letter, the subject of the greatest Red Scare in British political history which memorably disturbed the last days of the first Labour government in 1924. Allegedly written by Zinoviev, the President of the Communist International, to the British Communist Party, this sinister document contained apparent evidence of both Soviet subversion and Labour susceptibility to Communist pressure. A copy was leaked to the *Daily Mail* and published in the press four days before the general election of October 1924 which Labour lost. Though the letter did not lose Labour the election, at the time it was widely believed that it did. Its publication was the result of a plot between Conservative Central Office and retired intelligence officers, possibly assisted by one or more serving officers.[5] The Zinoviev Letter has been frequently mentioned as a precedent during the controversy aroused by Peter Wright's more recent allegations of a plot against the Wilson government in the mid-1970s. Wright himself twice refers to the Zinoviev Letter in *Spycatcher*. He gives two different dates for it (1928 and 1919); both are wrong.[6]

Lingering suspicions derived from the Zinoviev Letter episode help to explain why after the Second World War Clement Attlee passed over a series of able internal MI5 candidates (by no means all inveterate right-wingers) for the director-generalship and brought in an ill-chosen policeman, Sir Percy Sillitoe, to keep them in order. Attlee himself soon changed his mind about the Security Service and became the first Prime Minister to visit MI5 headquarters for discussions with senior officers.[7] Though there were unhappily a handful of Peter Wrights within the Security Service, the continued suspicions of some of Attlee's colleagues derived more from ignorance of its operations than from conspiracy by MI5. It never occurred to any Labour government to establish a body like the Security Intelligence Review Committee, able to confirm or refute continuing suspicions on the left that the Security Service confused subversion with socialism.

The reluctance of Harold Macmillan to authorize intelligence briefing for opposition leaders helped to ensure that Labour returned to power in 1964 after thirteen years of Conservative government with some of its traditional suspicions still intact. During the Wilson governments of 1964–70 and 1974–76 those suspicions produced occasional moments of black comedy more bizarre than any episode of *Yes Minister*. Lord Gardiner later admitted that, as Lord Chancellor from 1964 to 1970, he 'thought it more likely than not that MI5 were "bugging" the telephones in my office'. But he did not insist on a high-level enquiry to investigate his fears and remove the bugs, if bugs there were. Instead, he resorted to such desperate subterfuge as holding secret discussions with the Attorney-General, Sir (later Lord) Elwyn Jones while driving around London in his official car. This, Lord Gardiner explained, was 'because I knew the driver and I knew that she would never have allowed the car to be "bugged" without my knowledge'.[8] It is doubtful if British legal history contains any example of more bizarre behaviour by the two chief law officers of the Crown.

Despite his statesmanlike reserve in *The Governance of Britain*, Lord Wilson was himself subject to periodic alarms about plots involving, but by no means limited to, his Security Service. Two months after his resignation in 1976, Lord Wilson summoned two young BBC reporters, Barrie Penrose and Roger Courtiour, to his Lord North Street house. There they listened spellbound as the ex-Prime Minister urged them to investigate dirty tricks against him by MI5 officers and other ill-disposed persons. He told the young reporters and their tape-recorder:

I see myself as the big fat spider in the corner of the room.

13

Sometimes I speak when I'm asleep. You should both listen. Occasionally when we meet, I might tell you to go to the Charing Cross Road and kick a blind man standing on the corner. That blind man may tell you something, lead you somewhere.

At this and subsequent meetings with Penrose and Courtiour, Lord Wilson outlined a much broader array of conspiracy theories involving, in addition to MI5, the South African BOSS, the CIA, male model Norman Scott, Norman Scott's alsatian dog, a possible traitor at Number Ten Downing Street and the danger that anti-terrorist operations at Heathrow Airport might really be preparations for a military coup.[9] One wonders what the Security Intelligence Review Committee would have made of all that. In the two and three-quarter centuries since Sir Robert Walpole became Britain's first Prime Minister, no holder of that office has given more eccentric interviews than those recorded by Penrose and Courtiour.

In assessing the significance of Wright's more recent allegations of a plot against the Wilson government, it is worth remembering Karl Marx's observation at the beginning of his pamphlet, *The Eighteenth Brumaire of Louis Bonaparte*:

> Hegel remarks somewhere that all facts and personages of great importance in world history occur, as it were, twice. He forgot to add: the first time as tragedy, the second as farce.

If the Zinoviev Letter episode was tragedy, the Wright plot was farce. In *Spycatcher* Wright alleges that half of MI5 'were up to their necks in a plot to get rid of the Prime Minister'.[10] More recently, when interviewed on television, he changed his mind and said that the plotters consisted simply of himself and a few friends. When pressed further, he appeared to imply that the only plotter was himself.

Despite the undercurrent of suspicion on the Left, no major intelligence scandal, real or apparent, of the kind which led to the Congressional inquiries in the USA in the mid-1970s, the Hope Commission in Australia and the MacDonald Commission in Canada, has yet surfaced in Britain. Instead, there has been a series of minor scandals — some real, some imaginary — which have led to a succession of evasive actions and piecemeal reforms by government. The first post-war evasive action followed news in 1954 that Burgess and Maclean had surfaced in Moscow. (Though Burgess and Maclean had defected in 1951 there had hitherto been no hard evidence on where they had defected to.) A committee of Privy Councillors was set up to consider the case in private. The only public outcome was a White Paper so blatantly inaccurate that it has been used by Rupert Allason MP, alias 'Nigel West', to support the improbable hypothesis that its MI5 drafter, Graham Mitchell, must have been a Soviet mole. The White Paper was, however, not a Soviet disinformation operation but a traditional British cover-up.[11]

A decade later the Profumo scandal led to a much more reputable report by Lord Denning, followed by the creation in 1964 of the Security Commission, a non-statutory body which the government may summon 'to investigate and report upon the circumstances in which a breach of security is known to have occurred in the public service, and upon any related failure of departmental security arrangements or neglect of duty'.[12] Between 1965 and 1973 the Security Commission produced seven published reports on security breaches in Whitehall and the armed services, and on two cases of ministers consorting with prostitutes.[13] None of the reports, however, concerned the intelligence services themselves. By the late 1970s the commission was apparently moribund. Its creation left the old bipartisan intelligence taboos essentially undisturbed. The Security Commission has no powers of initiative; it springs occasionally to life only as the government decides and on issues of its choosing.

During the Thatcher decade, however, a series of public controversies involving the intelligence services gradually destroyed the bipartisan consensus which was still intact when the Conservatives returned to power in 1979, and led to a limited erosion of the traditional taboos which inhibit public and parliamentary discussion. The earliest intelligence controversy of the Thatcher years was the great public molehunt sparked off in 1979 by the unmasking of Sir Anthony Blunt as the 'Fourth Man'. Blunt's exposure forced the government to concede for the first time a security debate in the Commons of the kind previously denounced by Macmillan and Wilson as 'dangerous and bad for our general national interest'. Since then the hunt for further traitors has captured the imagination of publishers around the world. Such is the world-wide demand for stories of British moles in the Soviet service (preferably from good public schools and Cambridge University, with a record of sexual deviance) that when the supply of real moles began to dry up at the beginning of the 1980s, imaginary moles (all the victims of genuine mistakes) started to proliferate on airport bookstalls: among them Frank Birch, Arthur Pigou, Donald Beves, Guy Liddell, Andrew Gow, Sir Roger Hollis, Graham Mitchell (all dead), Sir Rudolf Peierls (who, despite claims that he, too, was dead, turned out to be alive and sued successfully for libel), Lord Rothschild (the victim until his death of innuendo rather than open accusation in case he also sued), and Dr Wilfred Mann (who did not sue but published a convincing explanation of his innocence). In 1989 Richard Deacon's *The Greatest Treason* carried the molehunt into the heart of the Royal Family. Prince Philip's uncle, Lord Mountbatten, was improbably exposed as a homosexual megalomaniac in league with the (imaginary) Soviet mole, Guy Liddell, in real life Deputy-Director General of MI5. 'Somehow', writes Deacon, 'I felt as if I was discovering a new version of *Alice on Wonderland* in which all the hidden violence and sexual perversion which some psychoanalysts have discovered in the old version had become terribly explicit'. The exposure in 1990 of John Cairncross as the (authentic) Fifth Man and of Leo Long as the unidentified Soviet spy codenamed 'Elli' seems unlikely to bring the long drawn-out literary molehunt to an end.

The most troublesome imaginary mole, so far as the government is concerned, has been Sir Roger Hollis, Director-General of MI5 from 1956 to 1965. After the publication of the first 'exposure' of Hollis in Chapman Pincher's *Their Trade is Treachery* in 1981, Mrs Thatcher, to her visible dismay, was forced to breach the traditional taboos once again, make a statement to Parliament, and declare Sir Roger innocent. Further government statements followed the conviction of a genuine mole, Geoffrey Prime of GCHQ, in 1982, and an apprentice mole, Michael Bettaney of MI5, in 1983. (Bettaney had tried hard to graduate as a mole by pushing top-secret documents through the letter-box of the KGB resident, Arkadi Guk, but without success. Guk believed Bettaney's actions were part of a bizarre trap for him set by MI5.) While periodically breaching Lord Wilson's dictum that the Prime Minister's remarks to Parliament on security and intelligence should be rare and 'uniformly uninformative', Mrs Thatcher struggled to keep the principle as intact as possible. She told the Commons in November 1986:

> I repeat [one of her favourite verbs]: the practice and the custom of all prime ministers of all parties is to adhere to the normal rule of not commenting on security matters. That practice is upheld in 'Erskine May' [the traditional guide to parliamentary procedure], and I shall follow it.[14]

In the light of the Thatcher government's departures from that principle, the Prime Minister's statement was almost as remarkable as some identifications of the 'Fifth Man'.

The second significant breach of the old intelligence taboos was caused by the Falklands conflict in 1982. Faced with opposition charges that the government had ignored intelligence warnings of an

Argentinian invasion, the government appointed a commission of six Privy Councillors headed by Lord Franks to carry out the 'Falklands Islands Review'. The Prime Minister did not do so willingly. According to David Owen, 'It was like dragging teeth out of her to agree to the Franks enquiry'.[15] Mrs Thatcher's reluctance was understandable. For by establishing the Franks Committee she virtually admitted the principle of parliamentary accountability which she continued to resist. The Franks Committee was not formally a parliamentary committee, but its six Privy Councillors included four members of the Lords and one of the Commons, two of whom were Labour politicians; all were given unrestricted access to intelligence files and personnel. Having accepted the Franks Committee's findings on the Falklands conflict and its recommendations on the structure of the Joint Intelligence Organisation in 1983, the Thatcher government could scarcely argue credibly that a parliamentary intelligence committee of similar composition would be unworkable the 1990s. It did, however, argue precisely that.

The third significant erosion of the intelligence taboos during the Thatcher decade concerns the use made of the Security Commission. Under previous governments it was used to report only on breaches of security within Whitehall and the armed services, and on sexual irregularities by ministers. Between 1982 and 1985, however, it produced, at government request, four major reports on the intelligence services: reviewing security procedures in the community as a whole after the allegations against Hollis and in GCHQ, the Defence Intelligence Staff and MI5 after the trials of, respectively, Geoffrey Prime, Lance-Corporal Philip Aldridge and Michael Bettaney. A summary of the first report's recommendations and the bulk of the other three reports were published. They pulled few punches. Though reassuring as regards operational effectiveness, the 1985 report on the Security Service called for 'a thorough-going re-examination of the personnel management services'.[16]

A fourth influence in eroding intelligence taboos has been that of the courts. By the mid-1980s British juries were reluctant to convict under the old discredited Official Secrets legislation. The government also came under pressure from the European Court of Human Rights. In 1984 the court upheld a complaint about the tapping of his 'phone by a British businessman, James Malone, who had been acquitted on a charge of receiving stolen goods. That judgment led directly to the passage of the 1985 Interception of Communications Act which provides for a tribunal and commissioner to monitor warrants for telephone tapping and investigate complaints. The most influential judgment of the European Court, little noticed by the British media, came in the Leander case of 1987 when a Swedish Communist complained about secret security vetting which had cost him his job. The court and the European Commission, though upholding the action of the Swedish security service, concluded that, in order to prevent abuse, all security services require their powers to be governed by legislation and their actions to be subject to some sort of oversight. That judgment was one of the reasons for the passage of the Security Services Act of 1989.

Probably the main force for recent change, however, has been the embarrassment caused to the government by Peter Wright and the *Spycatcher* case. The British government's civil action against Wright and his publisher in the New South Wales Supreme Court is certain to provide several entries in future editions of the *Oxford Dictionary of Quotations*, chief among them the admission of the Cabinet Secretary, Sir Robert Armstrong, that he had been 'economical with the truth'. Some parts of the proceedings combined the entertainment value of *Yes Minister* and *Fawlty Towers*. Faithfully following instructions, Sir Robert Armstrong declined to admit the existence of SIS. Reminded that he had already accepted a description of Sir Dick White as chief of SIS from 1956 to 1968, Sir Robert replied that he could not acknowledge that SIS existed either before 1956 or after 1968. Disconcerted by Mr Justice Powell's remarks during his summing up, the British QC Theo Simos observed politely: 'Your Honour's interventions are most helpful'. 'You liar', replied the judge cheerfully.[17] The end result of this sometimes bizarre trial, which for over a month was rarely off the front pages of the British press, left Whitehall with the conviction that things could not continue as before. The Master of the Rolls, Sir John Donaldson, implied as much when giving judgment in the action against British newspapers which had published banned extracts from *Spycatcher*. 'It may be', he said, 'that the time has come when Parliament should regularise the position of the Security Service.'[18]

And so it came to pass in the course of 1989. The Thatcher government deserves some credit for grasping two nettles avoided by all previous governments for the last quarter of a century and more: the legal position of MI5 and reform of the Official Secrets Act. The Denning report of 1963 drew attention to the embarrassing fact that MI5 had no place in either statute or common law. For the next 26 years successive governments averted their gaze. An Act of Parliament passed in April 1989 at last placed the Security Service on a statutory basis, provided for the issue of warrants for 'entry on or interference with property', for the review of these warrants by a commissioner

18

armed with extensive powers, and for a complaints procedure run by a tribunal or the commissioner. 1989 also brought the long overdue reform of the Official Secrets Act whose old, catch-all provisions made any unauthorized release or receipt of official information – right down to the type of teabags used in government canteens – a criminal offence. For a quarter of a century successive governments had reneged on promises of reform. Even the reforming Labour Home Secretary Roy Jenkins admits that he simply abandoned the attempt: 'I decided to apply what I think is a good old Conservative principle ... that if you cannot be fairly confident that you will improve matters, it is better to leave them as they are.'[19]

The question now is whether the 1989 Security Services Act and reformed Official Secrets Act go far enough. There is clearly no public outcry about either. With the gradual discrediting of Peter Wright's conspiracy theories and the absence of any major recent security scandal, the public and most MPs have for the time being largely lost interest. The attendance in the Commons during the passage of the Security Services Act never exceeded 42; in the case of the Official Secrets Act the maximum attendance was 69. Among the minority in Whitehall with a continuous interest in these matters and the larger number with a less constant interest, however, there has been a major shift of opinion over the last decade.

When I first put the case for a parliamentary committee on intelligence in 1977, the reaction of Whitehall was described by Peter Hennessy in *The Times* as akin to its response to an insulting reference to the Royal Family.[20] By the 1983 election some form of parliamentary accountability had become the official policy of the Labour and Alliance Parties. In December 1986, during the *Spycatcher* trial in Australia, the Commons debated for the first time a motion tabled by the Alliance to establish a joint committee of both Houses on the security and intelligence services. Though the government stuck to the traditional line, its closing speaker, John Biffen, ended the debate with the words: 'This is a serious and challenging problem. ... We are correct to believe that it will be a continuing debate.'[21] That debate and others since have also revealed growing support for some form of parliamentary accountability among the minority of Conservative MPs interested in intelligence matters. It was partly to meet their concerns that in 1987 the Prime Minister announced the appointment of an 'ombudsman' or 'staff counsellor' for the intelligence services to whom any of its members can take 'anxieties relating to the work of his or her service'.[22] A conference at Ditchley Park in October 1988 attended by a number of politicians from both sides of Parliament and retired Whitehall mandarins reached general agreement on the principle of external accountability for the intelligence community. Perhaps because of the presence of two persuasive Canadian supporters of the Security Intelligence Review Committee, greater interest was shown in the Canadian than the Australian model.

Probably the most striking aspect of the growing support for external accountability is the attitude of the Security Service itself. Jonathan Aitken MP, who is well informed on such matters, has claimed in the Commons: 'Three successive director-generals of the Security Service have supported independent oversight of some type for the Security Service'.[23] Other members of both Houses of Parliament have made similar claims about the Service as a whole.[24] It is, of course, impossible to speak with precision about the views of a body whose opinions are never made public. But there seems little doubt that the Security Service, like its counterparts in Canada and Australia, has become increasingly attracted by independent oversight as a means of protection against conspiracy theories which portray it as a sinister conspiracy against civil liberties. The Director-General of the Australian Security Intelligence Organisation (ASIO), Alan Wrigley, publicly welcomed the introduction in 1987 of the Joint Parliamentary ASIO Committee and the Inspector General of Intelligence and Security as ways of giving ASIO the public confidence it had visibly lacked in the 1970s.[25]

The British intelligence services are not, at present, the subject of intense public concern. But their public image has been somewhat tarnished by some real failures of security, notably those of Prime and Bettaney, and a larger number of ill-founded conspiracy theories such as those of Peter Wright. An intelligence committee of Privy Councillors, whether inside or outside Parliament, would doubtless offer a more balanced judgement. Largely unnoticed by the media, the signs are that during the 1980s the intelligence community had a series of major operational successes. After the Falklands conflict the Director-General of GCHQ, Sir Brian Tovey, sent 'high level' congratulations to all his staff. 'Never', he told them, 'has so much praise been accorded [by Whitehall].' My guess – and it cannot be more than that – is that Sigint will one day figure as prominently in histories of the Falklands conflict as it already does in histories of the Second World War. After the defection of the KGB resident in London, Oleg Gordievsky, in 1985, it was revealed that he had been working for SIS for the past 11 years – the longest and most successful intelligence penetration in KGB history. The relative containment of IRA and Middle Eastern terrorism as well as of Soviet bloc scientific and technological espionage in mainland Britain also suggests that the Security Service has had significant operational successes.

Oversight on either the Australian or the Canadian model would not, of course, be universally popular within the British intelligence community. Sigint officers have traditionally tended to regard the mere mention of their existence as a breach of security. Some no doubt still do. SIS doubtless continues to see some operational advantages in remaining officially unavowable. But it is reasonable to expect the Australian and Canadian experience to have an increasing influence on the British debate on intelligence oversight. American experience, because of the greater constitutional differences with Britain, may prove to be less influential. Stansfield Turner's dictum that 'If we want good intelligence in the long run, our only option is to make oversight work' remains, however, as compelling for Britain as for the United States.[26]

At present, the British government continues to deny the relevance of the Franks Committee precedent and to insist that a parliamentary or other independent oversight body would not work. According to the Foreign Secretary, Douglas Hurd: 'If the [oversight] body knew all, it would know that it could say little to the rest of Parliament without damaging results. If it knew little, it could say nothing with any conviction.'[27] That assertion takes no account of, inter alia, the Australian and Canadian experience. The British government response, thus far, is to argue that it is too early to pass judgement on either.[28] That is not an argument which can be maintained indefinitely by Mrs Thatcher's successors.

Policies on official secrecy in the rest of the English-speaking world may also have some influence on British practice. There are inevitable problems when intelligence allies who share as many secrets as Australia, Britain, Canada and the United States have different notions of what constitutes an official secret. At present Britain is clearly out of step. At a time when the Chairman of the KGB appears on Soviet television, writes articles in the press and gives interviews even to Western correspondents, the Whitehall tradition that the Director-General of the Security Service must remain officially anonymous is increasingly anachronistic. Glasnost in Whitehall still has far to go. The new Official Secrets Act, though in some respects a clear improvement on its predecessor, imposes an absolute duty of life-long confidentiality on all former intelligence officers in both war and peace. None may write anything about their past work 'without lawful authority'. The effect of the Act will depend on how much 'lawful authority' is granted. That is still unclear. One of the most interesting British intelligence memoirs published recently is Alan Stripp's *Codebreaker in the Far East*, which gave the first account of British wartime successes in breaking Japanese codes and ciphers. This kind of wartime memoir was authorized in 1978 by the then Foreign Secretary, David Owen. But *Codebreaker in the Far East* was rushed out at the beginning of 1989 because the author feared his book would be banned under the new Act.

There is growing support among MPs of all parties interested in official secrets legislation for decisions on the publication of intelligence memoirs to be taken not by the government but by an independent Publications Review Body appointed by the government. Though the passage of the 1989 Official Secrets Act occasioned only a minor Conservative back-bench revolt, 16 of the 19 back-bench speakers during the committee stage argued against the sections on security and intelligence.[29] The most liberal official indication of how the new Act will affect the publication of intelligence memoirs was given by one of the leading Tory 'wets', Chris Patten, when junior minister at the Home Office in December 1988:

> The sole criterion for authorising publication is whether part of a particular piece of information will jeopardise national security directly or indirectly. It is a judgement about considerations which are relevant today, not about past history or former embarrassments.[30]

There is still a striking contradiction, however, between Patten's assurances and the government's treatment of its archives. Even the earliest archives of the intelligence services remain completely taboo. The family of the first chief of SIS, Sir Mansfield Cumming (1909–23), has been informed that his pre-First World War diary remains so sensitive that not a single sentence, or any part of any sentence, can be declassified, or any date be set for declassification, for the foreseeable future. Even in the case of intelligence material which has been released to the archives, government policy remains riddled with anomalies. Though many wartime German intercepts, the most important part of the 'Ultra' secret, have been released to the Public Record Office, *pre-war* intercepts are withheld indefinitely. When asked to explain this anomaly by a Commons committee in 1983, Sir Robert Armstrong replied after three months' delay that the government considers peacetime intelligence documents, apparently irrespective of age, as more secret than even more recent wartime intelligence documents: a policy clearly derived from ancient taboos rather than current security needs.[31]

THE BRITISH VIEW OF SECURITY AND INTELLIGENCE

There are two possible ways of interpreting the significance of the Thatcher decade for the future of the British intelligence community. One possibility is that there will continue to be two major differences between Britain and its intelligence allies. First, in the name of national security, the government will continue to reject the systems of intelligence accountability pioneered in Australia, Canada and the United States. Second, again in the name of national security, the government will continue to remain sole judge of the extent of official secrecy in security matters – even if it means continuing to classify the pre-First World War intelligence archives.

There is, however, another interpretation which seems to me much more persuasive. The modest reforms of the Thatcher era represent, in my view, the beginning of a reluctant Whitehall progress towards a pattern of intelligence accountability and release of the intelligence archives not greatly different from that in Britain's intelligence allies. In ten years' time it will, I think, be clear that in the final quarter of the twentieth century the intelligence allies of the English-speaking world have been moving, albeit at different speeds, in the same general direction. Sadly, Her Majesty's Government in London has been slower to understand the course of intelligence history than Her Majesty's Governments in Ottawa and Canberra and their allies in Washington.

NOTES

1. *Parliamentary Debates (Commons)*, 15 Dec. 1924, col. 674.
2. An abbreviated version of Sir Michael Howard's comments appeared in the *New York Times Book Review*, 16 Feb. 1986, p.6. To be fair, HMG has not usually found it necessary to deny the existence of MI5 (unlike MI6/SIS), though until recently it has tried to avoid mentioning it.
3. Chapter 9.
4. *Parl. Deb. (Commons)*, 28 July 1977, col. 1223.
5. On the history and disputed authenticity of the Zinoviev Letter see Christopher Andrew, *Secret Service: The Making of the British Intelligence Community* (London, 1985), Ch. 10.
6. Peter Wright, *Spycatcher* (New York, 1987), pp.33, 369.
7. Andrew, *Secret Service*, pp.489–90. Wright, *Spycatcher*, p.33.
8. *Parl. Deb. (Lords)*, 19 May 1981, col. 858.
9. Barrie Penrose and Roger Courtiour, *The Pencourt File* (London, 1978), *passim*; quotation from p.13.
10. Wright, *Spycatcher*, p.371.
11. Nigel West, *Molehunt* (London, 1987).
12. K.G. Robertson, 'Accountable Intelligence – the British Experience', *Conflict Quarterly*, Vol. VIII (1988), No. 1, pp.20–3.
13. Cmnd. 2722 (June 1965), Cmnd. 2773 (Sept. 1965), Cmnd. 3151 (July 1966), Cmnd.

3365 (June 1967), Cmnd. 3856 (Nov. 1968), Cmnd. 5362) (May 1973), Cmnd. 5367 (July 1973).

14. *Parl. Deb. (Commons)*, 27 Nov. 1986, col. 428.
15. Cmnd. 8787 (Jan. 1983), *Parl. Deb. (Commons)*, 23 Nov. 1988, col. 150.
16. Cmnd. 8540 (May 1982), Cmnd. 8876 (May 1983), Cmnd. 9212 (March 1984), Cmnd. 9514 (May 1985).
17. On the *Spycatcher* trial see, *inter alia*, David Hooper, *Official Secrets: The Use and Abuse of an Act* (London, 1987), appendix 7, and Richard V. Hall, *A Spy's Revenge* (Harmondsworth, Middlesex, 1987).
18. *Parl. Deb. (Commons)*, 15 Dec. 1988, col. 1168.
19. *Parl. Deb. (Lords)*, 9 March 1989, col. 1614.
20. Christopher Andrew, 'Whitehall, Washington and the Intelligence Services', *International Affairs*, Vol. LIII (1977), No. 3: an argument further developed in subsequent broadcasts and newspaper articles.
21. *Parl. Deb. (Commons)*, 3 Dec. 1986, col. 987.
22. *Parl. Deb. (Commons)*, 2 Nov. 1987, col. 508; 3 Nov. 1987, col. 781.
23. *Parl. Deb. (Commons)*, 15 Dec. 1988, col. 1130.
24. *Parl. Deb. (Lords)*, 21 March 1989, col. 622. *Parl. Deb. (Commons)*, 3 Dec. 1986, col. 985.
25. Christopher Andrew, 'How Australia's Spies Came In From the Shadows', *The Daily Telegraph*, 11 May 1987. Idem, 'The Growth of the Australian Intelligence Community and the Anglo-American Intelligence Connection', *Intelligence and National Security*, Vol. 4, No. 2 (April 1989), p.25.
26. Stansfield Turner, *Secrecy and Democracy* (New York, 1985).
27. *Parl. Deb. (Commons)*, 15 Dec. 1986, col. 1136. Hurd was then Home Secretary.
28. Ibid., col. 1112.
29. *Parl. Deb. (Commons)*, 25 Jan. 1989, col. 1104.
30. *Parl. Deb. (Commons)*, 21 Dec. 1988, col. 538. Other government spokesmen have been less encouraging. Cf. *Parl. Deb. (Lords)*, 9 March 1989, col. 1666.
31. House of Commons: Education, Science and Arts Committee (Session 1982–83), *Public Records: Minutes of Evidence.*

3

The Soviet System of Security and Intelligence

JOHN J. DZIAK

The very title that the acronym KGB spells out – the Committee for State Security[1] – tells us something about how the USSR views the missions and roles of its premier security and intelligence service. First and foremost the KGB is a security service. This is not to say that foreign intelligence and various other covert actions are not central elements of Moscow's international activities. That dimension of the KGB's demeanor we know well from hard and repeated experience. But foreign activities, whether intelligence, 'active measures' or direct action were not the impetus for the creation of the CHEKA, the KGB's progenitor; preservation of the Communist Party's monopoly of power was. That still remains the overriding mission of today's KGB. This is especially true in this period of *glasnost* and *perestroika* which have set loose forces that have been suppressed for over 70 years by the very same state security which now finds itself called upon to monitor and channel those forces in a positive direction calculated to still perpetuate party rule.

This writer has advanced in other works the proposition that the Soviet Union, from its inception, can be viewed as the twentieth century's premier example of the 'counter-intelligence state'.[2] In such an enterprise the discovery and elimination of perceived conspiracies and enemies characterized the motives and behavior of an intermeshed party and state security apparat. It is no accident that the KGB has been officially labeled the 'shield and sword', and 'action arm' of the party. From the beginning the party-state security amalgam equated domestic opposition (and, under Stalin, even apathy) with treason, categorized whole classes of people as foreordained by history to destruction, and assigned to itself the responsibility to execute history's will on an international scale. Such an enterprise is pathological about enemies and makes the search for them and their discovery,

25

control or elimination an overriding state objective. Police and such uniquely Soviet counter-intelligence operations as mass arrests, extra-legal incarceration, assembly-line-like interrogation, penetration–manipulation–control, provocation and entrapment, deception and disinformation, grid-like informant networks, mass dossier compilation, spy mania, hate and denunciation campaigns, and so on, soon distinguished the behavior of the whole state structure, not just of the security organs. Domestic society was the first objective of these operations; the millenarian imperative of the Marxist-Leninist creed then carried such operations into the international system. Foreign intelligence, in certain respects, took on the dimensions of external counter-intelligence. The security service and foreign intelligence were the same organ of state, from the CHEKA to the KGB.

Only in 1989 in the wake of the unintended consequences of Gorbachev's effort to revivify his decaying party-state, have voices gone public for separating state security and foreign intelligence. But it is far too soon to tell if these reform noises are real, or just provocative initiatives from the 'organs' of the still existent counter-intelligence state. It should be recalled that several times in Soviet history name changes and apparent resubordinations of state security were publicized, one of their purposes being to assuage both internal and foreign opinion. But in none of these were the KGB's powers appreciably diminished. And only once before, with the creation of the KI, or Committee of Information (1947–51), was there an effort to consolidate all foreign intelligence under one roof, in this case the Council of Ministers. The attempt ended in failure; indeed the military partner in this odd three-way union, the GRU, was able to extricate itself 11 months from the start. The apparent purpose of this experiment had more to do with maneuverings among Stalin's top lieutenants, especially Vyacheslav Molotov, who himself headed the KI for a while, followed by Malik, Vyshinskiy and Zorin, all Foreign Ministry officials. The only meaningful leashing of KGB power occurred in the wake of Stalin's death, when in 1954 Khrushchev reduced it from a ministry to a state committee, followed by a purge of many of Beria's men.[3] But Khrushchev's intent was to ensure that state security was returned to its original purpose, the cutting edge and guarantor of party monopoly rule. It had degenerated under Stalin and Beria to a personal secret police answerable only to the 'Vozhd', or leader. By the time Andropov died in 1984 he had repaired the KGB's tarnished reputation with the party and had given it its most powerful voice since de-Stalinization.

In summary, even if reformist Soviet elements succeed in splitting the KGB into separate external intelligence and internal security services, it is the security service function which still matters most from the viewpoint of retaining and fostering the party's privileges and power in the Soviet system. It is the state security structure to which, as a final resort, the party would repair if sufficient elements felt that reforms were getting out of hand and threatening the party's claims and survival.

*　　*　　*

It would be appropriate at this juncture to consider just what constitutes the security and intelligence structure of the Soviet system. Basically, there are three institutionalized entities, all of which date back to the earliest days of Soviet history: the KGB, or Committee for State Security; the MVD, or Ministry of Internal Affairs; and the GRU, or the Chief Intelligence Directorate of the General Staff.[4]

THE KGB

The Committee for State Security, the KGB, is *the* premier security and intelligence organ in the USSR, a prominence it has retained since 1917. Its current title was acquired in 1954; however, it was refined in July 1978 when it was redesignated 'KGB of the USSR', succeeding 'KGB attached to the Council of Ministers'. This change was most likely a part of the rehabilitation initiated under Khrushchev and KGB chief Shelepin in 1959, and expanded under Andropov's long tenure as KGB Chairman from 1967 to 1982.

The service is organized in a series of Chief Directorates, Directorates and Departments under the Chairmanship of Army General Vladimir A. Kryuchkov, two First Deputies and seven Deputies.[5] Only one Chief Directorate, the First, or Foreign, Directorate, is explicitly dedicated to external operations. However, there are several other KGB elements whose duties involve foreign missions, such as the Eighth Chief Directorate (communications security and intercept), the Third Chief Directorate (armed forces counter-intelligence, which also works aggressively to penetrate foreign armed forces and foreign counter-intelligence) and the Border Guards, which run intelligence operations against foreign targets in adjacent border regions. But these activities are largely in support of the First Chief Directorate (CD) responsibilities; even the Second CD (internal counter-intelligence) supports the First by, among others, spotting and recruiting foreigners in the USSR who would then be run by the First CD when they returned home.

The overwhelming portion of the KGB's structure is dedicated to the internal role. Upwards of a quarter to a half million officers and enlisted personnel make up the KGB's strength. The Border Guards alone account for approximately 300,000 of the number,[6] the rest being spread through the various other Chief Directorates, Directorates, and Departments of the all-Union KGB and the fourteen Republic KGB organizations (the Russian Republic is serviced by the all-Union KGB). Of the internally targeted elements the most critical for this study are the Second Chief Directorate (internal counter-intelligence, the traditional heart of the secret police), the Fifth Directorate (dedicated to countering intellectual, nationalist, religious ferment, etc.), the Third Chief Directorate (penetration of the armed forces to ensure loyalty and counter foreign intelligence penetration) and the Border Guards (to keep Soviet citizens in and hostile foreign elements out; also the first line of defense against attack by land and from the sea.

Foreign operations of the First Chief Directorate likewise are executed through a series of Directorates, Services and Departments ranging from Illegals, Scientific and Technical, Active Measures (deception, disinformation, etc.) to Direct Action, Foreign Counter-intelligence, Reports/Forecasting, Geographic Operational Departments, Foreign Signals Intercepts, etc.

In short, the KGB is both a nation-wide security service and world-wide intelligence and covert action service. Because of its unique, symbiotic relationship with the party it is also much more than such descriptors can define. Its seven decades of extra-legal and quasi-legal operations, subject to no real constitutional constraints other than what the party allows or disallows, place the KGB in a unique and superior position relative to the other organs of the Soviet state. It has savaged every Soviet institution, including the party itself under Stalin. It has operated in an institutionally superior fashion to other state structures overseas (Foreign Ministry, GRU, Foreign Trade Ministry, etc.) because its relationship with the party requires that it penetrate these other organizations. Since Khrushchev's de-Stalinization it has suffered no assaults on its integrity and prerogatives such as have been visited by the party on the MVD, the military, the government apparat and even elements of the party itself. Only recently, in the heady atmosphere of growing popular criticism stemming from *glasnost* and worsening economic problems, has its exalted and previously sacro-sanct status come under direct assault from emboldened citizens.

THE MVD

The Ministry of Internal Affairs, or MVD, represents a second level of internal security capability in the service of party and state. In practice it is much more visible than the KGB in that it deploys the national and republic uniformed police. This police function makes the MVD the first and most obvious punitive authority the average Soviet citizen confronts in his daily life. The intimacy with the population at large makes it more susceptible to varying corruptive opportunities than the KGB, offering the MVD as a handy target for the party in deflecting public ire from itself and the KGB. It is no accident that the MVD has been the subject of many purges associated with the so-called anti-corruption campaigns begun under Andropov as General Secretary and continued under Gorbachev since 1985.

The MVD has no external intelligence functions, although historically its forces have been deployed outside the USSR in Eastern Europe during and after the Second World War, including Hungary in 1956, Czechoslovakia in 1968 and Afghanistan up until the Soviet withdrawal in early 1989. Which brings us to the subject of non-Ministry of Defense (MoD) military forces. The national and republic police, or Militia, are not the MVD's only punitive forces. The Administration of Correctional Labor Establishments runs the prison and labor camp systems – formerly the GULAG, so devastatingly portrayed by Solzhenitsyn. MVD officers and enlisted personnel staff this structure. Some of the more politically sensitive facilities, such as Lefortovo Prison, are actually KGB run.[7] Additionally, the KGB can make its authority and wishes known throughout the whole penal, camp and exile system of punitive measures.

The most important MVD military forces at this critical point in Soviet history are the Internal Troops, whose mission it is to contain or suppress riots, rebellions, insurrections, guerilla activities, or other civil disturbances beyond the abilities of the MVD's civil police, the Militia. These were the troops flown in to quell the disturbances in Armenia and Azerbaidzhan since 1988, the pogroms and rioting in the Fergana Valley in 1989 and the Abkhazian–Georgian clashes, also in 1989. The Internal Troops date to the special Party, NKVD and CHEKA troop formations formed during the Civil War and have a history of brutal repressions ranging from the suppression of the Kronstadt rebellion of 1921, the Basmachi uprising in Central Asia from 1918 to the early 1930s, the collectivization and state-induced famine in the early 1930s, the mass deportations of the 1940s, the

29

Katyn massacre of 1940, the mass executions of the Great Terror, the communization of Eastern Europe and combat duty in Afghanistan against the Mujahedeen, among others.[8]

As with KGB troop strength, estimates of MVD Internal Troop numbers vary. One commonly used Western source estimates 340,000 men organized in 30 divisions equipped with tanks and armored personnel carriers.[9] Recent Soviet sources are contradictory and wildly disparate. The Minister of Internal Affairs, Vadim Bakatin, said in early July 1989 that his ministry had responsibility for 700,000 'policemen' and 36,000 'troops'. In the same interview he stated that there was one policeman per 588 people – but that ratio would yield only 486,400 policemen.[10] His credibility as a statistician and reliable source is further impugned by one of his own subordinates who several days earlier said that the current numerical strength of the MVD internal troops totaled approximately 300,000. The source added that the figure was not rigid and hinted at a possible expansion depending on conditions in the country.[11] Given the geographically widespread nature of serious internal disturbances and historically consistent order-of-battle estimates of these forces, a third of a million men is a good bet.

The size of the MVD's Internal Troops underscores the contrasts between Soviet and Western approaches to security and intelligence. A third of a million men targeted on the nation's citizens says something about the party's faith in its own legitimacy and its trust in its subject. Yet given the widespread and growing disturbances and disaffection, 300,000 is nowhere near sufficient simultaneously to control or suppress current, probable and potential outbursts. Communist leaders are, if anything, prudent security planners. The Chinese Communist leaders had mustered comparable numbers of troops *in the capital region alone* to crush the student movement in June 1989. Minister Bakatin's '36,000' would be under severe strain just to cover a nation-wide coal strike; and 300,000 clearly would be insufficient to handle a restive Ukraine while simultaneously pacifying the fractious Caucasian nationalities, to say nothing about the rest of the empire.

Like their Polish counterparts, the party and security leaders are wary of using regular military forces to suppress the population. For one thing, a conscript army is closer to the people than the more politically reliable internal security troops. The Zomo, Poland's internal security forces, carried out the highly unpopular imposition of marshal law in 1981. The Polish military were used only as back-up. In Georgia in April 1989 it was the MVD Internal Troops who killed Georgians with sharpened shovels and gas. The regular army commanders ran for cover in the subsequent eruption of public outrage among the population and Congress of People's Deputies. Even the central party authorities in Moscow surfaced copies of communications purporting to show that the decision to use force against demonstrators was taken by local authorities, not the Politburo or Central Committee.

The authorities have apparently already decided to augment the stretched resources of the MVD to confront burgeoning civil unrest and avoid being forced into using regular (MoD) military forces. TASS has announced that a 'Moscow Detachment of Special Purpose' (*Otryad moskovsky osobogo naznacheniya* – a riot squad) was formed in Moscow in October 1988.[12] Reports of similar MVD units in other Soviet cities suggest a nation-wide force.

The MVD, and especially its Internal Troops, then, has been and still is the first-line public (as contrasted to 'secret police') punitive force serving the function of a twentieth-century praetorian guard. Periodically fused with and then broken off from state security, it had been a bludgeon in the hands of the counter-intelligence state to both intimidate the populace and impose Soviet-style socialism in newly conquered or annexed territories. Since de-Stalinization and especially under the long reign of Brezhnev it has come to be associated, along with party and government apparatchiks, with endemic corruption. Its most severe challenge comes at a point in Soviet history when real and profound popular unrest – not the paranoid fictions of the Stalin era – seriously threatens the very legitimacy of the party-state and, hence, its survival.

THE GRU

The Main, or Chief, Intelligence Directorate of the General Staff of the Ministry of Defense is the third principal instrument of the Soviet state charged with an intelligence or security mission (the full Russian title is *Glavnoye Razvedyvatel'noye Upravleniye*, hence GRU). But it is strictly a military intelligence service and has *no* internal security functions. Indeed, it does not even possess a counter-intelligence mission in the military, this being the province of the KGB's Third Chief Directorate. Nonetheless, it is a first-rate strategic, operational and tactical intelligence service with a respectable number of successes to its credit. Though penetrated by the KGB and politically and numerically inferior to it, it should not be viewed as a KGB creature or appendage. As a Chief Directorate (the Second) of the powerful and prestigious General Staff it is an important institution in its own right and wields significant influence in a military empire whose claims on the nation's wealth have been an overwhelming constant for most of the USSR's history.

Because of its military mission and subordination, the GRU's intelligence focus obviously carries a military–technical orientation; political intelligence is left largely to the KGB.[13] Its more military operational support activities are accomplished through an intelligence staff structure throughout the military district, fleets, groups of forces, theaters of military operations, etc.; an arrangement common to any major military establishment. At the strategic intelligence level it complements – and competes with – the KGB in acquiring signals intelligence, scientific and technical intelligence, warning intelligence and even more purely military intelligence. Satellite and aviation-based photographic and electronic intelligence is a GRU preserve, as are sea-based collection platforms. On the 'Humint' (human intelligence) side of intelligence collection the GRU operates much like the KGB, with several geographic elements at the GRU's center in Moscow controlling the GRU's legal residencies at Soviet embassies and other official establishments around the world. Also like the KGB it possesses an 'illegals' capability of deep cover networks and operatives independent of the official, and scrutinized, GRU's presence overseas.[14]

Generally speaking, the GRU has no responsibility for such purely non-intelligence operations as subversion, political action or political active measures. These belong to the KGB. However, it does share with the KGB another range of activities more commonly associated with darker aspects of KGB history, namely direct action: sabotage, assassinations, kidnapping, terrorist support, etc. Currently, the KGB's 8th Department of the First Chief Directorate is the party's principal instrument for foreign direct action missions of a political, economic or civil nature – although KGB operations in Czechoslovakia in 1968 and Afghanistan from 1979 point to military involvement as well.[15] But the overwhelming capability in this arena of specialized activity belongs to the GRU. The GRU commands a number of special-purpose brigades in the military districts and fleets, and in groups of forces outside the USSR – the *Voyska Spetsialnogo Naznacheniya* or Troops of Special Designation (or Purpose): more commonly recognized in the West by their Russian acronym, *spetsnaz*. The term *spetsnaz* historically has also been applied internally by both the KGB and MVD to similar forces under their control. The Soviets have shown a marked propensity for subordinating special operations forces to their security and intelligence services.

GRU *spetsnaz* have two broad sets of missions frequently interconnected in execution. The first is *razvedka*:

    ... a seamless web of intelligence, reconnaissance, surveillance and other activities associated with the collection and processing of information about actual or potential enemies ...

The second is less prosaic:

> ... they can also be used in direct action raids and demolition missions, to seize critical facilities in a *coup de main*, to supplant a victim's political military power, to negotiate garrison surrenders in the enemy rear, and other purposes.[16]

Recent history shows examples of how these missions were executed, Czechoslovakia in 1968 and Afghanistan since 1979 again being the prime cases. In both there was clear collaboration between the KGB and GRU *spetsnaz* in the early phases where surprise and decisiveness were critical to the achievement of the immediate political–military objectives. In Afghanistan, GRU *spetsnaz* were among the more effective of the Soviet forces in the country, and by the end of direct Soviet involvement in early 1989 had 'emerged as specialized light infantry in a broad range of counter-insurgency missions'.[17] While this type of utilization doesn't square with the mission profile of the *spetsnaz* brigades facing NATO, it is in keeping with the USSR's own long experience in suppressing insurgencies during and after the Civil War, the Basmachi uprisings, collectivization and in the Baltic and south-western Ukraine during and after the Second World War.

*　　*　　*

How is this massive apparatus directed and controlled? Just a few short years ago this was a rather straightforward question answerable with an equally direct and certain response. In some respects it still is, but the daily unfolding of unforeseen effects of Gorbachev's reforms and other initiatives introduces uncertainty. (It is doubtful that either Gorbachev or the KGB anticipated the nature of the response to his *glasnost* and *perestroika* initiatives. The admission of mass NKVD executions and the discovery of mass graves, the Molotov–Ribbentrop Pact of 1939 and its secret protocols, NKVD responsibility for the Katyn Forest executions of Polish officers, the stinging attack on the KGB by a deputy of the new Congress of Peoples' Deputies – these and other instances have put the KGB on the defensive internally. This *is* unique since the early 1920s.) Institutionally, the KGB, MVD and GRU have not diminished in power and authority, although, as we have seen, the MVD is still buffeted by a lengthy anti-corruption campaign. In foreign intelligence the KGB and GRU are even more aggressive in their response to Gorbachev's desperate efforts to prop up his disastrous economy and to tap Western high technology so he can divert some defense–industrial resources to assuage an increasingly restive populace. The phenomenon of intelligence assaults during an era of improved East–West relations is certainly not without precedent and actually dates back to the New Economic Policy of the early 1920s, which Gorbachev himself adduced as the prototype for his current efforts. The heightened espionage activity of the earlier period of *détente* under Brezhnev also comes to mind.

As for the continuities of control of the security and intelligence apparat, the party remains the locus of power. Before the events of fall 1988 when Gorbachev introduced several new party commissions which somehow are now interposed between the Politburo/Secretariat and the Central Committee Departments, the chain of command to the services was well established. The General Secretary was *the* party figure at the Politburo and Secretariat level who controlled the state security account. Nominal subordination of the KGB to the Council of Ministers was just that, nominal. Day-to-day control of the MVD and the GRU rested within their respective ministries but there was a special, intrusive party mechanism of monitorship and oversight because of the sensitivity associated with their missions and capabilities.

Additionally, at the Politburo level, the Chairman of the KGB had been either a candidate member or full-voting member of that body since 1967. But this ended with the accession in October 1988 of General Vladimir Kryuchkov to the KGB leadership. He is neither a full nor candidate Politburo member; nor is he a member of the Secretariat. He is, however, a voting member of the Central Committee. His predecessor, Viktor Chebrikov, retained his full membership in the Politburo and even assumed a Secretariat portfolio. Thus, for over 20 years the KGB chief was a participant in the highest political council of the system. He was also most likely a member of the Defense Council, an elite body comprising a 'rump' of the Politburo focusing on military and state security matters.[18] It was a cozy, and for the Western analyst, an analytically clean arrangement.

Below that level another series of party institutions served as transmission belts to the services. Foremost of these was the Administrative Organs Department of the Central Committee, which acted as the party's watchdog over all of the state punitive organs: KGB, MVD, Ministry of Defense, the Courts and the Procuracy. In the realm of foreign activities the Central Committee's International Department provided policy direction to the KGB, especially in the area of active measures and other covert work. Complementing this of course was the institution of party membership itself, an even more intimate or personal control device in that the officer members of the KGB, MVD or GRU are co-opted and socialized into the ethic and interests of the party as an all-embracing supra-institutional organism.

Still another tentacle in this interlocking skein of control was the KGB's Third Chief Directorate (mentioned earlier) which ran a highly structured network of informants throughout *all* of the military (not just the GRU) and into the MVD Internal Troops and even the KGB's Border Troops. This network, under the Third CD's Special Departments, or OO's (for *Osobye Otdely*), mirrored the networks run by the Second Chief Directorate in the country at large. Dating from the Civil War it represented, as far as the party was concerned, a reliable instrument for countering hostile intelligence penetration, but, more importantly, a key device for gauging loyalty in the armed forces – a deterrence, of sorts, to the party's perceived spectre of 'Bonapartism'.[19]

Finally, personal links have a bearing on how traditionally the party has controlled intelligence and security. Alexander Shelepin, an ambitious Komsomol chief, was personally selected by Khrushchev in 1958 to head state security. When Shelepin moved up to become a Party Secre-tary in 1961 he was succeeded by his Komsomol successor, Vladimir Semichastnyy. Neither man requited Khrushchev's loyalty as both were implicated in the 1964 palace coup that sent Khrushchev into retirement. However both were themselves unhorsed during Brezhnev's long tenure as General Secretary, Semichastnyy being replaced by Yuri Andropov in May 1967. Several months later Andropov was made a candidate member of the Politburo, acceding to full membership in 1973. He served as KGB Chairman until May 1982, whence he became a Party Secretary and, following Brezhnev's death in November, General Secretary. Andropov apparently had conspired against Brezhnev in the last year of his rule.[20] But Brezhnev had taken steps to prevent a repetition of what he had done to Khrushchev by placing his men (the notorious 'Dnepropetrovsk Banda') into key positions in the KGB and MVD in an apparent effort to box Andropov and limit his ambitions. One of Andropov's First Deputies was Semyon Tsvigun, Brezhnev's brother-in-law; the Minister of Internal Affairs was Nikolay Shchelokov, another member of Brezhnev's 'Banda'. Apparently this tactic worked, but only until 1982. In January of that year Tsvigun died in strange circumstances; suicide was rumored. Shchelokov was fired from the MVD by December 1982, being replaced by Vitaliy Fedorchuk, KGB chief from May to December. Shchelokov was also dropped from the Central Committee in June

1983 and it was reported that he later committed suicide. Viktor Chebrikov, one of Andropov's Deputies, assumed the KGB leadership in December 1982 and retained the post through Andropov's, Chernenko's and most of Gorbachev's tenures. In October 1988 he became a Party Secretary and was succeeded by Vladimir Kryuchkov, the first KGB Chairman to come from the foreign intelligence structure, the First Chief Directorate (more on the implications of this later).

That was how the organs were directed and controlled up to and into the first several years of Gorbachev's stormy tenure as General Secretary. Those years bore the imprints of Andropov's long stewardship over the KGB, which witnessed the steady rehabilitation of the service, an enhancement of its image and power internally, and an increased sophistication and expansion of its external operations.

In many respects that same structure and modality of control remain intact and the foregoing narrative need not have been cast in the past tense. But some dramatic developments in the last one-to-two years may force a different way of doing business and, indeed, may already have. The following are some reflections on these developments, though they represent by no means all of them.

For one, too much has been revealed about past and recent repressions at the hands of state security for either the KGB or the party to regain their privileged images. An example of deep popular contempt for the party and security organs would be that of Poland. This writer would not have suggested just two years ago that the CPSU and KGB could sink to such depths of popular disgust, but I am no longer so sure. The drumbeat of weekly and daily revelations of secret police atrocities and brutishness from *every* decade of the system's more than 70 years' history leaves no halcyon period to which Gorbachev or Kryuchkov could repair for moral uplift or in which they could take pride. Even Gorbachev's golden NEP era has been shown to be as much an incubator for Stalin's terror as the CHEKA's atrocities were during the Civil War. Herewith, a quick sampling:

- Mass graves in the Kuropaty Woods in Minsk in Byelorussia, with estimates of victims ranging from 20,000 to several hundred thousand, have been revealed in the Soviet press (*Izvestiya*, 27 November 1988; *Literatura i mastatstva* [Byelorussia], 3 and 24 June 1988; *Daugava* [Latvia], No. 9, 1988). The NKVD was identified as the executioner of the late 1930s victims. Other mass graves have been identified in the Leningrad area, in the Ukraine, in the Soviet Far East, Central Asia and other sites in Byelorussia. The fact that

36

the government sanctions this information – *Isvestiya* is a government organ – compounds the devastating effect of the revelations.[21]

- Moscow Television Service (12 May 1989) reports on a letter to the newspaper *Vechernyy Kiev* by a former NKVD executioner in the 1930s. He describes how he executed people at Babiy Yar on several occasions in 1934 and 1938. Babiy Yar was also the site of the massacre of hundreds of thousands of Jews and other undesirables by the Nazis. The former NKVD officer wished to repent and die in peace. The newspaper did not print the letter.
- Soviet television reports that Stalin's interpreter, Valentin Berezhkov, claims that Stalin praised Hitler for his execution of Ernst Rohm and others in 1934.[22]
- A Soviet film titled *Vlast' solovetskaya*, shown in Moscow in December 1988, portrayed the Solovki Special Purpose Labor Camp established in the early 1920s. Its message: long before Stalin terrorized the nation, the OGPU was imprisoning and executing its opponents, including (or especially) the non-Bolshevik Left (*Moscow News*, No. 43, 1988; *Izvestiya*, 21 December 1988).
- In an article on 31 March 1988 in *Izvestiya* it is revealed that the MVD has arrest quotas established according to work plans for the year, in this case 1988.
- In issue No. 13, 1988, of *Moscow News* a Soviet writer, Tamara Motylyova, attacks fellow traveller Roman Rolland as an accessory to the terror of the 1930s.
- A Hungarian writer, interviewed in *Komsomolskaya Pravda* (11 July 1989), stated that the NKVD archive was central to the Wallenberg mystery. His criticism of party and KGB obfuscation in the mystery is underscored by his statement that the 'NKVD devised the most detailed and sophisticated documentation system in the world', from which it was virtually impossible to remove or destroy anything.
- A mass grave in Leningrad, hitherto secret, was identified as the burial ground for over 40,000 NKVD victims. This was confirmed by the Leningrad Oblast KGB (*TRUD*, 26 July 1989).
- Mikhail Suslov, Brezhnev's chief of ideology who died in early 1982, was identified as the Party official responsible for the mass deportation of 64,000 Karachai from the Karachai–Cherkess Autonomous Oblast in 1943, according to *Sotsialisticheskaya industriya* (14 and 18 July 1989). Of these, 42,000 died.
- In an interview on West German television (23 July 1989), Valentin Falin, chief of the CPSU CC's International Department and member of the Congress of the People's Deputies commission to

evaluate the Molotov–Ribbentrop Pact, publicly acknowledged the existence of the secret protocols of the pact. Previously he claimed their existence could not be proven. This admission will exacerbate the Baltic situation and further complicate Polish relations.

- Earlier this year the Poles officially published a 1943 Polish Red Cross report on the Katyn forest massacre of Polish officers in 1940, which unequivocally links the NKVD to the atrocity. *Moscow News* on 21 May 1989 made strong hints in the same direction.

One could continue, but the above sampling gives a sense that both the KGB and the party stand seriously damaged.

Still other developments changing or affecting both the way state security works and its prestige in the system come from within the system itself. In the fall of 1988 the party announced the creation of six commissions which seem to somewhat supplant the Secretariat and at the same time sit between the Politburo and Central Committee departments and apparatus.[23] Viktor Chebrikov chairs the Legal Policy Commission, a post he received along with a Secretariat position when he was relieved of his KGB job. What is unclear at this point is the exact relationship of this commission to state security and the other punitive organs previously overseen by the Administrative Organs Department. Chebrikov and his Legal Commission now reportedly exercise control through the new State and Legal Department of the Central Committee; and apparently his commission has a broader mandate for internal matters than any of the other commissions. Yet, at the same time, some of these functions are supposed to pass to the newly empowered Supreme Soviet. To cap it all, Chebrikov has the reputation of one who views the reforms as potentially destructive of party control, yet he has been central to their execution!

On the foreign policy side, an International Policy Commission chaired by Aleksandr Yakovlev sits above the Central Committee's International Department headed by Valentin Falin. The latter element traditionally had been the party's policy overseer for certain of the KGB's foreign involvements, especially active measures. It is noteworthy that KGB Chairman Kryuchkov is a member of the International Policy Commission. Thus, while not sitting on the Politburo as did his predecessor, he is still in a position to exercise policy influence relative to the KGB's foreign activities.

One of the most unusual developments from within the system and which may have the potential – and I stress only potential – for affecting the way the KGB behaves, was the creation in June 1989 by the new Supreme Soviet of a Committee for Defense and State Security.

Inasmuch as its 44 members comprise some very senior officials from the military, defense industry and the KGB – for example, Marshal Akhromeyev and General Shabanov, Vladimir Lapygin (Chairman) and Academician Velikhov, and three KGB generals from Kazakhstan, Byelorussia and the Border Guards – it is unlikely that the military and the KGB will allow the Committee to become a Soviet version of US Congressional oversight.[24] To do its work it will be reliant on the KGB and the military for access to their secrets. It seems doubtful that they will collaborate in their own leashing. Stay tuned on this one, but don't hold your breath. For example, its chairman is reported to have declared that the USSR has no political prisoners.[25]

The biggest surprise over the last year or two is the vehemence with which the KGB and the military have come under attack in the media and from members of the Congress of People's Deputies and the Supreme Soviet. In the first couple of years of Gorbachev's tenure two entities enjoyed an immunity from overt attack: Lenin and the KGB (the military was never quite so sacrosanct). That has changed dramatically. It has been publicly suggested that Lenin's corpse be removed from public display and buried like that of any other human being. The assault on the KGB has come most assertively from within the new legislative structure itself. In a scathing attack on the KGB before the Congress of People's Deputies on 31 May 1989, Moscow Deputy Yuriy Vlasov, struck at the essence of the nation's problem – devastation wrought by the KGB and the fact that the KGB is beyond accountability:

> Every week television has shown the places where victims of mass repressions were buried ... the burial places of tens of thousands of our citizens. ... Undoubtedly, the members of the KGB can be of essential assistance in further searches. But even today, they are shut tight. ...
>
> With one wing, the KGB defends the people from the external enemy and *with the other, incomparably more powerful, it fulfills a particular specific function.* No, I don't mean the struggle against corruption. After the hard lessons of the past, with millions of people murdered, all of this with the direct involvement of the CHEKA and the KGB, the threat to democracy in our present day cannot be considered mythical. ...
>
> The KGB is removed from the control of the people. It's the most conspiratorial of all the Government institutions. ... The deep secretiveness which can be explained by the specifics of its activities insures that the KGB is practically uncontrollable. ...

When coming in conflict with the KGB, it is impossible to find the truth, and it is dangerous to seek it. Even now people considered dangerous by the apparatus are threatened with seizure for supposed mental imbalance. The democratic renewal in the country has not changed the position of the KGB in the political system. This agency exercises all-embracing control over society, over each individual.[26]

Vlasov added that the KGB was not just a service but an underground empire that, except for some excavated graves, had still to divulge its secrets. He called for the Congress to appoint the KGB's chairman and also to be informed of its size, budget and activities. Further, he wanted the KGB removed from its Dzerzhinskiy Square (Lubyanka) head-quarters, 'where, for decades, orders for the destruction and persecution of millions were sent out'. He drove home with the charge that the KGB 'sowed grief, cries, torture on its native land'.[27]

It is significant that Vlasov made a special effort to single out the KGB's internal structure and purpose as more powerful and dangerous than its external wing. This theme was picked up by the flamboyant Boris Yeltsin in the Supreme Soviet 'confirmation' debates on Kryuchkov as KGB chief in July. Yeltsin seemed to refer to foreign intelligence as counter-intelligence abroad (a feature of the counter-intelligence state); he observed that the KGB was *expanding* – a phenomenon inconsistent with restructuring – and proposed that a drastic reduction be made in the size of the organization.[28] Other deputies aggressively questioned Kryuchkov on historical and current KGB abuses, called for, along with Yeltsin, a separation of internal security (counter-intelligence) from foreign operations, and a law on state security.[29]

Yeltsin had indeed a point when it came to KGB expansion. As one student of the KGB has observed, Kryuchkov has more deputies than either Andropov or Chebrikov (Kryuchkov has nine; Chebrikov had eight in 1984, Andropov five in 1979).[30] In the KGB's bureaucratic ethos extra deputies connote expanded activities. As for Kryuchkov's response to the unprecedented grilling, he made many genuflections in the direction of KGB honor and restrained behavior. One important test of his truthfulness is seen in his answer to a deputy's question on internal spying: he formally assured the deputies that the KGB did not keep a network of informants, did not tap telephones and did not keep files on citizens who had not committed state crimes.[31] Just a few months earlier another KGB official, writing in *Izvestiya*, defended the use of informants ('the organization of work with citizens' written and verbal communications') as consistent with *glasnost*.[32]

*　　*　　*

Where does all of this leave the Soviet security and intelligence system and where is it headed? Probably neither Gorbachev, nor Kryuchkov, nor Chebrikov themselves are that certain, given the breakneck pace of revelations and the new-found assertiveness of citizens and Supreme Soviet deputies. There also is no guarantee that a halt would not be ordered and a reversion to 'old methods' would not ensue. The Chinese Communist leadership have shown how to do that. Like the Chinese, the party owns the guns, in the form of the KGB, the MVD and, as a final resort, the military.

The one area of the system largely unaffected by the internal ferment are the foreign activities of the KGB and GRU. If anything, these have intensified, as seen above. Some of the more vicious anti-US active measures campaigns occurred on Gorbachev's watch. If *glasnost* has impacted in this realm it is only in the lessening of the more egregious instances of direct action (*à la* KGB *spetsnaz* operation against Moscow's Afghan protégé, President Amin, in 1979).

Muting the justly deserved image of political criminality seems to be the tack the party and KGB leadership are now taking. A major public relations campaign, unmatched even by the Khrushchev/ Shelepin effort to rehabilitate the service's image, is under way with a vengeance. Kryuchkov was rather adept at his Supreme Soviet 'confirmation hearing' in parrying the pointed queries of the deputies. He was fully prepared with a dramatic answer to one particularly dramatic – and potent – question: did he 'consider it possible to preserve the *Stalinist–Brezhnevite structure of surveillance* of the Soviet people's thoughts? If not, then why is the present structure being maintained? Kryuchkov: 'No, comrades. The structure is not being maintained, and the subdepartment you are thinking of virtually no longer exists. New proposals have been drawn up in this respect.'[33]

Several things stand out about that exchange. First, the very phrasing of the question whereby the KGB under Brezhnev is qualitatively linked with the KGB under Stalin says something about the mettle and informed opinion of at least one of the Supreme Soviet deputies. Such a pregnant statement would be worthy of a Solzhenitsyn or a Western KGB critic. Second, it postulated that the Stalinist–Brezhnevite KGB system carried over into the Gorbachev era. Third, Kryuchkov did not challenge that premise; his answer implied that only recently did they begin to change the system. Fourth, Kryuchkov evidently was referring to the Fifth Directorate as the subdepartment going out of business. This is the structure created out of the Second Chief Directorate in the 1960s to deal with religious, nationalist, intellectual and other categories of dissent. Fifth, since the questions were prepared and submitted beforehand, and read off and answered before the assembled deputies, it is noteworthy that this particular one wasn't spiked before airing. And if it were tampered with or edited then the original would have had to have been a barnburner. Finally, Kryuchkov's response implicitly contradicts his other answer to the question of the KGB spying on its own citizens. He may be a good public relations man, but his client's track record does not lend itself to easy laundering.

In their attempts to proffer a new and reasonable image for the organs, Moscow is targeting two audiences, foreign and domestic. For the foreign audience, the accent is away from the notion of a secret police. By admitting to Stalinist and even recent repressions, Kryuchkov is fostering the notion of a complete break with a criminal past. At the same time he is arguing that the KGB is becoming an intelligence and counter-intelligence service such as one finds anywhere else.[34] He has taken a leaf from the book of Western critics of US intelligence and turned it to his use. In effect he is attempting to establish a moral symmetry between Soviet and Western intelligence. But in his view, this is a good thing. Since every nation practices intelligence and counter-intelligence to foster national survival, why should not the Soviet Union as well? Kryuchkov's PR sense is very adroit (those years in the First Chief Directorate were not wasted). In a response to one of the questions on separating intelligence from counter-intelligence, he allowed that for the West that worked well, given its concern with the concentration of too much power in one pair of hands![35] For the Soviet Union, however, such a de-coupling would have a negative effect on efficiency. In other words, foreign intelligence is still external counter-intelligence. The counter-intelligence state doesn't wither easily.

Also, the very selection of an intelligence officer in charge of foreign intelligence to head the KGB is itself a first, a message calculated to assuage both foreign and domestic concerns. Kryuchkov is the first KGB chairman not drawn from either the security elements or the upper ranks of the party. Again, the effort to foster the Western symmetry idea – which also plays to the notion of dispassionate and controlled professionalism.

Finally, Viktor Yasmann has come upon something which further highlights the KGB's newly-minted media agility.[36] He identifies a recent journal piece by a veteran KGB general which: (1) pays tribute to the need for legislative control over secret services to prevent their threat to peace and civil rights, and (2) portrays neutrally, and at times favorably, the CIA and CIA professionals, especially the Director of Central Intelligence, Judge William Webster. Yasmann concludes that a form of reverse psychology is at work here – the Soviet public simply assumes that whatever the CIA is charged with automatically fits the KGB.

This rush to generate a new image for state security demonstrates several unusual things about the current state of affairs in the USSR today. First, both the party and state security leadership have shown a sensitivity to their organs' image and a sophisticated approach to improving it never before seen in the USSR's history. Second, the truth about how criminal the KGB's and the party's history actually is, is so disturbing that these people have no choice but to devise a new legend and pedigree for these organs. Third, this writer senses that for the first time since the dark days of the early part of the Second World War when the system came close to collapse, party and state security leaders may detect a coming accountability – and retribution.

*　　*　　*

In conclusion, the Soviet system of security and intelligence is one which is characterized by a political/counter-intelligence thrust to ensure a monopoly of power. Until the creation of the Congress of Peoples Deputies and a Supreme Soviet that is something more than a fiction or rubber stamp, the KGB had no oversight outside of the party. It remains to be seen whether the new Supreme Soviet Committee for Defense and State Security can intrude on that privileged relationship. The last time the punitive organs were subject to any constitutional constraint in the twentieth century was under Nicholas II and then the Provisional Government. Since then state security has operated in a largely extra-legal fashion – but then again, so has the party. From this perspective, foreign operations of state security can be viewed as external counter-intelligence. Even the massive theft of Western technology may be regarded as such, since it really redounds to the maintenance of the party's monopoly of power internally.

NOTES

Research for this chapter was completed in late 1989 and does not reflect major 1990 developments. The views expressed are those of the author and should not be construed as representing positions of the US government.

1. In Russian, *Komitet Gosudarstvennoy Bezopasnosti.*
2. John J. Dziak, *Chekisty: A History of the KGB* (Lexington, MA: Lexington Books, 1988); John J. Dziak, 'The Study of the Soviet Intelligence and Security System', in Roy Godson (ed.), *Comparing Foreign Intelligence: The U.S., the U.S.S.R., the U.K. and the Third World* (New York: Pergamon Brassey's, 1988), pp.65–88.
3. Not all of Beria's cronies were executed, imprisoned, or thrown out. General

Serov, responsible for some particularly odious actions under Beria's tenure and patronage, was selected by Khrushchev to head the KGB in 1954. He was dropped in late 1958 and sent to run the GRU.

4. The CHEKA, the KGB's early predecessor, was formalized on 20 December 1917 (Gregorian calendar). The MVD's precursor, the NKVD was organized in November 1917. The start date for the GRU is somewhat murkier. In 1918 the new Red Army had an intelligence service known variously as the Third Section, and Registration Directorate until 1921, when the Intelligence Directorate (RU), or Second Directorate, of the Red Army General Staff was established. See Dziak, *Chekisty*, p.15.

5. It is worth noting that Kryuchkov's nine Deputies contrasts with five for Andropov (1979) and eight for Chebrikov (1984), an indicator of *increased* KGB activity under *glasnost* and *perestroika*. See Viktor Yasmann, 'Supreme Soviet Committee to Oversee KGB', Radio Liberty, *Report on the USSR*, 30 June 1989, pp.11–13.

6. John Barron puts the Border Guard figure at 300,000 to 400,000, in *The KGB Today* (New York: Reader's Digest Press, 1983), p.451. The *Military Balance, 1988–1989* (London, 1988) lists 230,000 KGB troops of all varieties.

7. The Ministry of Defense newspaper, *Krasnaya Zvezda*, in a fit of *glasnost*, ran a recent piece on how the KGB works today. It described how the all-Union KGB's Investigations Department occupies Lefortovo Prison as its headquarters, making sure to trace the building's pedigree back to Tsarist times (in this case one of 16 prisons built under Catherine the Great). The article denied that the building now housed a prison, but did allow that it contained 'some preliminary investigation isolator cells'. *Krasnaya Zvezda*, 10 March 1989.

8. For more details of NKVD–MVD military/security operations see John J. Dziak, 'Protracted Warfare: the Soviet Force Structure and C^3', in Richard H. Shultz, Jr. *et al.* (eds.), *Guerrilla Warfare and Counterinsurgency* (Lexington, MA: Lexington Books, 1989), pp.211–34. For a comprehensive examination of how NKVD–MVD elements have been used in special operations see William H. Burgess III (ed.), *Inside Spetsnaz: Soviet Special Operations Forces* (Novato, CA: Presidio Press, 1989).

9. The International Institute for Strategic Studies, *The Military Balance, 1988–1989* (London, 1988), p.44.

10. Radio Liberty, *Report on the USSR* 21 July 1989, p.46, quoting *TASS*, 10 July 1989.

11. *Krasnaya Zvezda*, 6 July 1989.

12. Radio Liberty, *Report on the USSR*, 14 July 1989, p.32, quoting *TASS*, no date given.

13. This does not mean that the KGB does not engage in scientific and technical intelligence collection. The party leadership, not over-stressed with cost efficiency in this business, tolerates and encourages redundancy. Western high technology is the payoff for this seeming duplication of effort. For the practical meaning of this investment and how it is managed from the highest party levels through the Military–Industrial Commission (VPK) and thence to the GRU and KGB, see: US Government, *Soviet Acquisition of Militarily Significant Western Technology: An Update* (Washington, DC: September 1985).

14. Unlike the KGB, the GRU is not blessed with a voluminous public literature. With fewer defectors and fewer still who write, the GRU presents some major research problems to students of Soviet intelligence. Viktor Suvorov (pseud.), a former GRU officer who defected in 1978, is one of the few just alluded to. See his *Inside Soviet Military Intelligence* (New York: Macmillan, 1984), from which this writer drew upon. For a Western account, see Pierre de Villemarest, *GRU: Le Plus Secret des Services Sovietiques, 1918–1988* (Paris: Stock, 1988).

15. See Dziak, *Chekisty*, Ch. 8; and Dziak, 'Protracted Warfare: the Soviet Force Structure and C3', in Shultz (ed.), *Guerrilla Warfare and Counterinsurgency*, Ch. 15.

16. William H. Burgess III, 'Assessing Spetsnaz', in Burgess (ed.), *Inside Spetsnaz*,

THE SOVIET SYSTEM OF SECURITY AND INTELLIGENCE

p.1. For more detailed statements of GRU *spetsnaz* missions, see Dziak, 'Protracted Warfare ...', and Jim Shortt, 'Organization, Capabilities and Countermeasures', in Burgess (ed.), *Inside Spetsnaz*, Ch. 13.

17. David C. Isby, 'Afghanistan', in Burgess, *Inside Spetsnaz*, Ch. 2.
18. On the role and membership of the Defense Council during the period under discussion see Dziak, *Soviet Perceptions of Military Doctrine and Military Power: the Interaction of Theory and Practice* (New York: National Strategy Information Centre/Crane Russak & Co., Inc.), Ch. IV.
19. Yet another control device for the GRU and the rest of the military is the Main Political Administration of the Army and Navy (MPA). Operating with the rights of a Central Committee Department it commands an independent structure of political officers who report upwards to the party through the MPA chain of command.
20. In early 1982 Andropov was believed to be the instigator of the *Avrora* affair, in which a journal by that name in Leningrad ran a lightly masked satire on aged leaders who would not step down. Andropov also was behind the investigation of Brezhnev's children for bribery, corruption, speculation and misuse of state funds. The real target clearly was Brezhnev and Andropov was accelerating the succession process.
21. For a full translation of the *Izvestiya* article see Robert Conquest, 'Unearthing the Great Terror', *Orbis* (Spring 1989), pp. 239–46. The author of the *Izvestiya* piece closes by calling for a public trial of Stalin.
22. Radio Liberty, *Report on the USSR*, 19 May 1989, p. 36. This confirms early NKVD defector Krivitskiy's story that Stalin not only praised Hitler but imitated him when he launched his own purges. See Dziak, *Chekisty*, pp. 62, 83–4.
23. They are: Agrarian Commission, Ideological Commission, International Policy Commission, Legal Policy Commission, Party Building and Cadre Policy Commission, and Socioeconomic Policy Commission.
24. See *Izvestiya*, 14 July 1989, for the full composition.
25. *The Washington Post*, 15 July 1989.
26. *The New York Times*, 1 June 1989. Emphasis added.
27. Ibid.
28. *Foreign Broadcast Information Service, Soviet Union* (hereafter *FBIS*), 17 July 1989, p. 47, reporting on Moscow Television Service, 14 July 1989.
29. Ibid., pp. 47–55.
30. Viktor Yasmann, 'Supreme Soviet Committee to Oversee KGB', p. 13.
31. *FBIS, Soviet Union*, p. 50.
32. Radio Liberty, *Report on the USSR*, 10 March 1989, p. 54.
33. *FBIS, Soviet Union*, p. 54. Emphasis added.
34. Yasmann, 'Supreme Soviet Committee to Oversee KGB', p. 12.
35. *FBIS, Soviet Union*, p. 54.
36. Yasmann, 'Supreme Soviet Committee to Oversee KGB', p. 13, quoting Oleg Kalugin, 'Razvedka i vneshnyaya politika', *Mezdunarodnaya zhizn'*, No. 5, 1989, pp. 61–71.

4

Strategic Intelligence: An American Perspective

LOCH K. JOHNSON

Strategic intelligence encompasses two meanings: first, the collection, analysis and dissemination of information about global conditions – especially potential threats to a nation's security; and, second, based on this information, the use of secret intelligence agencies to help protect the nation against harm and advance its interests abroad. Strategic intelligence is, in essence, information and response; the linkage that it provides in decision-making is a critical one in the face of modern doomsday weapons and fragile economic dependencies.

THE DISTINCTIVENESS OF THE AMERICAN EXPERIENCE

The modern American experience of strategic intelligence is unique in several aspects. The purpose of this essay is to suggest what is different about the American approach, what may be characteristic to Western democracies, and what virtually all nations with an intelligence apparatus may have in common regardless of the type of regime. The observations here are but tentative first steps into a region that has been little explored, for which the maps for the most part have been kept carefully folded and hidden by the national security establishments of every nation. It is difficult enough for this author to explore the practices of the US intelligence community, let alone to know much about the secret services of other regimes. Yet, despite the high risk of error, an improved understanding of strategic intelligence demands an attempt at comparative analysis. So what follows is offered in the spirit of exploration, in the hope that others will help readdress misdirections, separating out what may be correct from what is wrong, on the basis of their own research.

Comparing the Secret Services

Virtually every nation wishes to know more about dangers that might harm it from abroad (and about subversion from within, too, but that subject – internal security – lies outside this concentration on foreign intelligence). So America's intelligence apparatus, led by the Central Intelligence Agency (CIA, founded in 1947), is simply a variant of organizations found in sovereign states throughout the world. Some of the CIA's counterparts are large and fearsome in their aggressive capabilities, like the Soviet Union's KGB (which combines domestic and foreign intelligence duties in one entity – a CIA and a Federal Bureau of Investigation (FBI) wrapped into a single package with, among other tasks, responsibilities for the security of nuclear warheads as well) and its GRU (military intelligence, which is divided into several different entities in the United States). Others, in small nations, can be as rudimentary as the placement of a few intelligence officers under embassy cover in a foreign capital, directed to gather whatever information they can of use to their government.

Information, in a word, is viewed as valuable by all leaders, whatever their levels of sophistication and however prominent their countries in world affairs. This is why intelligence has had a long history (the 'second oldest profession'). Few nations are without enemies, real or imagined, current or potential; all take steps to protect themselves. This self-preservation instinct – the fundamental law of man and nature – is most readily observable in the world's flourishing and open commerce in arms. More hidden are the measures nations take secretly to protect themselves and to advance their global (or, for smaller nations, regional) interests through the methods of strategic intelligence; but take them they do.

Strategic intelligence, then, exists everywhere, and important differences can be noted in the organization, skills and objectives of the intelligence agencies between one nation and another. Strategic intelligence establishments – composed of a few, or of many, secret agencies – differ according to (among other things) their size and technical proficiency; their degree of institutional fragmentation and independence within the government; the extent to which they are closely monitored by internal and external monitors (overseers); and their adherence to, or rejection of, moral considerations in the conduct of intelligence operations – let us say, for short: their scope, pluralism, autonomy and ethics (see Figure 1).

FIGURE 1
DISTINCTIVE FEATURES OF US STRATEGIC INTELLIGENCE

Feature	Degree of Accentuation (Estimated)		
	High	Moderate	Low
Global Coverage (Scope)			
Size			
Personnel	USSR US		Most nations
Worldwide facilities	US USSR		Most nations
Technical capabilities	US USSR		Most nations
Pluralism	US	Democracies	USSR Autocracies
Accountability	US*/Canada	Democracies	Autocracies
Ethics		US*/Democracies/Autocracies	

* Since 1975.

The Scope of Strategic Intelligence

Despite its unhappy current trade balance and national debt, the United States continues to enjoy a robust economy. Its Gross National Product (GNP) remains the highest in the world. A quarter of its children may be undernourished (according to some studies) and its infant mortality rate is higher than that of many other industrialized nations, but America is by most measures a rich nation. The taxes derived from this wealth allow government officials to build a vast national security establishment. The United States has some 12,000 nuclear warheads, more than any other nation except the USSR (which has an equivalent number); though it comes second to the Soviet Union in several categories of conventional warfare (tanks and infantrymen, for example), America has more soldiers, weaponry and military bases distributed around the globe than any other nation.

Money: The Mother's Milk of Strategic Intelligence. The California politician, Jesse Unruh, once referred to money as the 'mother's milk of politics'. So, too, is wealth vital to the establishment of a sophisticated strategic intelligence apparatus. A sizeable portion of America's riches (some 13–20 billion dollars per annum) is channeled into its intelligence agencies, each equipped with the latest in technology. The headquarters of these agencies sprawl around the Washington perimeter, their Humint (human intelligence) and Techint (technical intelligence) tentacles reaching out across the globe. Nothing so distinguishes the American intelligence apparatus from other nations as its combination of size and technical proficiency, attributes which depend upon a nation's resource-capacity to recruit, train and support intelligence officials; to construct modern and secure buildings for their work; and – the most difficult challenge – to build advanced reconnaissance satellites, high-speed spyplanes with high-resolution cameras, and other collection 'platforms'. (This is without mentioning the need for sufficient resources to maintain universities and laboratories where advanced technical skills, foreign-language training and the like can be learned by would-be intelligence officers.) A primary indicator of a nation's strategic intelligence prowess, then, is likely to be its degree of wealth.

This is not to say that, with strategic intelligence capabilities, bigger is always better. Israel's redoubtable intelligence service (Mossad) is comparatively small, but has enjoyed much success as a result of experienced and brainy leadership coupled with skillful well-trained officers in the field. (The interception by its security branch of a suitcase bomb destined for an El Al flight in 1986 is one recent illustration.[1]) Even British intelligence is dwarfed by the US and Soviet global infrastructures, but Her Majesty's Secret Service has a long and worldly history to draw upon in the arts of espionage, counterintelligence and covert action; over the years, this experience has led to impressive intelligence successes where newer – and larger – services might have stumbled.[2] Appreciating this edge, America's fledgeling Office of Strategic Services (OSS, precursor to the CIA) relied heavily on tutoring from the British during the Second World War.

On balance, though, scope provides an important advantage for an intelligence service. Without its extensive inventory of satellites, reconnaissance airplanes, listening posts and the like, the United States (and the USSR) would be unable, for example, to verify with confidence strategic-arms locations, missile counts, opposition troop movements, and other vital indicators of military strength and intention. Take away these assurances, and it is possible that direct superpower confrontations might have been more likely in the post-war era (nuclear deterrence, of course, having continued to be a potent dissuader, too, along with the recollection of the horrors of the Second World War).

A Sense of Vulnerability. Yet wealth (and the scope it permits) is only a necessary, not a sufficient, condition for an effective, modern intelligence apparatus. Japan is one of the wealthiest nations in the world today, but its intelligence capabilities are limited compared with, say, the CIA or the KGB. The Japanese nation is less possessed by a sense of danger than either the United States or the Soviet Union – both important world leaders. Japan has the luxury of relying on America's military deterrent and intelligence shield; the United States will presumably look out for the safety of the Japanese, since it is in America's best interests to prevent Japan – with its imposing industrial capacity – from falling into the hands of powers hostile to the West. So, despite its imposing resource-base to create a vast, high-tech (indeed who better than the Japanese?) intelligence service, it does not need to – at least for now.

On the Persian Gulf, tiny Kuwait – with the highest per capita income of any nation – was also in a financial position to afford a more elaborate intelligence service than it possessed at the time of its forced annexation by Iraq in 1990. Instead Kuwaiti officials chose to rely primarily on diplomatic maneuvering as a means of fending off external threats (as when they skillfully persuaded the Reagan administration to flag and escort Kuwaiti oil tankers through the troubled waters of the Gulf). More attention to intelligence requirements might have forewarned Kuwait of Iraq's dark intentions.

Saudi Arabia enjoys even greater GNP wealth than Kuwait, but its global interests remain comparatively limited, too. Its intelligence apparatus has to be proficient mainly within the Middle East. In an age of expensive Techint hardware, however, national wealth is important even with limited regional objectives; few nations could afford the costly AWACS (Airborne Warning and Control System) for aerial reconnaissance recently purchased by the Saudis from the United States.

Israel represents a special case: a small country, but with considerable wealth, technical acumen – and many nearby enemies. It probably spends a higher proportion of its wealth on strategic intelligence than most other nations for one central reason: the people of Israel feel under siege from the sea of enemies in which they find themselves. Acutely sensitive eyes and ears, watching everywhere throughout the region and to some extent beyond, are mandatory to prevent a quick surprise attack from one of many contiguous foes. Intelligence warning-time in the Middle East is like the geographical distance between its capitals: short. Yet as least Israel is unburdened by the world-wide responsibilities shouldered by the United States and the Soviet Union – fortunately, for although well-to-do, Israel is by no means a major economic power; so, the Israelis can marshal their resources in defense against immediate regional vulnerabilities. (The limited schedule of El Al, for instance, simplifies Mossad's counter-terrorist problems.) Israel, however, has not altogether overlooked the advantages of a covert-action and counter-espionage capability to strike enemy terrorist factions based outside the region – reputedly with enviable success.

Compared with other nations, then, the United States has a uniquely comprehensive intelligence establishment, as measured by total funding, the possession of high-tech collection capabilities, the use of modern computer facilities for data-processing, a large staff of well-educated specialists (though in terms of sheer numbers of personnel the KGB and GRU are no doubt larger) and a global network ('infra-structure') of Techint and Humint resources. Half the floor space at the CIA is said to be covered with computers; the Agency has a highly selective recruitment program, hiring only accomplished PhDs and others with advanced training and experience; a spyplane will soon be ready for production that can travel at incredible speeds – from Los Angeles to New York City in ten minutes; the CIA has modern weapons for use in covert actions (like the Stinger missiles provided to Sivimbi in Angola and the Mujahideen in Afghanistan); the CIA alone (not to mention US military intelligence units) has had as many as some 7,000 assets in the field, mainly spying, but in place for covert action and counter-espionage operations as well; and, what perhaps most places the United States in a category by itself with respect to modern strategic intelligence, the nation's satellites and reconnaissance planes possess exceptional mobility and wide span, and produce high-resolution 'imagery'.[3]

Americans have invested in this extensive strategic intelligence capability for two major reasons. First, they can afford to (or, at least, think they can). Second, they feel widely threatened and seek information from every corner of the planet to protect themselves, especially data on Soviet weaponry and aggressive intentions (including Communist-inspired 'wars of liberation' in the developing world). The Kremlin adversary is strong; its missiles are only a sub-marine away in the Atlantic and Pacific Oceans; it can turn the United States into a medieval setting – or worse – within minutes. The perception of grave threat stirs a nation to defend itself in many ways; a nation's intelligence apparatus is apt to grow apace with its overt military establishment, since pre-eminently strategic intelligence serves as the warning shield of the commander-in-chief.

Money and anxiety: here are the driving forces behind a robust intelligence organization, and the United States has an abundance of each. A richness of resources, and the technical-scientific-engineering acumen which accompanies wealth, has allowed Americans to create a large and skillful strategic intelligence apparatus dedicated to the protection and advancement of their far-flung (and arguably over-extended) global interests and commitments. The apparatus consists of a vast high-tech array of listening and watching posts blanketing most of the globe, coupled with an aggressive capacity to intervene abroad with sophisticated weaponry, ubiquitous propaganda and agents of influence in every significant country – all fueled at the core by the instinct of self-preservation and, at present, the fear of a militarily still potent USSR and the sting of various terrorist and narcoterrorist factions.

From one American perspective (call it that of the 'realists' or 'strategists'), this capability may be viewed as an unalloyed 'good'. On the collection-and-analysis side, it enhances early-warning advantages; and, on the covert action/counter-espionage side, it tries – within the limited extent possible for nations and their leaders – to shape history toward more favourable outcomes for the United States. From another perspective, however (that of the 'idealists' or 'moralists'), this capability can be a 'bad'. It has been carried to extremes, idealists maintain, leading to an excessively intrusive interventionism abroad by the United States (chiefly in small, defenseless countries), not only with a thousand mirrors and microphones, but with black propaganda, bribery, coups, assassination plots and a Pandora's box of other horrors incompatible with the high-minded beliefs of Americans and their avowal to be different from – more honorable than – the totalitarian regimes.

Pluralism

Most countries have a tightly contained and hierarchically organized intelligence service. In the United States, however, the pluralism – that is, multiple centers of power – characterizing its political system is reflected in its intelligence community as well. Though more centralized than before the creation of the CIA, authority within the 'intelligence community' is none the less fragmented – probably more so than in any other major nation. The memoirs of Admiral Stansfield Turner, Director of Central Intelligence (DCI) from 1977 to 1981, are a vivid testimony of his frustrated inability to gain control over the scattered intelligence agencies – or even over his own Agency.[4] Turner found the National Security Agency (NSA), which he calls 'a loner organization', especially difficult to manage.[5] Another admiral, Rufus Taylor, concluded flatly, after his tenure as a CIA deputy director (1966–69), that the intelligence community was little more than a 'tribal federation'.[6]

This organizational fragmentation may be a 'good' from some vantage points. Competition within the community leads to a wider array of collection operations, sharpens minds, keeps the analysts honest, allows policy-makers a better sense of options and, most importantly, offers vital safeguards against a concentration of power that could evolve into the creation of a Cheka (secret police). It can be a 'bad', though, when it produces needless duplication, poor coordination, hostile bureaucratic in-fighting, individual agency entrepreneurship (for example, the Iran–Contra affair, when the NSA assisted Lieutenant Colonel Oliver L. North of the National Security Council (NSC) staff with his communications needs without the knowledge of the DCI or its other boss as a military intelligence unit, the Secretary of Defense[7]), and bureaucratic game-playing (for example, the Huston Plan episode, when various US intelligence agencies kept hidden from one another sensitive collection operations – as if their own sister agencies, not the KGB and the GRU, were the ones to guard against).[8]

Accountability

A third feature of the US strategic intelligence system seems distinctive: its degree of official internal and external accountability (that is, inside the CIA, as well as elsewhere within the executive branch, the courts and on Capitol Hill). 'We're the most scrutinized intelligence agency in the world', observes a CIA official with chagrin.[9] 'What we have is covert action by national consensus!' adds another, lamenting the layers of decision-making now required for approval of the so-called quiet option.[10] Only Canada's Security Intelligence Review Committee seems to match America's seriousness of intent in watching its secret service; and, arguably, in some respects Canada goes beyond the current degree of rigorous oversight in the United States, especially with the SIRC's reported use of surprise, random program audits.[11]

Certainly the number of intelligence overseers in the United States is remarkable – at least since the Year of Intelligence (1975) when government investigators concluded, in the light of their discovery of improper domestic spying operations, that tighter supervision had become necessary. Before then, the CIA and the other agencies were largely left alone to carry on as they saw fit their secret Third World War against the Communists, without much supervision from the White House or kibbutzing from Capitol Hill.[12]

Covert action offers an illustration. Beginning in 1975, all important covert action proposals have had to run a daunting decision gauntlet.[13] Before an operation receives a green light, it has to be reviewed serially by various individuals and entities: by CIA field personnel, who conceive of some 85 per cent of all covert action operations (the major checkpoint at this level is the Agency's chief-of-station, or COS, and the ambassador is usually consulted, too); by the Covert Action Staff (CAS) and Special Operations (SO) units within the Operations Directorate at Agency Headquarters; by the Department of State (for propaganda themes); the Intelligence Directorate (the analytic shop of the CIA); the Comptroller, the General Counsel's Office; the Legislative Counsel; the DCI; and by an NSC inter-agency review group; then it goes back to the DCI; on to the NSC itself; the President; the legislative oversight committees (as many as eight in the 1977–80 period, reduced to two in 1980); back to the CIA; then out to the field for implementation.

Along the way, strong criticism can lead to the modification or abandonment of a proposal. The NSC staff-review stage has become the primary sepulcher for questionable proposals. During the Carter and Reagan administrations, over 50 per cent of all covert action schemes reportedly perished on the tabletops of these overseers; and most of the successful proposals were modified in one way or another based on NSC staff suggestions. Another 15 per cent met their demise at the hands of Presidents; and occasionally, congressional overseers have demurred – most visibly with the series of Boland Amendments in the 1980s to curb paramilitary operations in Nicaragua.[14]

A few exceptions to this close scrutiny have occurred. During the Carter years, the administration delayed reporting to Congress until after its attempted operations to rescue Americans in Tehran had run their course, for fear a leak might jeopardize the plans (and at the insistence of the Canadian government, which assisted in some aspects of the effort). These exceptions took place before passage of the 1980 Intelligence Oversight Act, however, with its insistence on prior notification to Congress.[15]

Then, in a more notorious exception to established procedures (and occurring after the passage of the 1980 Act), the Reagan administration elected to bypass most of the checkpoints inside the CIA – and all of them on Capitol Hill – in its Iran-Contra operations (1984–86), raising funds privately at home and abroad towards the financing of an 'off-the-shelf, self-sustaining, stand-alone' covert action capability.[16] In the opinion of its critics, 'privatization' of the quiet option represented a sharp blow to constitutional government in the United States.[17] The

54

perpetrators on the NSC staff were eventually indicted in 1987; and, two years later, a jury found the first to be tried – Lieutenant Colonel North – guilty of improper conduct.[18]

The Iran-Contra scandal reminds us that even strict controls can be avoided by officials determined to have their own way, regardless of established laws and procedures. The attitudes of men and women in office – especially their respect for the law – will always be of over-mastering importance in any system of accountability. In the over-whelming majority of the cases, however – some 99.9 per cent – the new procedures seemed to have worked in the United States. Congress's hold of the purse-strings has been a powerful consideration. As former DCI Colby comments, 'In order to persuade the CIA to abandon a proposed covert action, a Committee chairman needs only to say to the DCI at the end of the briefing [required since the passage of the Hughes–Ryan Amendment in December 1974]: "Write down in your notebook $100 million, because – if you go ahead – that is what is coming out of your CIA budget next year."'[19] Moreover, beyond the official instruments of oversight within the government, the American media have played a much stronger role in monitoring the secret agencies than appears to be the case in other nations; indeed, news-paper exposés in December 1974 were responsible for triggering the official inquiries leading to the new era of vigorous oversight.[20]

How one evaluates the New Oversight in the United States depends, again, upon one's point of view. Some intelligence professionals (as well as outside observers) complain bitterly of 'micromanagement' by legislators who insist on inserting themselves in the small, delicate wheels of secret operations. They complain, too, of delays and timidity brought about by layers of supervisors waving executive orders, com-mittee reports and statutes in the air. 'The intelligence agencies need *horsepower*!' says an exasperated former CIA official.[21]

Others, though – inside and out – welcome the idea of an executive–legislative partnership for intelligence policy, replacing the ambiguous boundaries of earlier days. 'With today's supervision, and with the command structure trying to keep things straight, the people in CIA know what they should do and what they should not do – as distinct from the 1950s, in which there were no particular rules', remarks William Colby. 'If CIA people today are told to violate their limits, or if they are tempted to violate those limits, one of the junior officers will surely raise that question and tell the command structure, and, if not satisfied there, he will tell the Congress, and, if not satisfied there, he will tell the press, and that is the way you control it.'[22] In a similar vein, DCI Turner informed his senior staff and Agency stations around the world in 1978:

'Oversight can be a bureaucratic impediment and a risk to security. It can also be a tremendous strength and benefit to us. It shares our responsibilities. It ensures against our becoming separated from the legal and ethical standards of our society. It prevents disharmony between our foreign policy and intelligence efforts. It helps build a solid foundation for the future of our intelligence operations.'[23]

The American experiment in intelligence accountability remains in its early stages, having seriously begun only in 1976. This infancy has been marked by distress. The Carter administration – despite the President's ardor for intelligence reform as a candidate for office – successfully rebuffed attempts at an omnibus oversight law[24]; and the Reagan administration displayed an outright contempt for accountability with its Iran–Contra operations and its bluff, anti-Congress DCI (William J. Casey, 1981–87). The Iran–Contra scandal 'fractured' the existing oversight relationship between the branches, according to a leading member of the Senate Intelligence Committee.[25] Since then, an atmosphere of wariness toward the CIA lingers on Capitol Hill, though Casey's replacement (William H. Webster, 1987–) has been more skillful in his dealings with legislators. Moreover, President George Bush is well-liked and respected in Congress (both he and his father were once members) for his knowledge of intelligence matters, having himself served – uniquely among US presidents – as DCI between 1976 and 1977.

Despite the willingness to give Webster and Bush the benefit of the doubt during the 'honeymoon period' (the House of Representatives withdrew a new intelligence oversight bill already passed overwhelmingly by the Senate, in no small part because of the friendship ties between Bush and then-Speaker Jim Wright, Democrat, a fellow Texan and former colleague),[26] an Era of Distrust has displaced – for the time being at least – the Era of Uneasy Partnership that preceded the Iran–Contra scandal. In the United States, the search continues for the proper balance between, on the one hand, the effective conduct of the strategic intelligence missions so vital to the defense of the nation, and, on the other hand, their democratic accountability, so vital to the freedom of American citizens.

Ethics

Moral considerations sometimes enter into questions of strategic intelligence. This is an extraneous issue in most countries – indeed virtually all when it comes to espionage. Secretary of State Henry L. Stimson's moral injunction in 1929 (as he closed down his Department's cryptanalytical section) that 'Gentlemen don't read other people's mail' is, one suspects, universally viewed among major governments as a quaint but naive outlook on world affairs (one from which Stimson himself soon retreated).[27] In the United States, the question of morality usually took a back seat (or, more likely, was banished to the trunk) with respect to intelligence operations in the post-war period – that is, until 1975.

The prevailing philosophy of this earlier era is captured well in a passage from the once top-secret Doolittle Report (1954) to President Eisenhower:

> It is now clear that we are facing an implacable enemy [the USSR] whose avowed objective is world domination by whatever means and at whatever cost. There are no rules in such a game. Hitherto acceptable norms of human conduct do not apply. If the U.S. is to survive, long-standing American concepts of 'fair play' must be reconsidered. We must develop effective espionage and counter-espionage services. We must learn to subvert, sabotage and destroy our enemies by more clear, more sophisticated and more effective methods than those used against us. It may become necessary that the American people will be made acquainted with, understand and support this fundamentally repugnant philosophy.[28]

An official change in ethical standards for America's intelligence agencies (in contrast to the sporadic criticisms of some private citizens and individual officeholders throughout the post-war era) came in reaction to newspaper exposés and official inquiries into the CIA during 1974–75. Evidence that the Agency had spied on American citizens (Operation Chaos), tried to overthrow the freely elected President of Chile (Allende) and planned assassination plots against foreign leaders led to widespread calls for reform.[29] With the Watergate scandal and high-level mendacity over Vietnam War policy as an immediate backdrop, these latest revelations of wrongdoing brought forth a fresh concern for the morality of public affairs.

In December 1975, President Ford signed an executive order prohibiting assassination as an instrument of US policy, as did President Carter and Reagan in succession.[30] Also in 1975, former top officials recommended sharp cut-backs in the use of covert action, while reform-minded legislators lambasted the unsavory practices of the CIA and moved to institute closer supervision of the intelligence community.[31] The New Morality had its limits, though. Efforts to pass an anti-assassination law failed in Congress in 1976; and a long litany of moral objectives codified in the proposed Omnibus Intelligence Act of

1978 (which included prohibiting the creation of epidemics of diseases, the creation of water shortages or floods and the use of chemical and biological weapons) drew sharp criticism from 'realists' for locking the intelligence agencies in moral handcuffs, while America's adversaries roamed free. The bill attempted to stretch the new ethical boundaries, and failed.[32]

'Must the United States respond like a man in a barroom brawl who will fight only according to Marquis of Queensberry rules?' asks a realist. Must the United States 'fuzz the difference between ourselves and the Soviet Union ... [yielding to] a childish temptation to fight the Russians on their own terms and in their own gutter ... and throw away one of our great assets?' responds a moralist.[33] As with the tug-of-war over micromanagement-versus-accountability, the struggle goes on between realists and moralists over the proper balance between protecting the nation's interests and maintaining its virtue. The merits of both schools aside, the debate is in itself unique; no other nation has devoted so much time and public attention to the question of ethics and intelligence. Almost everywhere else, the moralist's argument has been roundly dismissed as quixotic.

The influence of the moralist school in the United States should not be overstated, however. Of late, US policy-makers have been more squeamish than in the past about ordering certain operations (notably assassinations) – but not much more. Compared with whom, though, is an appropriate question here, as throughout this analysis. Kidnapping terrorist leader's relative, castrating him, stuffing his testicles in his mouth and shooting him in the head in revenge for hostage-taking, as the KGB has reportedly done, or blowing up an ecology protest-ship in Auckland harbor, killing a crew member, as French intelligence has done, are inconceivable operations for US intelligence agencies, at least in present climes (and a pity, too, might add a hard-core realist).[34]

The moral ground is notoriously slippery. While intervention abroad can lead to excesses, intervention often seems the proper course to take if, in the end, it promises to help an oppressed people find freedom. This was a strong motivation behind America's support for the Mujahideen, which even moralists seem to support; yet, ironically, this objective was also a strong motivation for US involvement in Vietnam, which most moralists ultimately opposed.

The recommendations of policy-makers who have thought deeply about these dilemmas offer few specific guideposts. During the 'intelligence wars' of 1975, Senator Frank Church (Democrat, Idaho), chairman of the most extensive congressional investigation into strategic intelligence policy ever conducted in the United States, could conclude only that covert action should be resorted to when 'consistent either with the imperative of national survival or with our traditional belief in free government'. For Clark Clifford, a former Secretary of Defense, covert action should be used only when it 'truly affects our national security'. For Cyrus Vance, then a former Deputy Secretary of Defense (and later Secretary of State), covert actions had to be 'absolutely essential to the national security'.[35]

While considerations of what is good and bad about strategic intelligence will continue to be difficult and contentious, one conclusion seems reasonable: a strong linkage should exist between accountability and morality. More than the President and his agencies alone should help decide these difficult questions. Elected representatives of the people in Congress – or, at any rate, those serving on the two intelligence committees and in times of emergency at least the top four-to-eight congressional leaders – should be consulted, in advance and in executive session, about the moral as well as the practical wisdom of secret intervention. As Gregory F. Treverton puts it succinctly, 'Don't evade process ...'[36] Individuals who have served on these committees – Anthony C. Belienson (D, California), David L. Boren (D, Oklahoma), William Cohen (R, Maine), Wyche Fowler (D, Georgia), Lee H. Hamilton (D, Indiana), George Mitchell (D, Maine), Sam Nunn (D, Georgia), Arlen Specter (R, Pennsylvania) – among others, have much to bring to these judgements.

THE COMMONALITIES OF STRATEGIC INTELLIGENCE

The preceding section focused on the distinctiveness of US strategic intelligence. A second broad set of comparisons is appropriate: the extent to which America's experience is like that of other nations. From a longer list, three commonalities are presented below, one from collection-and-analysis, another from covert action, the third from counter-intelligence.

The Information and Understanding Gaps

Among the many features of strategic intelligence shared by nations, one stands pre-eminent: every country must endure a gap between what it may need or want to know and what it actually knows or can know. The world is too large – for any nation – to scour thoroughly (the Grenada problem). In 1989, most countries seemed to have been surprised by the student rebellion at Tiananmen Square in Beijing and the harsh crackdown by the Chinese regime. Further, some information one would like to have is simply too inaccessible (such as the activities of small and elusive terrorist factions – the Abu Nidal problem). The CIA remains unable to find out the location of American hostages in the Middle East, some of whom have been held for years. Then comes the added problem of appreciating and understanding the information one does have, without misperceiving or otherwise distorting its meaning (the kill-the-messenger problem). Even if no distortion occurs, do a nation's leaders have the wisdom to judge accurately the implications of the data placed before them? Every nation – large or small, rich or poor – confronts these hazards; certainly no nationality has a monopoly on wisdom.

The Beguiling Quiet Option

My hunch is that every nation with a capacity for covert action finds it a virtually irresistible alternative at times to more overt instruments of foreign policy, such as overt war and diplomacy. Open warfare is always too noisy and formal; diplomacy is often too slow and frustrating. Covert action holds out the temptation of a behind-the-scenes quick fix – though it rarely works so easily, for the currents of history are strong and resist the feeble efforts of human beings to change its course. In democracies, executive officials also find covert action attractive because it avoids debate with annoying legislators (the Iran–Contra problem – 'I didn't want any interference', testified NSC staff director Vice Admiral John N. Poindexter).[37]

In the United States (and, one suspects, elsewhere) covert action almost seems to take on a life of its own, irrespective of existing overt policies. This, one may hypothesize, occurs for two major reasons. First, the CIA may have its own policies which it carries out, and which may or may not conform to the President's publicly stated objectives. Or, and I think this is the correct interpretation, the White House has tended (like 'White Houses' in other nations) to have two foreign policies: one overt and one covert – the latter frequently in pursuit of objectives (under order of secret NSC directives) that, paradoxically, may run counter to the former. When the United States has sought more peaceful relations with the Soviet Union (détente), the subterranean Cold War fought by America's (and the Soviet Union's) secret services has continued its own course, unabated.

Though but crude estimates, the trend lines in Figure 2 depicting the relationship between US–Soviet diplomatic relations and CIA expenditures on covert action (with their Pearson's correlation of only .02 – virtually no relationship) suggest the existence of two American foreign policies, one overt and one covert, often headed in separate directions, a hidden Cold War in the midst of avowed peaceful intentions.[38] On a normative note, one cannot help but wonder whether the overt overtures might have been more successful if the United States (and the Soviet Union) had thought more about the limiting effects of secret warfare on serious diplomacy.

The Security Gap

Under present conditions, few nations feel secure. No nation can boast of perfect counter-intelligence. Each is vulnerable to the Abu Nidals of the world; no one knows for sure if a Semtex-filled Toshiba Boombox lies ticking in the baggage compartment of the airplane or in the bread truck outside the embassy. Further, every nation will suffer defections, false defectors, penetrations and other security breaches. The more technologically advanced nations have an advantage in this regard, with their embassy-break-in, remote surveillance and other advanced espionage capabilities; but on this conflict-riven globe, the counter-intelligence task (including its counter-terrorist and counter-narcotics dimensions) is as difficult to address successfully as that of collection.

Moreover, one suspects, every nation wrestles like the United States with the proper organizational approach to counter-intelligence: a tightly centralized corps of specialists (with the risks of isolation and the virtues of security), as practiced in the CIA under the legendary CI Chief James Angleton (1954–74), or a more decentralized approach that makes counter-intelligence a part of every intelligence officer's responsibilities (with the risks of penetration and the virtues of broader coverage).[39] This serious management problem is likely to remain a part of the internal counter-intelligence debate in most countries.

STRATEGIC INTELLIGENCE IN THE TWENTY-FIRST CENTURY

What has been the significance of strategic intelligence in the Nuclear Age, and what lies ahead? By way of summing up, this conclusion offers some brief observations on these large questions.

Pluses

On the positive side, strategic intelligence has made the world a much safer place. Modern methods of surveillance have allowed the major nations a greater sense of security against becoming the victims of military surprise; no guarantees are assured in this unpredictable world, but as the Nuclear Age weds the Age of Surveillance, the likelihood of surprise is far less than it used to be. Further, more and better information about world affairs has, one would suppose, improved the quality of decision-making within the various capitals.

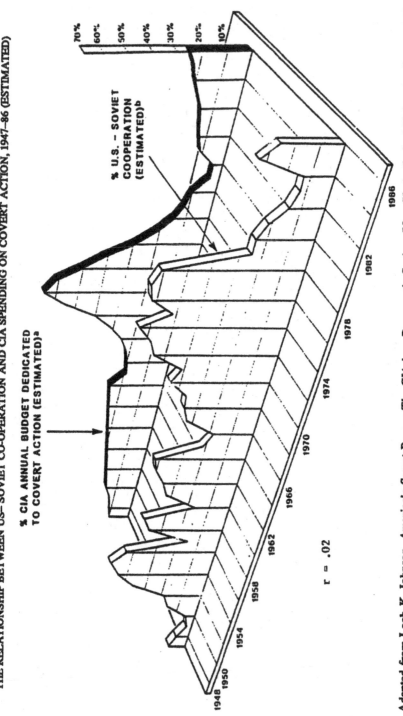

FIGURE 2

THE RELATIONSHIP BETWEEN US–SOVIET CO-OPERATION AND CIA SPENDING ON COVERT ACTION, 1947–86 (ESTIMATED)

% CIA ANNUAL BUDGET DEDICATED TO COVERT ACTION (ESTIMATED)[a]

% U.S. – SOVIET COOPERATION (ESTIMATED)[b]

r = .02

1948 1950 1954 1958 1962 1966 1970 1974 1978 1982 1986

70% 60% 50% 40% 30% 20% 10%

a. Adapted from Loch K. Johnson, *America's Secret Power: The CIA in a Democratic Society* (New York: Oxford University Press, 1989), p. 103.

b. For the 1947–80 period, adapted from Charles W. Kegley, Jr., and Eugene Wittkopf, *American Foreign Policy: Pattern and Process* (New York: St. Martin's Press, 2nd ed., 1982), p.58, which in turn is based on data assembled by Edward Azar and Thomas Sloan; for the 1981–86 period, the author's own judgements, based on general media sources and discussions with colleagues.

Policy-makers are less apt to decide too quickly and rashly, with gaping holes in their understanding of world events. For the United States, the Cuban missiles crisis is perhaps the most vivid example (though it was hardly without its ambiguities – and, even in this modern era, America has endured major intelligence fiascos like the Bay of Pigs in 1961 and the *Mayaguez* incident in 1975).

In its more judicious use of covert action, the United States has also had some positive results. In Greece immediately after the Second World War and in Afghanistan in more recent years, US intelligence aided groups who sought to drive out Communist intruders; and CIA covert propaganda has brought a more accurate understanding of American policies to people sealed off by totalitarian rule than reliance upon overt communications alone would allow.[40]

Counter-intelligence has enjoyed pluses, too: protecting vital secrets, as well as penetrating foreign intelligence services, terrorist factions and narcotics traffickers to help thwart their harmful operations directed against the United States. As for accountability, on the whole – Iran–Contra is a troubling exception – the intelligence community has accepted the New Oversight and these new arrangements (not everybody will agree) have introduced greater thought and better planning into America's covert operations.

Minuses

Sometimes America's collection and counter-intelligence missions have run awry. Over-zealous managers and officers have, in cruel irony, directed their awesome technologies against the very people they were meant to protect: American citizens, whose only 'crime' might have been to criticize the Vietnam War, to have marched with Dr Martin Luther King, Jr or to have questioned the merits of US involvement in Nicaragua or El Salvador. Operations Chaos, Shamrock, Minaret, Cointelpro, Cispes – the list goes on.[41] Here is the ultimate danger of the secret services, brought to life darkly even in a nation with strong democratic traditions.

Moreover, according to critics, covert action has also done at least as much to damage the reputation of the United States as it has to help. 'When we choose our weapons, let's choose ones we are good at using – like the Marshall Plan – not ones that we are bad at – like the Bay of Pigs', writes Roger Fisher. 'To join some adversaries in the grotesque world of poison-dart guns and covert operations is to give up the most powerful weapons we have: idealism, morality, due process of law, and belief in the freedom to disagree, including the right of other countries to disagree with ours.'[42] Ferdinand Mount laments the abandonment of 'friends' abroad whom the United States has encouraged to take up arms against a common foe: Ukrainian emigrés, Meo tribesmen, South Vietnamese intelligence assets, the Khambas, the Kurds and others – all 'so many causes and peoples briefly taken up by the CIA and then tossed aside like broken toys ...'.[43]

Finally, America's experiment in intelligence accountability has been uneven. It failed dismally in the Iran–Contra episode, and has sputtered forward at other times according to the degree of determination and courage busy legislators were prepared to invest in this task.[44]

Bottom Lines

Today, America's intelligence agencies are distinctive in several ways: they are large and technically sophisticated, dispersed in their organization and management, watched closely by overseers (at least compared with most nations) and guided by some moral signposts. America's secret service also shares common traits with counterparts abroad, among them an inability to collect all the data policy-makers may need; the distortion of information by analysts and policy-makers; and excessive attraction to covert action, even when these operations may undermine or diminish publicly stated diplomatic initiatives; and failures of counter-intelligence.

If these characterizations are accurate, they suggest several future directions. In the United States (and elsewhere), the size and technical development of the secret service warrants further support, if properly supervised and directed chiefly toward foreign-intelligence collection. The more nations can reduce uncertainty about the capabilities and intentions of their adversaries, the more likely they can avoid conflicts resulting from a fear of surprise attack or from other mistakes. Strategic intelligence, in short, can have a stabilizing effect on world affairs.

The pluralism in the US intelligence community remains excessive and, within limits, the authority of the DCI ought to be increased – especially over collection tasking. The system of intelligence accountability in America remains in a state of flux; more thought and dedication to this responsibility is necessary on Capitol Hill and, as legislative investigators recently urged, an improved 'spirit of good faith with Congress' must be forthcoming in the executive branch.[45] The intelligence missions need greater moral definition, too, particularly in sorting out 'acceptable' covert actions. The defeated Grand Charter of 1978 no doubt went too far in this direction, but currently the agencies have too little guidance; the abandoned ethical provisions of the Charter deserve another look, for some of the ideas had merit (the prohibition against crop-destruction, for one).

As for common problems touching all nations, leaders should begin to consider more seriously the possibilities of openly sharing some types of strategic intelligence data with other foreign leaders. While some countries already engage in sharing to some extent (Britain and the United States, for instance)[46], a greater pooling of information – say, on ecological and natural-resource problems, not just political and military threats – would help remove ambiguities and build bridges of international co-operation. Further, just as treaties are signed on arms control, so should nations begin to prohibit some aspects of covert action, trying collectively to resist its strong tug. Covert action is unlikely to be banished any time soon; but efforts at better international supervision are warranted, including resistance to the use of covert actions which directly contradict overt diplomatic initiatives and understandings – in essence, driving with the brake on.

Even the murky world of counter-intelligence lends itself to some forms of international co-operation, most obviously in joint combat against the drug epidemic and terrorism. Here, indeed, may be the most promising starting point for nations to work together solving common problems of strategic intelligence. Though some national leaders actually profit from the drug trade and have no interest in co-operation – or are too intimidated by narcoterrorists – most want to save the souls of their young.

What each of these initiatives requires is will, wisdom, and intelligence of a different kind. The rising interest in questions of strategic intelligence among scholars, policy-makers, and, most importantly, the general public encourages hope.

NOTES

1. See John Newhouse, 'Annals of Intelligence: Changing Targets', *The New Yorker*, 10 July 1989, p.77.
2. See, for instance, the skillful handling of Col. Penkovsky by the British, discussed in David C. Martin, *Wilderness of Mirror* (New York: Harper & Row, 1980). The British, of course, have also had their mistakes – most painfully and obviously in the counter-intelligence field, with such major defectors as Kim Philby.
3. Interviews with CIA officials, 1980–89. See, also, James Bamford, *The Puzzle Palace* (New York: Houghton Mifflin, 1984); William E. Burrows, *Deep Black: Space Espionage and National Security* (New York: Random, 1986); Jeffrey Richelson, *The U.S. Intelligence Community* (Cambridge, MA: Ballinger, 1985); and Victor Marchetti and John Marks, *The CIA and the Cult of Intelligence* (New York: Knopf, 1974).
4. Stansfield Turner, *Secrecy and Democracy: The CIA in Transition* (Boston, MA: Houghton Mifflin, 1985).
5. Stansfield Turner, 'Foreword', in David D. Newsom, *The Soviet Brigade in Cuba; A*

Study in Political Diplomacy (Bloomington, IN: University of Indiana, 1987).

6. Quoted by Marchetti and Marks, op. cit., p.70.
7. See testimony of Secretary of Defense Casper Weinberger, *Hearings*, Senate Select Committee on Secret Military Assistance to Iran and the Nicaraguan Opposition and House Select Committee to Investigate Covert Arms Transactions with Iran, US Congress (24 July 1987), hereafter the Inouye–Hamilton Committees (after their respective chairmen, Daniel K. Inouye, D, Hawaii, and Lee H. Hamilton, D. Indiana).
8. See Loch K. Johnson, 'Mr. Huston and Colonel North', *Corruption and Reform* 3 (1988), p.224.
9. CIA analyst Arthur S. Hulnick, public lecture, University of Georgia, Athens, Georgia, 20 Nov. 1984.
10. Loch K. Johnson, 'Covert Action and Accountability: Decision-Making for America's Secret Foreign Policy', *International Studies Quarterly*. 33 (March 1989), pp.81–110.
11. Remarks by Canadian political scientists, Panel on 'Controlling Intelligence', Annual Meeting, American Political Science Association, Chicago, 1 Sept. 1987.
12. Johnson, 'Covert Action and Accountability', op. cit., and, 'Foreign and Military Intelligence', *Final Report*, Book I, Select Committee to Study Governmental Operations with Respect to Intelligence Activities, US Senate (26 April, 1976), pp.163–76, hereafter the *Final Report*, Church Committee (after its chairman, Frank Church).
13. See Loch K. Johnson, *America's Secret Power: The CIA in a Democratic Society* (New York: Oxford University Press, 1989), Ch.6.
14. Ibid., p.294, n.45. For a discussion of the six Boland Amendments passed between 1982 and 1986, see *Report*, Inouye–Hamilton Committees, op. cit., and, Henry A. Kissinger, 'A Matter of Balance', *Los Angeles Times*, 26 July 1987.
15. See Loch K. Johnson, 'Controlling the CIA: A Critique of Current Safeguards', *Harvard Journal of Law & Public Policy*, 12 (1989), n.134, and 'Intelligence Policy in the Carter and Reagan Administrations: From Reform to Remission', *Southeastern Political Review*, 16 (Spring 1988), pp.73–104. For the 1980 Oversight Act, see 94 Stat. 1981, title 4, sec.501, 50 U.S.C. 413 (formally, the Accountability for Intelligence Activities Act).
16. See the testimony of Lt. Col. Oliver L. North, *Hearings*, Inouye–Hamilton Committees, op. cit., pp.240–41.
17. See William C. Cohen and George J. Mitchell, *Men of Zeal* (New York: Viking, 1988); and, Elizabeth Drew, 'Letter from Washington' (22 March 1987), *The New Yorker*, 30 March 1987, p.111.
18. A year later another jury found North's boss, Vice Admiral John N. Poindexter, guilty also of perjury before Congress and other crimes.
19. Remarks, 'Secrecy and U.S. Foreign Policy', Tufts University Symposium (27 Feb. 1988). For the Hughes–Ryan Act (co-sponsored by Senator Harold Hughes [D, Iowa] and Leo Ryan [D, California] and passed on 30 Dec. 1974), see 30 U.S.C. 403.
20. See Loch K. Johnson, *A Season of Inquiry: Congress and Intelligence* (Chicago: Dorsey, 1988), pp.9–10. Particularly influential was the reporting of *New York Times* reporter Seymour M. Hersh throughout December 1974.
21. Dr Ray S. Cline, former CIA Deputy Director for Intelligence, remarks, Panel on 'Controlling Intelligence', Annual Meeting, American Political Science Association, 1987, op. cit.
22. William E. Colby, 'Gesprach mit William E. Colby', *Der Spiegel*, 23 Jan. 1978 (author's translation).
23. Loch K. Johnson, 'The CIA: Controlling the Quiet Option', *Foreign Policy*, 39 Summer 1980), pp.143–52.
24. Senate bill (S.) 2525, introduced on 9 Feb. 1978, formally entitled the National Intelligence Reorganization and Reform Act. For the text, see the *Congressional Record* (9 Feb. 1978), pp.3110–41.

25. Sen. Patrick Leahy [D, Vermont], interviewed by David Brinkley, ABC television, 'This Week with David Brinkley', 14 Dec. 1986.
26. See 'Intelligence Oversight Act of 1988', *Report No.1000–276*, Select Committee on Intelligence, US Senate (27 Jan. 1988); 'Intelligence Oversight Act of 1988', *Report No.100–705*, Permanent Select Committee on Intelligence, US House of Representatives; and, the *New York Times* (1 Feb. 1989). Wright may have also sought to deflect attention from CIA allegations that he had leaked classified information on Agency operations in Nicaragua – a persistent news story at the time, despite Wright's denials.
27. Marchetti and Marks, op. cit., p.67.
28. Final Report, Book I, Church Committee, op. cit., p.9.
29. Johnson, *Season of Inquiry*, op. cit., William E. Colby and Peter Forbath, *Honorable Men: My Life in the CIA* (New York: Simon & Schuster, 1978).
30. For these executive orders (respectively, E.O. 11905, E.O. 12036, and E.O. 12333), see: *Weekly Compilation of Presidential Documents*, 12 (Washington, DC: Government Printing Office, 1976), pp.234–44; *Public Papers of the Presidents of the United States: Jimmy Carter, 1978, Book 1* (Washington, DC: Government Printing Office, 1979), pp.194–214; and, *Public Papers of the Presidents of the United States: Ronald Reagan, 1981* (Washington, DC: Government Printing Office, 1982), pp.1128–29.
31. See the *Hearings*, Church Committee, op. cit. 4 and 5 Dec. 1975.
32. On reasons for the failure of S.2525, see the testimony of David Aaron, 'Congressional Oversight of Covert Activities', *Hearings*, Permanent Select Committee on Intelligence, US House of Representatives (22 Sept. 1983), p.98; and, Anne Karalekas, 'Intelligence Oversight: Has Anything Changed?' *Washington Quarterly*, 6 (Summer 1983), pp.22–30.
33. See 'Should the CIA Fight Secret Wars?' (a round-table discussion with several national security experts) *Harper's*, Sept. 1984, pp.39, 44.
34. For this account of KGB practices, see Bob Woodwood, *Veil: The Secret Wars of the CIA, 1981–1987* (New York: Simon & Schuster, 1987), p.416. The bombing of the Greenpeace ship, *Rainbow Warrior*, occurred in 1985.
35. *Hearings*, Church Committee, op. cit., 4 and 5 Dec. (1989), p.42.
37. Testimony of Vice Admiral John M. Poindexter, *Hearings*, Inouye–Hamilton Committees, op. cit., Vol.8, p.159.
38. For the 1947–80 period, the degree of cordiality in US–Soviet relations depicted in Figure 2 is adapted from Charles W. Kegley, Jr, and Eugene Wittkopf, *American Foreign Policy: Pattern and Process*, 2nd ed. (New York: St. Martin's Press, 1982), p.58, which in turn is based on data assembled by Edward Azar and Thomas Sloan; the 1981–86 estimates are the author's own judgements, based on general media sources and discussions with colleagues. The covert-action budget estimates are based on the author's interviews with intelligence officials (see Johnson, 'Covert Action and Accountability', op. cit.).
39. On CIA squabbles over counter-intelligence, see John T. Elliff and Loch K. Johnson, 'Counterintelligence', *Final Report*, Book I, Church Committee, op. cit.; Loch K. Johnson, 'Seven Sins of Strategic Intelligence', *World Affairs*, 146 (Fall 1983), pp.192–3; and Roy Godson, (ed.), *Intelligence Requirements for the 1980s: Counterintelligence* (Washington, DC: National Strategy Information Center, 1980).
40. For an illustration, see the testimony of former ambassador L. Dean Brown, 'The CIA and Media', *Hearings*, Subcommittee on Oversight chaired by Les Aspin [D, Wisconsin], Permanent Select Committee on Intelligence, 1979, p.168.
41. *Final Report*, Books I–III, Church Committee, op. cit.; Johnson *Season of Inquiry*, op. cit.
42. Roger Fisher, 'The Fatal Flaw in Our Spy System', *Boston Globe* (1 Feb. 1976).
43. Ferdinand Mount, 'Spook's Disease', *National Review*, 32 (7 March 1980), p.300; on the abandonment of intelligence assets in South Vietnam, see Frank Snepp,

Decent Interval (New York: Random House, 1979).

44. See Loch K. Johnson, 'Congress and the CIA: Monitoring the Dark Side of Government', *Legislative Studies Quarterly*, 5 (Nov. 1980), pp.77–99, and 'Legislative Reform of Intelligence Policy', *Polity*, 17 (Spring 1985), pp.549–73.

45. *Report*, Inouye–Hamilton Committees, op. cit., p.383.

46. For examples, see Jeffrey Richelson and Desmond Ball, *The Ties That Bind: Intelligence Cooperations between the UKUSA Countries* (Boston: Allen & Unwin, 1985).

PART TWO

Canadian and Comparative Perspectives

5

Introduction

DAVID STAFFORD

In Canada, the shadow of the McDonald Commission report has hovered over most public discussion of intelligence and security issues for the last decade. Only now, as we enter both a rapidly changing era of international politics and learn to live with the new national security apparatus put into place in 1984, are the terms of the debate beginning to change. The essays in Part Two both reflect and discuss that evolution.

Faced with violent separatism in Quebec in the early 1970s, the Security Service, then under the control of the federal policing authority, the Royal Canadian Mounted Police (RCMP), launched a series of counter-subversive operations, many of which were either illegal or broke accepted democratic norms. Although public exposures in the mid-1970s revealed that the RCMP had often been profoundly ineffectual in Quebec, the subsequent McDonald Commission enquiry focused principally on the wrongdoings and how to prevent them in the future. As Peter Gill points out in the first of the essays in this section, the Commission was certainly concerned with *effective* security. But its report, when published in 1981, 'made clear that, whenever there was a clash between the interests of efficacy and propriety, then the latter should prevail'. The 1984 parliamentary act establishing the Canadian Security Intelligence Service (CSIS) embodied most of the central principles recommended by McDonald: a separate civilian agency with a clearly defined mandate subject to legal control and accountable both to ministers and to outside review – although by an appointed review body, the Security Intelligence Review Committee (SIRC), rather than, as McDonald had recommended, by a parliamentary committee. It is worth noting that the first attempt at a bill – Bill C157 – encountered strong criticism both inside and outside Parliament on the grounds that it strayed too far from the McDonald Commission's concerns with propriety. Such was the strong climate of opinion at the time in favour of strengthening judicial and political control over the Security Service, that the government had to yield on many of these issues.

71

The 1984 CSIS Act required that there should be a parliamentary review of its workings after five years. That review began in the fall of 1989, and a central purpose of the conference organized by the Canadian Association for Security and Intelligence Studies (CASIS), on which this volume is based, was to contribute to that exercise. At the time of writing [May 1990], parliamentary hearings were still under way, and the special committee's report was not expected to appear until some time in the fall of 1990. Whatever it recommends, however – and it seems unlikely to lead to any fundamental changes in the systems established in 1984 – it is clear that the five years preceding the review were an important period of transition. We now find ourselves firmly in a post-McDonald era where the focus of debate is less on propriety than on efficacy – and, as Reg Whitaker notes, on the even more basic question of efficacy at *what*. For with the Gorbachev revolution in the Soviet Union and the disappearance of Moscow's allies in Eastern Europe, Canada, as an integral part of the Western intelligence community, has to evaluate the meaning for its security intelligence system of the changing nature of the traditional Soviet threat. To continue with Cold War paradigms, Whitaker notes, is not only outmoded but perverse, because it could well lead to a neglect of new and dangerous threats. Here, Frank Cain's analysis of the Australian Security Intelligence Organization (ASIO) usefully reminds us that Cold War concerns profoundly affected the evolution of the security system in another Commonwealth country. Created at the height of the East–West conflict in 1949, ASIO was envisioned as 'the means for convincing the US, the British and the Australian electorate, that the government was reliable and firmly anti-communist in all aspects'. Dr Cain's article also underlines the importance of scandals in generating enquiry and reform in security matters. Obviously true for Canada in precipitating the McDonald Commission report, it has also been true for Australia. The first Hope Commission began its work in 1974 amidst considerable public controversy about ASIO, and the second was launched in response to the Combe affair and had its final recommendations influenced by the ASIS/Sheraton affair. The result is that Australia now has an Inspector-General of Intelligence and Security and a Joint Parliamentary Committee on ASIO – reforms that, as in Canada, were resisted by 'insiders' within the intelligence community. To what degree the Australian intelligence community can flexibly adapt from the Cold War paradigm that literally led to its creation remains to be seen.

Canadians, of course, have been recent tragic victims of threats from non-traditional and 'non-Cold War' sources. To mention only the most obvious case, the destruction of the Air India flight bound from Canada to Bombay in June 1985 took the lives of over 300 Canadians, and responsibility for the tragedy is generally ascribed to terrorist action on Canadian soil. This was only one of several incidents that troubled the early years of CSIS and led to heavy public criticism that its creation marked little or no improvement over the days when the RCMP ran security intelligence. In retrospect, we can see that much of this debate on security intelligence issues was inevitable, given both the continuity of personnel employed by the Service – most simply transferred from the RCMP – and the fixations of the media on the wrongdoings of the 1970s. In retrospect, too, we can see that it was bound to pass once the Service's teething problems were over and public legitimacy for its operations was firmly grounded. In establishing the latter, the Security Intelligence Review Committee played a major role.

The essay by John Starnes reflects some of the fears felt by 'insiders' within the Canadian intelligence community about the establishment of this external review body. SIRC members are Privy Councillors appointed by the Prime Minister, and they have full access to CSIS material in making their reports and conducting investigations. When SIRC was established by the 1984 Act, strong fears were expressed from some quarters that access to secret material by outsiders could destroy the trust of Canada's allies, lead to a drying up of vital sources of intelligence, and paralyse the country's security system. There is no evidence that this has happened, and SIRC has been leak-proof. None the less, it has remained a focal point of concern for those uncomfortable with the new regime. This is not to suggest that Mr Starnes, who became Director of the RCMP Security Service after long experience in intelligence matters at the Department of External Affairs, is opposed to the existence of SIRC. What concerns him, rather, is the role SIRC has been trying to establish for itself. Mr Starnes sees this as going beyond the mandate laid down by the legislation. While the focus of his essay is on SIRC's use of the concept 'oversight', which he correctly points out has a distinct meaning, at least in English, from 'review', he also takes SIRC to task for floating in public such issues as the desirability of establishing an independent Office of National Assessment, the need for a Canadian Foreign Intelligence Service and the importance of bringing such agencies as the Communications Security Establishment (CSE) also under external review. These, Mr Starnes feels, are issues that lie outside its purview. 'The proper course, surely, is to raise [them] privately with ministers and senior officials', he writes.

Mr Starnes is an experienced and thoughtful observer in all these matters. But this plea for private rather than public discussion of sensitive issues of security and intelligence seems out of step with the climate of the times, and, it could be argued, if followed, would almost certainly be a guarantee of inaction. For as he himself notes elsewhere in his essay, on many of these important issues discussion in Canada has been stifled 'by ministerial indifference, inertia and inaction'. The legitimacy that SIRC has helped so importantly to confer on the conduct of security intelligence affairs since 1984 is surely due, many observers would argue, to its demonstrated concern with a whole range of interlinked issues that require informed public debate. If this has involved a generous interpretation of the mandate, then, many critics would argue, this is all to the good.

Interestingly enough, one of the issues brought up for discussion by SIRC for which it earns Mr Starnes' criticism provides a measure of the distance that has been travelled since the days of the McDonald Commission report and its dominating concerns with propriety. The idea that Canada should have its own foreign intelligence service was briefly floated in the McDonald Commission report. But it never rose to the surface of public debate, so dominated was this by the mood of scepticism and hostility towards anything that smacked of clandestinity – a climate that was also affected, it should be borne in mind – by revelations and controversies south of the border about CIA wrong-doings and mistakes in Vietnam and elsewhere. That it should now be the very agency at the centre of the system of accountability that has raised the issue again – and, indeed, that it has received a respectful hearing from individuals and quarters most deeply concerned not so long ago about propriety issues surrounding the Security Service (including CSIS) – is perhaps a small but significant measure of the changing climate of the times.

The debate over means has been overwhelmed, at least temporarily, by a debate over ends. Yet it is important that they be kept clearly distinguished one from another. It is vital to identify and respond to changing threats. But this makes efficacy and propriety no less important than in the past. Indeed, as Peter Gill suggests, together they are guarantors that future needs in security and intelligence will best be met.

6

The Evolution of the Security Intelligence Debate in Canada since 1976

PETER GILL

A major theme of the security intelligence debate in Canada has been the perceived need to find some balance between the security requirements of the state and nation on the one hand and the civil rights and liberties of individuals on the other. The former demand that the nation's security intelligence agencies must operate effectively; the latter, that the agencies are accountable and operate properly within the law. For brevity's sake, throughout this essay these two dimensions will be referred to respectively as efficacy and propriety. Efficacy is used as a synonym for effectiveness, which, it should be noted, is distinguished from efficiency. Propriety refers to behaviour which is not just lawful but which is also consistent with accepted democratic standards; not all actions which might be considered improper will actually be unlawful.

Some progress towards being able to judge the effectiveness of security intelligence arrangements in Canada was made with the passage of the Canadian Security Intelligence Service Act 1984. The Act defined publicly the duties of CSIS: collecting, analysing and retaining information respecting activities reasonably suspected of constituting threats to the security of Canada.[1] These threats were in turn defined in Section 2 of the Act and are generally referred to as espionage, sabotage, foreign influence, terrorism and subversion. Measuring efficacy, however, remains highly problematic. It might be argued that an overt absence of these threats would indicate highly effective security intelligence operations; but for some, this absence would merely indicate that such activities were being carried on more covertly. Similarly, does the expulsion of foreign diplomats indicate effectiveness (the uncovering of espionage attempts) or ineffectiveness (a failure to turn the diplomats into assets)? In the case of propriety the

75

meaning of the concept itself is contested: may security intelligence agencies use any means which are not explicitly unlawful, or should they aim for a higher standard of ethical behaviour? This essay will, first, try to place this debate within the context of some major aspects of the intelligence process. Then the main contributions will be discussed briefly, categorized as those emphasizing propriety, those emphasizing efficacy and those seeming to emphasize both equally. The concluding section discusses the relationship between efficacy and propriety.

THE INTELLIGENCE PROCESS

Fundamentally the debate about the efficacy and propriety of security intelligence operations is one specific example of the general concern of democratic theory with securing public consent to the operations of the state. For example, state policy should be determined, at least indirectly, by competitive elections and specific policy decisions should be made by politically responsible ministers rather than by appointed officials. The reality – how it actually works – indicates the tenuous extent to which state practice in fact reflects public consent. In the area of security intelligence, the issue is compounded by the frequent absence of any recognition that democratic restraints should exist even formally. Security intelligence issues become public only in association with serious intelligence failures or scandals and therefore 'debate' is inevitably lop-sided. These issues have not been the stuff of elections, and between elections, ministers have preferred not to know of operations for fear of having to take difficult decisions. In turn, security intelligence agencies themselves have preferred to keep ministers in ignorance in order to preserve 'plausible deniability' and to avoid embarrassment to ministers or themselves.[2]

Formally, the intelligence process can be seen as consisting of five stages: planning/targeting, collection, processing, production/analysis, and dissemination. If the revelations of abuse in domestic security intelligence operations in North America, Europe and Australia during the last 20 years have achieved anything, it has been to dispel the myth that it was best in the public interest for such operations to remain beyond the ken of elected politicians. This was a matter of both efficacy and propriety. The enormous embarrassment caused to governments by improper security activities produced a virtual consensus – at least outside of the British government – that greater political control must be exercised in order to minimize the chances of recurrence and at the same time brought the realization that, left to themselves, security intelligence agencies were no more likely

76

to be effective than any other public sector bureaucracy. During the same period security intelligence requirements were seen to become much more complex as events demanded the replacement of the one-dimensional Cold War security intelligence paradigm with a multi-dimensional one incorporating population movements, political violence and environmental threats. The new issues had a much higher potential for electoral impact and therefore clearer political direction of security intelligence became necessary.

It is now better appreciated that the internal logic of the information collection process is expansionist and limited only by resource con-straints. To the extent that information is collected on the principle that 'we don't know today what we might need tomorrow' this may pay no heed to criteria of efficacy – targeting realistically according to some clear notion of priorities and the seriousness of threats – or to propriety – surveillance may spread as widely and as intrusively as resources permit. For example, the first part of the CSIS mandate in the Act is to collect information '... to the extent that it is strictly necessary'.[3] On the face of it this is directly contrary to the internal logic of the process, particularly when one considers the highly future-oriented nature of some of CSIS's targets, for example, 'activities ... intended *ultimately* to lead to the destruction or overthrow by violence of the consti-tutionally established system of government in Canada'.[4] Is it possible to determine today what information is strictly necessary concerning activities with such long-term intentions?[5]

The stage of information processing is normally seen as a relatively technical question and one which has given rise to less debate than other stages of the overall process. However, there is one factor which in Canada has given rise to both efficacy and propriety concerns: the languages issue. Certainly during the early years of CSIS the failure to treat French equally and the carry-over of Anglophone dominance from the RCMP meant that both the efficacy of the organization and, as far as Francophones were concerned, the propriety of its behaviour were inadequate.[6]

Two issues at the production/analysis stage seem particularly relevant to this discussion. First, the status of analysts within security intelligence organizations. In order that the stages of collection and analysis do not unduly contaminate each other, people carrying out these roles have tended to be separated and collectors have generally enjoyed higher status than analysts. To the extent that the quality of analysis suffers as a consequence of this, the problems of a lack of political direction and co-ordination of all security intelligence agencies within a government will be increased. Secondly, another theme running through this discussion is whether the product is 'operational' or 'strategic'. The former is seen as being essentially case-oriented and often, by implication, relatively short-term in significance while the latter is seen as longer-term, wider in scope and produced for a more general government audience.[7]

Hence to the final stage, dissemination. Here a major issue, and one which received considerable attention at the Canadian Association for Security and Intelligence Studies (CASIS) conference in September 1989, is the contribution made by intelligence to policy-making. Most of the contributions to the panel on Strategic Planning and Effective Policy were to the effect that, in the words of Robert Jervis's paper, the connections between good intelligence and good policy 'are highly mediated'.[8] Oral contributors were somewhat blunter, suggesting that, to the extent that the two can be distinguished, intelligence contributes little to the making of policy but perhaps more to its implementation.

EMPHASIS ON PROPRIETY

It is hardly surprising that the public debate and academic contributions concerning the security intelligence question in Canada from 1976 onwards were dominated, at least for the subsequent decade, by concerns for the propriety of security intelligence operations. It was, after all, revelations that RCMP Security Service officers had been involved in bombings, burnings, break-ins and thefts rather than some spectacular intelligence failure that precipitated first the provincial inquiry in Quebec and then the federal inquiry under McDonald.

Therefore, although great care was taken by the McDonald Commission in discussing efficacy issues more thoroughly than they had been discussed before, the commission's reports maintained propriety as the essential value to be upheld. In the case of the three special studies published separately by the commission in 1980 this assessment is tentative because none of them addressed the question directly; it is rather in the nature of the subjects they discussed that concern mainly with propriety issues can be discerned.

J. Ll. J. Edwards' study centres on ministerial concern with the propriety of police or security operations and prosecutions, rather than the efficacy of those operations. For example, 'Where no evidence is brought to light of dubious police methods it is natural that the principle of non-interference remains sacrosanct.'[9]

C.E.S. Franks' study of Parliament points out that if parliaments fail to tackle the question of legislative mandates for security intelligence agencies so that the agencies enjoy no more legal powers than other citizens (what he calls the 'closed season' approach), then they may well find that governments will knowingly break the law ('poaching').[10] This study of the Canadian Parliament, which, like others, has limited time and access to relevant information, finds that the discussion of security matters was 'spotty and partial', but that Parliament had shown 'a consistent concern for the civil rights aspects of cases of security matters', if not for efficacy issues.[11]

M.L. Friedland's study of the legal dimensions of national security acknowledges both that attempts to meet security threats may themselves threaten civil liberties and that the law is only a part of the solution.[12] Although legal provisions might be seen as facilitators of effective security intelligence, the vagueness and uncertainties of the existing law were criticized primarily because they made it difficult for the police to obey the law.

The major report of the McDonald Commission itself was published in 1981. It said:

> Effective security within a democratic framework – that is the fundamental precept which has guided our diagnosis of past failures and wrongdoings in Canada's security system, as well as our prescription for reform of the system.[13]

Therefore it might seem inappropriate to allocate McDonald to this section of analyses in which propriety concerns predominate. The reason for so doing, however, is that McDonald made clear that, whenever there was a clash between the interests of efficacy and of propriety, then the latter should prevail:

> Where a choice must be made between efficiency in collecting intelligence and the fundamental principles of our system of government, the latter must prevail. It would be a serious mistake – indeed a tragic misjudgement – to compromise our system of democratic and constitutional government in order to gather information about threats to that system: this would be to opt for a cure worse than the disease.[14]

Once the CSIS Act was passed in 1984, early analyses of the Act continued to emphasize issues of propriety over those of efficacy. For example, Jean-Paul Brodeur, in one of the papers written for a seminar organized by the Security Intelligence Review Committee (SIRC) in October 1985, argued that the very nature of the threat assessment process was such that complete accuracy could be achieved only by massive invasion of civil freedoms, and therefore SIRC's job must be to secure the public accountability of CSIS rather than to concern itself with threats against Canadian security.[15]

Also in 1985, Geoff Weller concentrated on those aspects of the government of security intelligence which were associated with legislatures in Canada and the United States. As with Franks' study referred to above, this led to a predominant concern with propriety issues. Weller pointed out the strength of the argument, particularly in parliamentary systems, that the executive needs to be free from legislative interference in the security intelligence area in order to ensure effectiveness.[16] When he discussed the need for the development of criteria by which the performance of the intelligence services could be evaluated, and criticized the CSIS Act for its generality and limited coverage in terms of security intelligence agencies,[17] implicitly the emphasis was on propriety rather than efficacy.

Similarly, Murray Rankin discussed the particular impact of information policy on the security intelligence debate in two papers. In the first he noted that the traditional deference of Canadians aggravated the problems which were inherent in the development of 'national security' states with their obsessional secrecy.[18] In the second paper Rankin noted that the House of Commons Justice and Solicitor-General Committee had recommended the elimination of class exemptions from the Access to Information Act and their replacement by a test of 'significant injury'; also that the committee had made a similar recommendation for the removal of class exemptions from the Privacy Act. However, noting not only the real demands of national security but also the unparalleled concentration of power in the state, the tendency of national security agencies to cry wolf regarding disclosure, their excessive classification and the use of national security as an all-purpose cover for political embarrassments,[19] the author's argument was clearly that the system of official information is far too skewed towards efficacy values and away from propriety values.

The final examples within this section come from the Office of the Inspector-General. Established by the CSIS Act as one part of the external review structure for CSIS, its role has been primarily concerned with the propriety rather than the efficacy of CSIS actions. This emerged from this author's interviews with the first Inspector-General, Dick Gosse, and the then Acting Inspector-General, Michael de Rosenroll, in April 1988. The Inspector-General's own paper on the interpretation of the 'strictly necessary' criterion for CSIS information gathering reiterated this priority:

If there is any doubt about whether or not an investigation is 'strictly necessary' that doubt should be resolved in favour of the privacy of the individual and the investigation should *not* be conducted.[20]

Similarly, Joseph Ryan's study pointed out that suggesting ways of improving CSIS

is not a primary function of the Inspector General, however, and arises incidentally to his other tasks. That is, in the first instance, the Inspector General is mainly concerned with the propriety, rather than the efficacy, of the Service.[21]

However, the Inspector-General's contribution to efficacy is potentially significant. In the Act he is to review the Service's operational activities and report on any unreasonable or unnecessary exercises of power, which clearly relates to propriety, but he is also to monitor the Service's compliance with its operational policies and report on contraventions,[22] which is arguably as much about efficacy as it is about propriety. In his first Certificate Gosse noted that he might need to look at recruitment, training, resources and management in terms of their impact on operational activities,[23] and in his third Certificate he referred to his review of an internal economy, efficiency and effectiveness audit.[24]

EMPHASIS ON EFFICACY

Given the climate of the times following the revelations of abuses by RCMP agents, it is not surprising that public contributions to the security intelligence debate that took a position favouring efficacy over propriety were not numerous. However, given that the intelligence community itself has historically operated beyond the public gaze, it is reasonable to assume that the case for elevating effectiveness concerns was put strenuously within government circles, where, apparently, it received a sympathetic hearing.

In 1979, however, John Starnes, who was the first civilian head of the RCMP Security Service between 1970 and 1973, published a short piece in which he identified the urgent need for a review of Canada's existing internal security system. His list of what he saw as essential matters for new legislation included the machinery for independent audit,[25] which indicated that propriety issues had not been forgotten, but there was no discussion of the major propriety issues of surveillance methods and their control. The author concluded that 'the *overriding* issue [was] the nature of an effective Canadian internal security service'.[26]

When McDonald's main report was published in August 1981 the government issued a statement in which it announced that it had accepted the recommendation regarding separation of the Security Service from the RCMP; it also took issue with some of McDonald's conclusions. Throughout the statement efficacy considerations predominated. The main reason for the separation decision was the need for a specialized organization to respond to the 'increasingly sophisticated nature of threats to our security'.[27] A Planning and Transition Group was to plan in accordance with five basic principles: the first was to ensure an 'effective security-intelligence agency'; the second was to develop an adequate legal framework so that the agency could operate within the Rule of Law while recognizing the right of democratic dissent.[28] In contrast to McDonald, who had taken the view that activities not specifically authorized by law should not be undertaken by an agency (that is, discretion should be used narrowly), the government argued that, unless conduct was prohibited by law, it was not unlawful and 'in proper circumstances ... may be necessary and appropriate'[29] (that is, discretion may be interpreted broadly). The Commission's interpretation of the application of the rule of law, said the government, 'raises very serious questions for the effectiveness of law enforcement across the country'.[30] This statement was argued by some to be an attempt to discredit McDonald.[31] For the present purpose, it showed clearly where the government's priorities lay.

These were evidenced further when Bill C-157 was introduced into the Commons in May 1983. On a range of significant points it departed from McDonald's model: in particular both ministerial and external controls of the Security Service were weakened. With respect to the former, applications for judicial warrants for intrusive surveillance would not require ministerial approval, and, while the Minister could issue general directions to the Service, he could not override the Director's decisions on targeting or Service reports to the government.[32] In response to this attempt to institutionalize ministerial ignorance, Peter Russell commented: ' "Plausible deniability" should not be erected into a statutory principle'.[33] Perhaps the clearest example of the elevation of efficacy over propriety , however, came in Section 21 of the Bill:

> The Director and employees are justified in taking such reasonable actions as are reasonably necessary to enable them to perform the duties and functions of the Service.

In summary, C-157 set out to legalize those security intelligence activities, the legality of which had hitherto been in doubt, and to do so in a way that did not seriously impinge upon the autonomy of the Security Service either from political control or from external review. Since the government clearly believed that the controls proposed by McDonald would hinder effectiveness, it proposed a weaker set. Whereas McDonald proposed, first, an Advisory Committee on Security and Intelligence (ACSI) to review propriety issues, a Joint Parliamentary Committee to review issues both of efficacy and of propriety, and a Security Appeals Tribunal (SAT) to hear appeals against adverse clearance decisions, the Bill proposed an internal reviewer – the Inspector-General, whose brief would be primarily propriety issues – SIRC, which would combine external review and appeals functions, and no parliamentary committee. This structure was apparently designed as much to prevent ministerial embarrassment as to control the Security Service. The Bill's reception was so contentious that the government did not provide for a second reading debate in the Commons, instead sending it to the Senate. Their discussion is considered in the next section.

At SIRC's seminar in October 1985 David Charters' paper concerning the problem of accurately assessing foreign threats was the only one which dealt predominantly with efficacy. In part this may have been because of the general presumption that propriety issues do not weigh as heavily with foreign nationals as with one's own citizens.[34]

The first comprehensive examination of the efficacy of the new arrangements came, not surprisingly, from within government. In the wake of SIRC's third, and highly critical annual report and the exposure of the Boivin case,[35] the Solicitor-General appointed an Independent Advisory Team to examine two specific issues relating to CSIS: first, the impact on its efficacy of its recruitment, training and personnel management; and, second, its targeting, especially regarding the counter-subversion programme and the need to balance the needs of the state and the rights of individuals.[36] Space does not permit a detailed resumé of the Team's 34 recommendations but, for present purposes, it is significant that the majority (19) of them concerned essentially efficacy issues (nos. 1–7, 9–14, 17, 27–31), nine concerned issues which concerned both efficacy and propriety (nos. 8, 19–23, 32–34), and just six dealt with propriety issues alone (nos. 15, 16, 18, 24–26).

A number of writings in 1989 indicated a growing interest in efficacy issues. The Mackenzie Institute published a contribution to the debate that clearly takes the view that efficacy issues are the central ones. Its case is that CSIS's powers are inadequate and the restraints on it too severe, but the argument is somewhat flawed by the fact that evidence both of apparent CSIS successes – the refusal of visas and *persona non grata* declarations – and apparent failures – no solving of Air India, failure to detect agents of influence – is taken to support that. Confidence in the argument is further undermined when it declares that:

> Canada needs an intelligence service with the necessary powers and means to gather intelligence. In appropriate circumstances, electronic surveillance, intercept, confidential access, surreptitious search and related activities are essential for success, and should be recognized as such by Parliament.[37]

because Section 21 of the 1984 CSIS Act gave CSIS precisely these powers.

In a better argued piece, Ken Robertson notes that, from the overall perspective of the Canadian intelligence community, CSIS's product is relatively peripheral when compared with that of National Defence and the Communications Security Establishment (CSE) and that analysts' concentration on the political and external control of intelligence gathering has ignored efficacy issues. Robertson notes that inadequate attention has been given to the mechanism for the centralization and co-ordination of setting intelligence priorities, and thus the integration of CSIS into the community has been slow. Of the two subcommittees reporting to the Interdepartmental Committee on Security and Intelligence (ICSI), the Intelligence Advisory Committee (IAC) has co-ordination and task-ing responsibilities, while the other, the Security Advisory Committee (SAC), does not, meaning that CSIS has been self-tasking.[38] McDonald did not find this distinction between the two committees,[39] which suggests at the least some confusion at the top about precisely who is doing what. Robertson recommends that either the IAC or the SAC should play this co-ordinating role – in the light of his comment regarding SIRC's lack of efficacy concern,[40] it might be noted that SIRC has made a similar proposal in its recommendations to the five-year review.[41]

More recently, a number of contributions to the CASIS Conference in September 1989 signalled a similar interest – the papers by both Jean-Paul Brodeur and Robert Jervis concerned themselves with the nature of good intelligence and its integration into more effective security operations, including the relationship between intelligence work and law enforcement.

EQUAL EMPHASIS ON EFFICACY AND PROPRIETY

In the course of the debate, there were a series of pieces which attempted to give equal weight to both efficacy and propriety issues. In 1978 Richard French produced the first academic commentary on the revelations of 1976–77 and concluded:

> Thus the jerry-built network of half-hearted programs, rigid traditionalism, fragments of law, pious hopes, and a lot of whistling in the dark, which we laughingly called security policy, collapsed into a bitter aftermath of civil liberties violated, public confidence shaken, and the effectiveness of the Security Service eroded.[42]

Issues of efficacy and of propriety were seen to be inextricably bound up. For example, the organizational principles of need-to-know and plausible deniability which are at the heart of security intelligence agencies might serve to maintain the secrecy and effectiveness of operations but they also restricted the flow of information and thereby reduced the quality of decisions.[43]

The special Senate Committee which deliberated on the unpopular C-157 actually called its Report 'Delicate Balance' to indicate its conviction that issues of efficacy and of propriety were inseparable. Just as McDonald swung the pendulum of debate to the propriety side of the balance, and the government swung it to the other side in C-157, so the Senate committee sent it back again towards the propriety side, though not as far as McDonald's position. The Senate report is included in this section not because its position was particularly well thought out, but rather because it attempted to cover all the possible angles. For example,

> There is a very basic tension between the concepts of collective and individual security, and it must be addressed at virtually every stage of the formation and operation of a security intelligence agency. To a significant degree, it must be noted, individual rights depend upon maintenance of collective security. Both ends are desirable, but they also make competing demands on the institutions of a democratic state. Either end, by itself, could be easily attained, but at great expense to the other. The crucial task is to arrive at an appropriate balance of the two.[44]

This raises as many questions as it answers. Is it being consistent to argue that individual rights depend 'significantly' on collective security, while arguing that there is a 'very basic tension' between the two? Can either collective security or individual rights be 'easily' attained? More fundamentally, while there are certainly numerous examples of individual rights being sacrificed to notions of 'collective security', are there examples of collective security being sacrificed by an excess of individual rights? Surely while the excessive demands of the former have been seen to *necessarily* sacrifice individual rights, 'excessive' individual rights do not necessarily endanger collective security. The final sentence in the quotation above reflects the Senate's acceptance of the common notion that efficacy and propriety are in a constant sum relationship, an issue which will be taken up in the conclusion.

In one of the papers written for SIRC's 1985 seminar, Stuart Farson took up this very point and argued that this 'balance' perspective was wrong since compromises between efficacy and propriety issues were inherently dangerous and might simply achieve neither. It would be better, he suggested, to see both as objectives to be attained (implicitly, therefore, they are in a variable sum relationship), which was the approach adopted by McDonald.[45] Farson regretted that the legislative structure failed to enact McDonald's proposals because, for example, it was uncertain at that time to what extent, if at all, the Inspector-General and SIRC would examine issues both of efficacy and of propriety.[46]

The following year Geoff Weller did attempt some preliminary assessment of the new structure both in terms of efficacy and of propriety and concluded that the changes were likely to have a 'marked beneficial effect on the efficiency of the CSIS in the long run ... [and] are also likely to enhance accountability'.[47] Although some of his comments about recruitment and liaison with other agencies were to prove a little optimistic in the light of the events of 1987, they were based on a variable rather than constant sum view of the relationship between efficacy and propriety.

A more recent assessment has been produced by Stuart Farson, in which he restates his earlier argument that efficacy and propriety are in a reciprocal relationship. The failure to understand this, he argues, has resulted in an overemphasis on formal methods of organizational control to the exclusion of informal methods. Thus the pendulum might have been swung back from pre-McDonald days, but to the extent that efficacy has been relatively ignored, this might have adverse longer-term consequences for civil liberties.[48] A specific example of the argument is the closure of CSIS's Counter Subversion Branch in 1987. Farson argues that this might well reduce the noticeable amount of abuse, but for the wrong reasons. It will do so because counter-subversion operations will lose out in the competition for organizational resources, and not because the hearts and minds of people within the organization have changed.[49] It might be argued that this dichotomizes unnecessarily the explanations of organizational change. Structural and cultural change are not necessarily counterposed to one another; notwithstanding the well-researched ability of the organizational culture in police and security organizations to subvert formal reforms, in so far as both types of change work in the same direction they can reinforce each other in the longer term.[50]

Finally, what of the contribution to this debate of SIRC itself? Clearly, not all will agree with the proposition that SIRC has given equal attention to issues of efficacy and of propriety.[51] There is evidence to sustain the argument, however. As we have seen, McDonald foresaw that the Advisory Committee would concentrate primarily on issues of propriety, especially since he proposed that the Parliamentary Committee deal equally with issues of efficacy and of propriety. With no Parliamentary Committee established in 1984 there might have been some expectation that SIRC would take on efficacy issues (along with appeals) but this expectation would be more likely to be fulfilled to the extent that SIRC adopted a variable rather than constant sum view of the efficacy/propriety relationship. Its statutory mandate certainly has the potential to examine both issues: Section 38 'to review generally the performance' of the Service includes implicitly both efficacy and propriety. Section 40 discusses the review of Service actions to ensure that they comply with regulations and involve no unnecessary or unreasonable exercise of powers, which leans towards propriety issues. Section 41 providing the mandate to hear complaints could imply effectiveness issues but is more likely in practice to concern propriety.

To the extent that SIRC reacts to public concerns then its agenda will be dominated by efficacy or propriety issues in proportion as they become public and, since SIRC's credibility depends on its ability to allay public concerns, it cannot really determine whether efficacy or propriety issues predominate. If one looks at SIRC's own proactive agenda of review, then it is arguable that, during the last five years, it has concerned efficacy as much as propriety. The counter-subversion study conducted during 1986–87 concluded that the branch responsible should be disbanded, and did so primarily on propriety grounds, although it might have been argued that it was hardly effective for organizational resources to be diverted to what were minimal threats.[52] On the other hand, the following year's counter-terrorism study began with four questions: first, is CSIS effective in identifying terrorist threats; second, is CSIS working within the law; third, is CSIS unreasonably or unnecessarily using its powers; and fourth, is the statutory framework appropriate for CSIS activities?[53] The first of these raises an efficacy issue, the second and third raise propriety issues, and the fourth has an element of both.

SIRC's first annual report had identified six priority areas for research, in only one of which (exchange of information with other agencies) did SIRC specifically identify a concern with propriety. The other five all raised as many issues of efficacy as of propriety: personnel recruitment/training, use of human sources, use of open sources, budgetary priorities and statistical analysis of resource allocation.[54] The following year's annual report summarized the year's work by dealing briefly with some propriety issues – CSIS compliance with the law and targeting – and then predominantly with efficacy issues – recruitment, civilianization, relations with the RCMP, bilingualism and personnel management (especially in Quebec) and security screening.[55] The following year's annual report set out to present a more overall view of CSIS operations and was also the most critical to date, particularly on counter-subversion targeting and civilianization.[56] It was this that led directly to the establishment of the Independent Advisory Team, as we have seen, and can be seen to concern issues of efficacy as much as those of propriety.

In 1987 SIRC published other reports which bore directly on efficacy questions. First, it produced an expurgated copy of a paper it had prepared setting out the constituent parts of Canada's security and intelligence community.[57] As we have seen, various writers have argued that the failure of the 1984 structure to incorporate all of the community has been a factor inhibiting both the efficacy and the propriety of security intelligence operations. The second was a special report to the Solicitor-General concerning two main issues: the status of French within CSIS and staff relations in Quebec. While the first might appear to be essentially a propriety issue, in a bilingual nation it had also major implications for organizational effectiveness; the second was clearly an efficacy issue.[58] SIRC's special report on the Boivin case, on the other hand, was entirely propriety-oriented since it attempted no evaluation of the efficacy of human sources and concentrated on the propriety of CSIS's actions.[59] Finally SIRC has made its recommendations to the five-year parliamentary review of the CSIS Act.[60] As with the IAT Report, no effort will be made here to examine those in detail, but a tentative classification is offered: of the 31 recommendations, five relate to efficacy issues (4, 7, 13, 25, 26), seven to mixed issues (1, 2, 10, 19, 22–24) and 19 to propriety issues (3,

5, 6, 8, 9, 11, 12, 14–18, 20, 21, 27–31). At the last this appears to dent the overall argument and the wisdom of placing SIRC's contribution in this category, but taking into account all of SIRC's contributions over the last five years the judgement still appears defensible.

CONCLUSION

First, the debate between those for whom the efficacy of security intelligence operations is the priority and those for whom propriety is the fundamental value will continue. If for no other reason, this is because too many of the concepts at the centre of the debate – propriety, democracy, subversion, threat – are essentially contested. Their meaning has an evaluative component and there is no 'scientific' way of establishing some 'essential' meaning.

Second, whether issues of efficacy or propriety are being discussed, the statutory framework established in Canada is deficient in one central respect, that is, its coverage is limited to just one security intelligence agency and therefore assists neither the internal co-ordination nor the external control of that community.

If the first point regarding the futility of pursuing some 'final' resolution is accepted, then what is to be done? Left to itself the debate will develop as a series of temporary solutions to the situation prevailing at the time the solution is called for. As we have seen, the public debate in Canada in the early years was dominated by propriety concerns and the passage of the Canadian Security Intelligence Service Act 1984 reflected one temporary resolution of it. The new institutions have developed since then in ways which have made further contributions to the debate and now the 1990 review of the Act will mark another temporary resolution. What happens will depend on the balance of political forces at the time. In 1983–84 the 'insiders' (government and security service) were unable to enact their preferred measure (C-157) because of the still greater concern with propriety following McDonald. One might predict that, barring any major revelation of impropriety during 1990, the insiders may then be able to achieve more of their objectives.

The debate about security intelligence, therefore, will, and in a democracy should, always be a political one, but can that debate be advanced somewhat by a more analytical approach? This essay has covered a number of different perspectives concerning the debate between propriety and efficacy; can we at least clarify what the argument is about so that the way ahead might become more apparent?

First, 'what you see depends on where you sit'. Other things being equal, outsiders are likely to be relatively more concerned with propriety. Joe Fletcher found that, contrary to expectations generated by work on 'democratic elitism', elite groups were more likely to support wiretapping, however minimal the threat, than citizens in general.[61] Insiders might well explain this in terms of outsiders' relative ignorance of the needs of government in general and security intelligence in particular, but we should expect that the people with the greatest stake in the institutions and procedures of the state are likely to have the greatest faith in their workability and concern with their efficacy.

On closer examination, of course, we find that not all insiders share precisely the same view. At its most basic we need to be aware of the likely differences between people in policy or supervisory roles compared with those in lower-level operational positions. Once some degree of accountability has been established we might expect to find greater concern with propriety at senior levels, where contact with influential outsiders is most likely and political responsibility is higher. At operational levels we would expect to find, as with policing, a much greater concern with 'getting the job done', if necessary by application of the Ways and Means Act.

Other distinctions emerge when it comes to consideration of the sources of information and the intelligence product. Although there is a general recognition that security intelligence agencies need both covert and open sources of information, the recommendations of commissions and policy-makers reflect their belief that agencies make inadequate use of the latter while conversely at an operational level it would appear that greater faith is invested in the former. Similarly, while senior levels and politicians emphasize their preference for more strategic intelligence, the agencies themselves, especially at the operational levels, seem much happier preparing case-oriented intelligence.

A final dimension required in order to clarify the debate is that of time. When people have been at cross-purposes in this debate, it has often been because of the different time-scales implicit in their arguments. At the risk of over-simplifying, if one takes a short-term view of security intelligence operations then it is possible to point to a basic incompatibility between efficacy and propriety. If an officer does not break a speed limit and loses contact with a target, it is not efficacious. If intercept tapes are erased in order to comply with a 'strictly necessary' standard for the retention of information so that the tapes cannot be reviewed at a later date for other purposes, that is not efficacious.

On the other hand, if one takes a long-term view then there can be no incompatibility between efficacy and propriety in security intelligence operations because the former depends largely on the latter. In a democracy this may seem rather obvious but it is worth restating: without the trust of citizens that police or security officers will act properly, the flow of information upon which they largely depend will diminish steadily. As it does so, the pressure on those officers to get results leads them to use ever more coercive or intrusive methods in an attempt to compensate. More frequent impropriety, in turn, causes a further decline in citizen trust and so a vicious downward spiral is established.[62]

In summary, aggregating these various distinctions, we find that a crucial problem has been the assumption that efficacy and propriety are to be found on a single dimension, so that movements toward one inevitably lead away from the other – a constant sum relationship. Rather, it becomes clear that separate dimensions are required for efficacy and for propriety. The first is characterized by the short-term, insider (especially lower-level operational personnel) perspective which emphasizes the value of covert rather than open sources and produces operational intelligence. This perspective is closer to that found in policing and views the main effect of oversight mechanisms as inhibiting operations. Hence the relationship between efficacy and propriety is seen as constant sum.

The second is characterized by the long-term, outsider (plus more senior, managerial personnel) perspective which places much more value on open sources and prefers to produce strategic intelligence. This is further removed than the first from police models of intelligence, and external oversight mechanisms are seen as valuable since they enhance the legitimacy of intelligence agencies. Hence the relationship between efficacy and propriety is variable sum; increases in one do not necessarily reduce the other and they may actually both be increased. These two dimensions illustrate two dominant perspectives on security intelligence.[63] Clearly these are meant to indicate major tendencies rather than hard and fast distinctions.

It is to be hoped that the implications of this argument are clear. As Canada – and other democracies – assess their security intelligence requirements for the 1990s, the siren call of the proposition that propriety may have to be traded in order to achieve effectiveness must be resisted. While there is no certainty that such a trade will pay off positively in the short term, it is certain that in the long term the pay-off for democracy will be negative.

NOTES

I would like to thank Ken Robertson and Joe Sim, who commented very helpfully on an earlier draft of this piece.

1. *Canadian Security Intelligence Service Act*, 32–33 (1984), Ch. 21, s. 12.
2. For example, see Justice D.C. McDonald, *Commission of Inquiry Concerning Certain Activities of the RCMP*, Second Report: *Freedom and Security Under the Law* (Ottawa: Minister of Supply and Services, 1981), pp. 101–2. (Hereafter referred to as McDonald.)
3. *Canadian Security Intelligence Service Act*, s.12.
4. Ibid., s.2.
5. This question is discussed in Inspector General, ' "Strictly Necessary": a legal constraint in the section 12 mandate of the Canadian Security Intelligence Service', April 1987.
6. Security Intelligence Review Committee, *Closing the Gaps: official languages and staff relations in the CSIS* (Ottawa: Minister of Supply and Services).
7. Security Intelligence Review Committee, *Annual Report for 1987–88* (Ottawa: Minister of Supply and Services), pp. 35–6.
8. R. Jervis, 'Strategic Intelligence and Effective Policy', paper presented to CASIS Conference, Ottawa, 1989, p. 5.
9. J. Ll. J. Edwards, *Ministerial Responsibility for National Security as it Relates to the Offices of Prime Minister, Attorney General and Solicitor General of Canada* (Ottawa: Minister of Supply and Services, 1980), p. 97.
10. C.E.S. Franks, *Parliament and Security Matters* (Ottawa: Minister of Supply and Services, 1980), pp. 3–4.
11. Ibid., p 65.
12. M.L. Friedland, *National Security: the Legal Dimensions* (Ottawa: Minister of Supply and Services, 1980), p. 123.
13. McDonald, p. 47.
14. Ibid., p. 841.
15. J-P. Brodeur, 'On Evaluating Threats to the National Security of Canada and to the Civil Rights of Canadians', presented to SIRC Seminar, Meech Lake, Oct. 1985, pp. 7–11.
16. G.R. Weller, 'Legislative Oversight of Intelligence Services in Canada and the United States', presented to the American Political Science Association, New Orleans, Aug. 1985, p. 16.
17. Ibid., pp. 21–5.
18. M. Rankin, 'National Security: Information, Accountability, and the CSIS', *University of Toronto Law Journal*, Vol. 36, No. 3 (Summer 1986), pp. 249–85.
19. M. Rankin, 'Reporting on National Security: the "Delicate Balance" Revisited', presented to Conference on Domestic Security, Osgoode Hall Law School, May 1987, pp. 11–17.
20. Inspector General, 1987, op. cit., p. 29, emphasis in the original.
21. J.F. Ryan, 'The Inspector General of the CSIS,' *Conflict Quarterly*, Vol. IX, No. 3 (Spring 1989), p. 40.
22. *Canadian Security Intelligence Service Act*, s. 30 and s. 33(2).
23. *Certificate of the Inspector General of the CSIS*, 1985, p. 17.
24. *Certificate of the Inspector General of the CSIS*, 1987, p. 26.
25. J. Starnes, 'Canadian Internal Security: The Need for a New Approach, a New Organisation', *Canadian Defence Quarterly* (Summer 1979), pp. 22–3.
26. Ibid., p. 26, emphasis added.
27. Solicitor General of Canada, *Statement of the Government of Canada on the Publication of the Report of the Commission of Inquiry Concerning Certain Activities of the RCMP* 25 Aug. 1981, p. 3.

28. Ibid., p. 4.
29. Ibid., p. 5.
30. Ibid., p. 6.
31. M. Mandel, 'Discrediting the McDonald Commission', *Canadian Forum*, Vol. LXI, No. 716 (March 1982), pp. 14–17.
32. *An Act to Establish the Canadian Security Intelligence Service* (May 1983), ss. 6–7.
33. P.H. Russell, 'The Proposed Charter for a Civilian Intelligence Agency: An Appraisal', *Canadian Public Policy*, 9 (1983), p. 334.
34. For example, see Canadian Civil Liberties Association, *Brief regarding Bill C-9*, House of Commons, Standing Committee on Justice and Legal Affairs, April 1984, Issue No. 11A, p. 13. D. Charters, 'Real or Perceived Threats to the Security of Canada: By What Criteria Should the Threat be Assessed?', presented to SIRC Seminar, Meech Lake, October 1985.
35. A.S. Farson, 'Old Wine, New Bottles and Fancy Labels: The Rediscovery of Organizational Culture in the Control of Intelligence', in G. Barak (ed.) *Crimes by the Capitalist State* (New York: State University of New York Press, 1989); P. Gill, 'Defining Subversion: The Canadian Experience', *Public Law* (Winter, 1989), pp.617–36.
36. Independent Advisory Team on the CSIS, *People and Process in Transition* (Ottawa: Minister of Supply and Services), p. 1.
37. A. Kavchak, *Canadian National Security and the CSIS Act* (Toronto: Mackenzie Institute, 1989), p. 15.
38. K.G. Robertson, 'Canadian Intelligence Policy' (University of Reading, 1989), pp. 2–12.
39. McDonald, 1981, p. 849.
40. Robertson, op. cit., p. 12.
41. Security Intelligence Review Committee, *Amending the CSIS Act: Proposals for the Special Committee of the House of Commons* (Ottawa: Minister of Supply and Services, 1989), pp. 16–18. This issue is addressed further in Stuart Farson, 'Propriety, Efficacy and Balance: A Preliminary Appraisal of Canada's "New", "Improved" Administrative Security Program', in P. Hanks and J.D. McCamus (eds.), *National Security: Surveillance and Accountability in a Democratic Society* (Cowansville, Quebec: Les Editions Yvon Blais Inc., 1989), pp. 144–6.
42. R.D. French, *The RCMP and the Management of National Security* (Toronto: Institute for Research on Public Policy, 1978), p. 76.
43. Ibid., p. 39.
44. Special Committee of the Senate on the CSIS, *Delicate Balance: a Security Intelligence Service in a Democratic Society*, para. 23.
45. A.S. Farson, 'Countering the Security Threat in the 1980s: McDonald's legacy and the need for effective and efficient control', presented to SIRC Seminar, Meech Lake, October 1985, pp. 2–3.
46. Ibid., pp. 33–4.
47. G.R. Weller, 'Democracy, the CSIS and the Future', presented to the Association for Canadian Studies in Australia and New Zealand, Brisbane, May 1986, p. 21.
48. Farson, 'Old Wine', op. cit., pp. 12–13. In another article Stuart Farson develops his argument regarding efficacy and propriety in the particular context of Canada's developing administrative security program: 'Propriety, Efficacy and Balance', op. cit., 1989.
49. Farson, 'Old Wine', p. 37.
50. For a different perspective on the closure of the Counter Subversion Branch see Gill, 'Defining Subversion', op. cit.
51. For example, Robertson, op. cit., p. 12. For an evaluation of SIRC's performance up to 1988 see P. Gill, 'Symbolic or Real? The Impact of the Canadian Security Intelligence Review Committee, 1984–88', *Intelligence and National Security*, Vol. 4, No. 3 (July 1989), pp. 550–75.
52. Security Intelligence Review Committee, *Annual Report for 1986–87* (Ottawa:

Minister of Supply and Services, 1987), p. 40.

53. Security Intelligence Review Committee, *Annual Report for 1987–88*, op. cit., pp. 27–28.
54. Security Intelligence Review Committee, *Annual Report for 1984–85* (Ottawa: Minister of Supply and Services, 1985), p.21.
55. Security Intelligence Review Committee, *Annual Report for 1985–86* (Ottawa: Minister of Supply and Services, 1986), pp. 4–10.
56. Security Intelligence Review Committee, *Annual Report for 1986–87*, op. cit.
57. Security Intelligence Review Committee, *The Security and Intelligence Network in the Government of Canada: A Description*, (Expurgated Copy), (SIRC, January 1987). Later published as Appendix C in SIRC, *Annual Report for 1987–88*, op. cit.
58. Security Intelligence Review Committee, *Closing the Gaps*, op. cit.
59. Security Intelligence Review Committee, s.54 *Report to the Solicitor General on CSIS Use of its Investigative Powers Regarding the Labour Movement*, March 1988.
60. Security Intelligence Review Committee, *Amending the CSIS Act*, op. cit.
61. J.F. Fletcher, 'Mass and Elite Attitudes about Wiretapping in Canada: implications for democratic theory and politics', *Public Opinion Quarterly*, 53 (1989), pp. 225–45.
62. This might be compared with the three models of domestic security intelligence agencies: (1) 'bureau of domestic intelligence', (2) political police', (3) 'internal security state' developed by William W. Keller, *The Liberals and J. Edgar Hoover* (Princeton: Princeton University Press, 1989, esp. Chs. 1 and 5. Similarly, for example, Ken Robertson discusses how clear threat identification both helps the effectiveness of the agency and may also prevent abuses of power in 'Intelligence, Terrorism and Civil Liberties,' *Conflict Quarterly*, 7 (Spring 1987), p. 58.
63. This is similar to the split between 'public' and 'private' discourses suggested by Farson, 'Propriety, Efficacy and Balance', op. cit., pp. 129–30.

7

Review versus Oversight

JOHN STARNES

This essay probably would not have had to be commissioned if the Security Intelligence Review Committee (SIRC) in their annual reports had not used the word 'oversight' instead of 'review'. In the 1985–86 report the word is used 26 times in 45 pages, in the 1986–87 report 25 times in 69 pages and in the 1987–88 report 14 times in 60 pages. Altogether, the word was used 65 times in 174 pages. I suppose one can take encouragement, however, from the fact that the incidence of the continued use by SIRC of the inauspicious word appears to be diminishing rather than increasing.

The word 'oversight' is not used once in the legislation which created SIRC, whereas the word 'review' is used extensively, and Part III of the Act which, *inter alia*, sets out the mandate of SIRC, is headed 'Review'. It should be noted that the original Act (Bill C-9) has now been split into two separate pieces of legislation: Bill C-23, 'an Act to establish the Canadian Security Intelligence Service (CSIS Act), and Bill S-7, 'an Act respecting enforcement in relation to certain security and related offences' (Security Offences Act). This has resulted in a re-ordering of paragraphs and parts. For example, Part IV of C-23 is now entitled 'Review by Parliament' and has become paragraph 56(1) and (2).

It seems quite clear that SIRC's use of the word oversight has been deliberate, although their reasons for seeking to change the intent of the legislation and their mandate for doing so in such a way, and at such a relatively early stage in their term of office, are far from clear. The matter deserves discussion, especially at a time when the membership (including the chairmanship) of the committee has changed and the governing legislation is being reviewed in accordance with Section 69 of the CSIS Act.

SIRC apparently have tried to argue that the word 'oversight' is synonymous with 'review'. Indeed, I understand they even sought and obtained a legal opinion to that effect. However, instead of a legal opinion they should have sought the advice of a qualified etymologist. It is difficult to argue convincingly that 'review' is identical and co-extensive in sense and usage with 'oversight' in the face of the very different definitions given to the two English words in various reputable dictionaries. The Random House (unabridged edition, 1981), Webster's and Oxford dictionaries make this clear. All three dictionaries define 'review' to mean to view again, to survey again and to take a retrospective view, and 'oversight' to mean supervision, management or control. Indeed, one US dictionary uses the word to describe 'an elected administrative officer in some States, often a member of a board governing a county'.

A member of SIRC (Mr Blais), at the 1988 annual conference of the Canadian Association for Security and Intelligence Studies held in Windsor, raised the matter in the following terms:

> A mild controversy has arisen relating to our responsibilities. It relates to the timing of our inquiries in relation to the CSIS role. Is the Committee, in discharging its responsbilities, limited to a 'review process', an *ex-post-facto* revisiting of CSIS activities, or is it a 'watchdog' over the ongoing activities of the Service? The Committee has viewed its responsibilities as indeed being retrospective, but having an immediate dimension as well. Since a review of the performance of the Service clearly requires ongoing investigation of the activities of the Service, it would be unacceptable to Parliament, in our view, to refrain from probing ongoing activities of the Service. In addition the Statute requires that we must 'review directions issued by the Minister' to the Service relating to the management and control of the organization. It would be difficult to review such directions if we were unable to follow through on their implementation in ongoing operations. The complaints process may well bring us to review active field operations as they are being conducted. It would be irresponsible for the Committee, or indeed for the Service, to suggest that they be suspended pending our findings unless the evidence of improper activity is available at the outset. Other examples can be given of like nature showing that while the Act may speak of 'Review', it does not limit our activities to closed files, or completed operations.

It seems to me this statement evades the real issue: the difference between 'review' and 'oversight'. If SIRC believe the two words to be synonymous, why did they bother to act in a manner calculated to raise doubts about the proposition? The use of the word 'review' throughout the legislation does not seem to have inhibited their work, nor have they argued in any of their reports that it has. There is nothing in the Act that has prevented SIRC from making any inquiries about CSIS's activities or denied them access to its staff, files, *modus operandi*, or ongoing operations. Their reports are eloquent proof of this.

SIRC's persistence in this matter suggests there may be more at stake than a mere question of semantics or a rather silly attempt to argue that the word 'review' really means 'oversight' and vice versa. Ineluctably one is drawn to the conclusion that members of the committee may have hoped that their continued use of the word 'oversight' to describe their role eventually might become generally accepted and reflected in whatever changes may be made as a result of the five-year review of the CSIS Act.

At the same time there have been strong hints from their actions that SIRC may be interpreting their self-given 'oversight role' as meaning they have the right (and the duty) to make comments and recommendations on any matters touching upon security and intelligence questions affecting Canada. This certainly was not the intention of those legislating for the establishment of SIRC and there are sound reasons for opposing the idea.

There also have been hints in their reports that they may envisage a future role for SIRC, within the context of oversight, well beyond that provided for in the governing legislation. For example, in their 1986–87 Report they wrote:

> Another issue we can already see on the horizon is the oversight function itself. The CSIS Act broke new ground when it created this Committee to monitor the service. But there are other major players in the Canadian security and intelligence community and they are not in the purview of any independent oversight.

In their 1985–86 Annual Report they gratuitously raised the question of whether CSIS should, 'be allowed to conduct information-gathering operations abroad', rather naively suggesting this might be accomplished by a simple amendment to the CSIS Act. More recently, I understand, SIRC have commissioned, with public money, a study of the pros and cons of a Canadian Secret Intelligence Service, an agency which would be akin to the British SIS, the American CIA or the First Chief Directorate of the KGB.

In their 1987–88 annual report they spread wide their umbrella of 'oversight' to include a superficial discussion of the pros and cons of establishing an independent Canadian Office of National Assessments similar to the Australian Office of National Assessments. Wisely, they have been cautious in raising a matter that so clearly lies outside their legislated terms of reference. On this score they wrote:

We want to make it clear that we are not at this point recommending imitation of the Australian model. We have not had an opportunity to examine this matter thoroughly enough for that. We also recognize significant differences between APB's role in CSIS (the Analysis and Production Branch of CSIS) the ONA's role in Australia. But we believe a separate agency is an option the Government might consider if it shares our view that it needs more basic intelligence.

There are, of course, various other options.

Among other things, one is struck by the assumption, implicit in the statement, that SIRC can make recommendations for a major restructuring of the government's arrangements for using and assessing information/intelligence from all sources to produce reports and assessments relevant not only to Canada's internal security but to a wide range of international political, military, scientific, economic and environmental matters at both tactical and strategic levels.

As members of SIRC would have discovered had they had more time to reflect on the matter, the question of establishing an Office of National Estimates (similar to the US body), whether in the Cabinet Offices, as an independent agency or within an appropriate government department, such as External Affairs, has been discussed for years. Certainly, when I was the Chairman of the Canadian Joint Intelligence Committee between 1958 and 1962 the matter was actively debated, although never resolved, largely because ministers never felt an urgent need for it and because of interdepartmental rivalries. Perhaps things have changed in the intervening years, although I rather doubt it.

Wearing their 'oversight' bowler hat, SIRC also sought to explain to the public, in an appendix (C) to the 1987–88 annual report, what they have chosen to call 'The Intelligence Network in Canada'. As they correctly point out, the Canadian Security Intelligence Service has certain responsibilities spelled out by legislation, while a key player is none the less only a part of the network. The appendix is based on a paper prepared by officials in 1987 for SIRC to help them to understand better how CSIS fits into the Canadian security/intelligence community. SIRC 'thought it would be of interest to the public'. As they point out, the material presented is by no means comprehensive; 'drastic trimming was required because much of the information in the original paper is secret'.

Despite censorship, Appendix C to SIRC's 1987–88 Annual Report is useful and informative. However, the question is whether it was wise and appropriate for SIRC to have become the medium between the government and the public for informing Canadians on matters lying well beyond its authority and competence. In my view, such an official paper should be issued only under government auspices, probably under the imprimatur of the Privy Council Office.

One is left with the distinct impression that present members of SIRC rather fancy dealing with mysterious matters of this kind, which now clearly lie outside their remit, and that they may be thinking of a greatly enlarged role for the Committee; a kind of super-oversight body. If a 'watchdog' or 'oversight' role is to be taken to mean that SIRC also should have statutory responsibility for commenting on and making recommendations about such diverse, complex matters as the creation of a Canadian Secret Intelligence Service, an Independent Office of National Estimates, or the intelligence activities of agencies and departments other than CSIS, such as CSE, then I strongly object on grounds of principle and for quite pragmatic reasons, to be discussed later.

It seems clear to me, having spoken to a number of the legislators who participated in the drafting of the CSIS Act, that with the exception of one senator who mentioned a role for SIRC akin to that carried out by US House and Senate intelligence committees and the President's Intelligence Oversight Board, there was little enthusiasm for the American concept of oversight when it was discussed behind closed doors. When the language of the Act was being considered, therefore, the choice of the word 'review' appears to have been quite deliberate. It is worth noting, also, that none of the witnesses appearing before the Special Senate Committee proposed an oversight role or even raised the question.

My objections to the use of the word 'oversight' rather than 'review' to describe and govern the Committee's activities are twofold: (a) the use of the word 'oversight' is an ill-considered attempt to borrow from the Americans an executive and congressional oversight structure inappropriate to the Canadian parliamentary system of government and, (b) the concept of oversight as opposed to review inevitably tends to draw SIRC into policy and operational decisions which, in the Canadian system, properly should remain those of the executive arm of government, thus gradually making it increasingly difficult for SIRC to carry out their primary task of independent, unbiased audit.

There are important differences between the roles of the US legislative committees and the President's Intelligence Oversight Board and the role Parliament assigned to SIRC, just as there are important differences between the political and constitutional settings in which the US and Canadian committees work. The US committees and the President's Oversight Board have the concept of oversight firmly embedded in their mandates. These legislative bodies and the President's Oversight Board are empowered to approve budgets and to become directly involved in operational and management decisions, before the fact. SIRC members are not legislators, perform no budgetary function *vis-à-vis* CSIS and are empowered only to carry out reviews after the fact.

The US legislative oversight structure has been in place for over ten years. On the whole it appears to have worked reasonably well, although there now are signs of uneasiness about the burgeoning bureaucracy supporting the structure and the inevitable lobbying, not just to expand their power and budgets, but also to use them for political purposes. However, on the central issue of working out appropriate, practical ways of monitoring the activities of the various intelligence and security agencies by the executive and the legislative branches of government, the Americans have succeeded. Public confidence has been restored and new ideas and a sense of direction have been brought to the US intelligence community's work.

In the introductory chapter to their 1986–87 Report SIRC stated:

> Oversight does not mean that we are a kind of board of directors for CSIS. We do not hesitate to give advice, privately when circumstances dictate and publicly, when we can, through our annual reports and in testimony before Parliamentary committees. ... But we do not set policy or issue orders. Nor would we want to, for that would make us active players in security intelligence and remove the freedom to criticize that is our *raison d'être.*

Yet, if the US concept of 'oversight' was to become entrenched in the Canadian legislation, either by substituting the word 'oversight' for 'review' or in other ways, the unique character of the Canadian experiment represented in the CSIS Act would be destroyed. That would be a great pity. Indeed, in some respects I think the Canadian legislation may be regarded in other countries as a paradigm.

I believe the Canadian experiment has been worthwhile and should be allowed to develop untrammelled by the experience south of the 49th parallel by an intelligence community, fifty times larger, richer and more complicated and varied than the Canadian community. SIRC have performed a very useful task at a time when the new security agency experienced a number of problems. I am convinced SIRC's reports have helped to restore public confidence in CSIS and to improve the organization in various ways. However, SIRC would be committing a disservice to the Canadian public if they were to suggest that the Committee should be empowered to approve budgets and become any more involved than they now are in policy, operational and management decisions.

In seeking to offer public comment and recommendations on matters outside their mandate such as whether Canada ought to have a Secret Intelligence Service to collect information outside Canada, an independent Office of National Assessments or whether there should be independent supervision of the intelligence activities of various departments and agencies other than CSIS (for example the Communications Security Establishment in National Defence or the Political and International Security Branch in External Affairs), SIRC are probably only trying to fill a vacuum largely created by ministerial indifference, inertia and inaction. In my view SIRC did not show good judgement in yielding to the temptation to fill the vacuum and to use their annual reports to float such ideas before the public. The idea for the creation of a Canadian Secret Intelligence Service, for example, if it ever were to be acted upon, would represent a major foreign policy decision; perhaps one of the more important such decisions taken in the last two decades. It hardly seems appropriate for such an important suggestion to be floated in an offhand manner in an annual report made by a body created principally to ensure the Canadian Security Intelligence Committee acts within its mandate and the law and to provide a quasi-judicial forum for hearing complaints relating to security matters. If SIRC feel strongly on some point which comes to their attention through this work on CSIS, but which obviously lies outside their purview, the proper course surely is to raise it privately with ministers and senior officials. Only the government has the power to take the executive action necessary for the first step toward implementing of ideas such as the creation of an agency covertly to gather intelligence outside Canada or an Office of National Assessments.

If the government were to decide it was in the public interest to have some means of carrying out independent audit of the activities of other intelligence bodies such as the Canadian Security Establishment, it seems unlikely that they would favour having this done by SIRC. There are obvious differences between the tasks performed by CSIS and CSE, as illustrated in Appendix C to SIRC's 1987–88 Annual Report, calling for skills and knowledge on the part of those chosen to review their work different from the attributes of those chosen to review CSIS's work.

CSE is described by SIRC as having a twin mandate; 'signals intelligence and the security of communications and data processing in federal agencies'. In the wicked world in which we live the task of providing secure communications within Canada and abroad for all Canadian government messages requiring secrecy is probably the more urgent, if not the more important, part of their mandate. If Canada did not already have a well-established capability in this area it would have to invent it. The two tasks are intimately connected; to create safe ciphers one has to know all there is to know about breaking them. It is not a field for amateurs. It is highly technical, complex and constantly changing as new technology is being invented and brought into service. The same considerations, of course, apply to the security of computer banks, the communications linking them and the more exotic alternative means of communications now being developed.

Similarly, if the government ever were to establish an agency for the covert collection of intelligence outside Canada and decided its activities should be independently reviewed it seems unlikely they would chose SIRC for the task. Chapter 7 (International Dimensions) of the Second Report, Volume I of the McDonald Commission, states:

> It would be unwise to combine very different intelligence collection agencies within a single agency. In addition, there is a danger of creating a security and intelligence monolith in a democratic state. Demarcation lines between the two services, dealing with the foreign and domestic overlap of the two, would have to be carefully drawn.

I agree wholeheartedly with the observations. The same principles should apply when considering what external or independent review mechanisms (if any) should be set in place for such an agency. That is to say, the review mechanisms for an agency established to collect intelligence in other countries should be quite separate from those established to review CSIS activities.

The idea of a monolithic supra-departmental 'oversight committee' to review the activities of the various, disparate intelligence and security activities of the federal government has no apparent merit, and particularly if the committee was empowered to approve budgets, monitor and veto covert intelligence, counter-intelligence and counter-espionage operations at home and abroad as well as exercising all the other considerable powers granted SIRC under the CSIS Act. Given the considerable span of control which a 'super-oversight committee' would enjoy, inevitably it would be drawn increasingly into becoming a part of government rather than providing the kind of independent criticism which is needed or, worse, it could become a new kind of player who occasionally may be opposed to government and in reality is responsible neither to Parliament nor to ministers.

At the conclusion of their 1987–88 annual report SIRC say:

> We believe the Act is basically sound and in most ways it works well as a framework for carrying out the basic principles articulated by the McDonald Commission. ... A civilian agency whose mandate is spelled out in law rather than by executive order, with clear political and judicial control and independent review, remains the appropriate model for security intelligence in Canada.

I agree with the statement and I hope SIRC simply get on with the excellent job they have done to date without agitating further for 'oversight', American-style, or straying into areas of government responsibility outside their mandate. There is much for SIRC still to do without looking for more or different work.

8

Accountability and the Australian Security Intelligence Organization: A Brief History

FRANK CAIN

The Australian Security Intelligence Organization (ASIO) was established on 16 March 1949 by an administrative order issued to Mr Justice G.S. Reed of the South Australian Supreme Court by the Prime Minister, J.B. Chifley. It was a very inauspicious start to the founding of an organization that was never expected by the Labor Party leader to be very large. By the early 1980s, however, its staff had billowed to 800, and its annual budget in 1985–86 was $38.5 million.[1] This chapter attempts to explain briefly why ASIO was established and how it functioned before analysing the several attempts at making this burgeoning intelligence organization accountable to the Australian community.

Intelligence organizations are political bodies established to solve political problems and their accountability likewise involves questions of politics. They have been established to maintain conformity with what are perceived as essential values of that society. They have become a type of policeman of unwritten laws and political values – and, until recent times, how these policemen-figures went about their tasks has rarely been analysed. This article traces the political origins of ASIO and examines how the political culture that informed its policies became inappropriate after two decades. It illustrates how intelligence organizations are incapable by definition of re-programming themselves to adapt to rapid political change.

Accountability has become an important concept in all functions of democratic countries in the last two decades. While its application to most organs of government has a direct path and obvious relevance, accountability and intelligence organizations make strange bedfellows. In Australia, courts, parliaments and the bureaucracy have attempted to make ASIO accountable, producing a series of political and semi-legal institutions whose true efficiency has yet to be fully tested. This article provides no answers to the question of how accountability should function, but by exploring the political and administrative means by which the present position has been reached it is hoped that it will contribute to a better understanding of the question.

Intelligence collecting for political reasons was conducted by the state police forces in Australia until the First World War, at which time the Military Intelligence section of the Australian Army took over such activities to pursue those opposed to the government's war policy, such as the Industrial Workers of the World (IWW), anti-conscriptionists and pacifists. Mail openings, reporting speakers' comments at meetings and the use of informers were some of the techniques used to compile a large collection of dossiers on numerous Australians. At the end of the war the activities of Russian immigrants, who pestered the Commonwealth government to help them to return to Russia, plus the natural suspicion of non-Labor governments toward militant trade unions and socialist groups then debating about how to establish a Communist Party of Australia (CPA), provided sufficient reason for the Australian government to establish its first intelligence organization, named the Investigation Branch and attached to the Attorney-General's Department.

In these post-war years the Investigation Branch, establishing a pattern later intensified by ASIO, began watching closely every activity of the CPA and looking for a Communist-inspired motive in every industrial action undertaken by militant trade unions. The CPA was reported on, its annual conferences were infiltrated and a comprehensive index compiled of all its members. The travels of its officials overseas were monitored and their baggage searched on their return in order to examine what literature and funds they had allegedly brought with them from Moscow. This watching was frequently undertaken in conjunction with MI5 as many officials passed through London. This established another surveillance tactic later extended and expanded by ASIO, that of using overseas and fraternal intelligence agencies to keep watch on radical Australians overseas.[2]

The non-Labor governments, and particularly John Latham, who was frequently the Attorney-General, made amendments to the Commonwealth Crimes Act to provide for greater restrictions on the CPA. By 1935 the government obtained a court order to have the CPA banned, but a counter order sought by the CPA and the Friends of the Soviet Union (FOSU) had this lifted. In 1940 the ban was finally imposed under wartime emergency legislation and the Investigation Branch assisted the state police forces to seize the CPA's papers, membership lists and the printing presses, which were made forfeit to the Crown. After the Australian Labor Party (ALP) took office in 1941 the ban was lifted by its Attorney-General, Dr H.V. Evatt.

The post-war years witnessed labour unrest fuelled by pent-up demands from the war years and expectations of higher living standards. The CPA was believed to be behind the growing militancy and the Investigation Branch, now renamed the Commonwealth Investigation Service (CIS), expanded its staff and brought its dossiers on CPA officials up to date. At this time Australian political life was feeling the effects of the expanding Cold War. A faction centred on the Catholic Church began organizing to seize control of the trade unions, ostensibly to eliminate CPA officials. The non-Labor political parties began attacking the ALP government for being too soft on the CPA and not banning it, as it promised to do if elected. It was against this complex of dissension at home and problems abroad that the Chifley government established ASIO in 1949.

But the ramifications of the establishment of the Soviet embassy in Australia produced the most compelling reasons for the government creating ASIO. After negotiations between Dr Evatt and Mr Molotov which culminated on 14 July 1942, diplomatic relations were established with an exchange of ministers, and they were raised to ambassadorial level on 22 May 1948.[3] Intelligence authorities viewed the arrival of the large diplomatic staff amounting to 52 (including wives and children) plus six couriers as similar to a Soviet Trojan Horse arriving in Canberra, from which would flow propaganda material and funds to aid the CPA. The CIS, in conjunction with MI5, watched the embassy and, allegedly through the decryption of radio traffic between the Canberra embassy and Moscow by British and US intelligence, it was established that the Soviets had spies in the Department of External Affairs.[4] Other evidence indicates that a radio transmitter was not used and that the embassy exchanged communications with Moscow by filming the material, which was then transported by couriers. Other material was sent via post office cables in diplomatic code – probably one-time pads.[5] How or indeed why British intelligence uncovered this alleged Soviet spying connection with Australia remains one of the many unsolved mysteries of Australian intelligence history.

News of this alleged message decryption was brought to Chifley by the Director-General of MI5, Sir Percy Sillitoe, in May 1948. It is unclear what material Sillitoe produced as evidence, but it does seem that a list of codenames, invented by the Soviets to identify Australians, was handed over. One document of little importance, given by the British to the Australian Post-Hostilities Section of the External Affairs

Department, seems also to have been identified. Suspicion, for some undisclosed reason, fell upon an External Affairs official, Ian Milner. An inquiry was conducted and the Secretary of the Department, Dr Burton, cleared Milner of any wrongdoing and Chifley wrote to Attlee on 9 June 1948 saying that there was no 'evidence of any irregularity'. The codenames remained a riddle for ASIO to stew over.[6]

The vetting procedures for military staff and all public servants who came in contact with defence material in the Prime Minister's Department, Treasury and External Affairs were expanded by the CIS and, by June 1949, 2,400 military and 200 civilians had been checked and cleared. The opposition, scenting electoral victory in the offing, increased its attacks on the government for not suppressing Communism and charged it with disloyalty to the British and US allies. When the US Defense and State Department embargoed the transfer of all classified information to Australia in May 1948, the opposition believed it had the government cornered.

This cut-off of information arose from the establishment of the so-called Joint Project between Australia and the UK to construct a testing and research facility at Woomera and Salisbury for the manufacture of guided missiles. The US Defense Department was reluctant to help its British competitor to build the weapon of the future and the embargo arose from this as much as jealousy between the three US services. Australia was judged to be 'a poor security risk' because of the discovery of the alleged spy in the External Affairs Department. There had been no leak of information from the Joint Project. The CIS had been vetting all the staff from its commencement. It controlled the Peace Officer Guard which guarded all defence establishments and a Long Range Weapons Board Security Organization had been established which, by June 1949, consisted of 77 members, 20 Peace Guards and 10 Army Provost members.[7]

The CIA distributed a monograph in April 1949 with the title *The Communist Influence in Australia*, indicating that the CPA dominated the maritime industry in Australia and nearby countries, that two cabinet members were 'probably Communists' and 'another cabinet member and the Speaker of the House, Communist sympathizers'. The establishment of ASIO was envisaged as the means for convincing the American, British and Australian electorates, that the government was reliable and firmly anti-Communist in all aspects.[8]

The plan did not work. The Secretary of the Defence Department, Sir Frederick Shedden, was sent to Washington to negotiate the lifting of the embargo, but the Truman administration seemed fixed in its idea that Australia was a security risk and the embargo remained until after the general election in December 1949 when the government lost office. Two weeks later the new coalition government led by R.G. Menzies was informed that the embargo would be raised to allow the exchange of information at the 'confidential' classification. Soon after this, an agreement was prepared for the exchange of defence information between the two countries plus Britain although under very restrictive conditions.[9]

R.G. Menzies was no less aware than Chifley that ASIO was to be a hallmark by which Australia was to demonstrate its trustworthiness as an anti-Communist member of the western alliance to which, given the clashes between returning European colonialism and Asian nationalism, plus the rise of a Communist China, the Menzies government believed it was necessary to attach itself. Whether internal forces required an organization like ASIO was beside the point. Its establishment, and imprimatur from a body like MI5, was to be the principal means of Australia being readily accepted into the defence and military alliances it believed it must join for reasons of self-defence. Menzies was also aware that actions speak louder than words in international politics and this, along with domestic electoral factors, helps to explain why he initiated a fierce and prolonged anti-Communist crusade in which ASIO was to figure. As part of this new policy, Menzies advised Justice Reed that he could return to his court in South Australia and replaced him with the Director of Military Intelligence, Colonel C.C.F. Spry.[10] Having witnessed what happened to the Chifley government on the international level for what was seen to be the failure to deal firmly with Communism and take seriously the establishment of intelligence and security organizations, Menzies could not be condemned for his heavy-handed anti-Communist policies.

The CPA was banned in 1950 with a legislative measure that placed the onus on people to prove that they were not Communists. The vast material collected by ASIO and its predecessor, the CIS, was to be used in rebutting claims from Communists bold enough to assert that they were not party members. The protection of ASIO's informants was another reason why this obligation of proof was placed on the defendant. The Act was challenged in the High Court of Australia and in March 1951 was judged to be unconstitutional. The government thereupon held a referendum in September to amend the Australian constitution to allow for the banning. But the referendum was lost, although only by the narrow majority of 0.5 per cent.

ASIO began watching those groups whose membership would overlap with that of the ALP, such as peace groups, the Unemployed Workers Movement and anti-conscription groups established in response to the government's introduction of universal compulsory military training. Immigrants from certain countries who were expected to have Communist leanings were also watched by ASIO, but most of its surveillance resources went into watching trade unions. Field officers were allocated to union-watching, and strikes and union elections were monitored. Informants in the unions, newspaper reports and especially branches of the states' police forces were all tapped for information, particularly concerning those unions that had CPA members on their executive. ASIO published a monthly summary of all industrial disputes for ministers and permanent heads, and this continued until 1973.[11]

The Australian labour movement was aware that ASIO had assumed the role of industrial policemen from the CIS. ASIO recruited its officers from the state police forces or from among retired military officers, and the trade union organizers were aware of their presence at union meetings. What brought ASIO into the greatest odium with the labour movement were the ramifications of the Petrov affair. Vladimir Petrov was Third Secretary at the Soviet embassy, where he worked as cipher clerk and his wife as a book-keeper. One of ASIO's important roles was then, and still is, to monitor the Soviet embassy closely. It had one of its part-time agents, a Russian-speaking Polish medical practitioner, befriend Petrov on his frequent visits to Sydney from Canberra and entertain him in the flesh-pots of Sydney night life. This continued from 1951 until early in 1954 when Petrov defected. The defection was on the eve of a Federal election when the electoral tide was not running in the government's favour. ASIO believed Petrov to be an MVD agent and asked him to bring papers from the embassy for which he was paid $10,000.[12] It was hoped by ASIO that these papers might reveal the membership of the spy ring in the External Affairs Department, which was one of the main reasons for establishing the organization in 1949. The excitement of defection helped to have the government returned in May 1954, and the Royal Commission into Espionage, which was suspended during the pre-election weeks, resumed sitting to examine the Petrov papers in fine detail.

The Leader of the ALP, Dr Evatt, who was also a leading barrister, appeared before the commission because members of his staff were named in the documents. He believed that the affair had lost him the election and now he believed that ASIO and the Royal Commission were conspiring to undermine the Labor Party and his career. Such feelings were shared by many in the Labor movement, who blamed ASIO and the non-Labor government for manipulating events to this end. Natural suspicion surrounded ASIO because it played a central role in the commission hearings. It held Petrov and his wife in safe houses; it produced evidence it had collected from them in these houses; and the commission heard ASIO submissions only in sessions held in camera. After ten months' inquiry the commission closed, but no spies were detected and no prosecutions launched. Although the affair turned into a damp squib, thereafter ASIO's name was blackened in the eyes of the ALP, for whom the accountability of ASIO became an important issue.

The Director-General, C.C.F. Spry, was aware of this ALP hostility, and because ASIO was still functioning on the basis of a Prime Ministerial directive he sent Menzies a copy of a Bill he had drafted to make ASIO a statutory body. Spry claimed that the future of ASIO and the continued employment of his specialized staff was in jeopardy. 'In view of the attitude of the present Leader of the Opposition', he wrote, 'their position would be precarious, to say the least, should he, or the party he leads, become the government'.[13]

The Bill to establish ASIO legally was put before Parliament in October 1956. It was a short Bill endowing the Director-General with powers for total control of the organization. He was to collect intelligence and distribute it, as he considered, 'in the interests of security'. He could hire and fire staff, who were not to be under the Public Service Act, meaning that they would not necessarily enjoy the same conditions and wages as applied to normal public servants although they now became eligible to join the Commonwealth Superannuation Fund, thereby giving them a pension on retirement. The Bill represented a successful attempt at converting an intelligence institution directed by one individual, and exercising wide independence under a Prime Ministerial directive, into a type of statutory body where the director's independence was endowed with legal sanction while the staff he had selected gained no improvement in working conditions but did obtain rights to a pension.

Spry provided Menzies with a second-reading speech, most of which he adopted including the phrase 'The attacks made on our own Security Service during the course of the Royal Commission on Espionage have convinced the Government that it is necessary for the protection, and therefore also for the efficiency of the Security Service ...' to give it a statutory basis.[14]

The ALP offered to support the Bill on condition that three amendments were made. These were to provide for ministerial responsibility for ASIO; to have officers of ASIO given the same rights of appeal for promotion and against dismissal as other public servants; and to provide for appeals against adverse ASIO security assessments. There were few precedents the opposition could draw upon for making an intelligence service accountable. There was no mention of the Petrov affair, but the ALP members expressed concern that a large well-funded intelligence body had to be accountable and based their proposals on British constitutional grounds. These included such principles that departments must be responsible to a minister, that public servants must be granted equal access to public service rights of appeal, and that an Australian citizen had the right to clear himself of allegations made by a security service.

E.G. Whitlam, one of the speakers, offered the US loyalty boards as one example where people could clear their names in circumstances where faulty documentation was used by the intelligence bodies. Another example was the Australian wartime regulation allowing internees to appeal to a tribunal which could inspect army records and explain to the detainee the reasons for internment.[15] The government refused to accept the amendments, and the beginnings of accountability for ASIO had to wait until after Whitlam formed his own government.

Meanwhile ASIO continued monitoring the militant trade unions and immigrant groups from Communist countries, as well as building links with overseas intelligence bodies including the CIA. ASIO joined with Australia's spying service, the Australian Secret Intelligence Service (ASIS), in the 'combined section', and in 1954, when the CIA appointed a liaison officer, it expanded its links with the western intelligence brotherhood. The Vietnam War witnessed a confrontation with the numbers of Australians opposed to the war. ASIO agents with cameras attended with police Special Branch officers to monitor demonstrations and many middle-class Australians were confronted for the first time with the business-suited and anonymous persona of the Australian secret intelligence operative. The Campaign Against Political Police (CAPP) was established in Melbourne and with an approach of humour and satire turned the tables by photographing ASIO agents and publishing names of alleged ASIO officers.[16]

Labor members of parliament experienced at first hand the arbitrariness of ASIO. Many migrant groups supported the ALP, and when two politically active migrants, one from Greece and one from Italy, sought naturalization in Melbourne and were refused on security grounds by ASIO, the ALP took up their case during the term of the Whitlam Labor government and naturalization was granted. Both men were subsequently elected as Labor members to the Parliament of Victoria.[17]

The capricious and unaccountable nature of ASIO drew many

criticisms from the ALP and these collectively found expression in the 1971 National Conference of the ALP, the national policy-setting organ of the ALP, in a motion to dissolve ASIO. It was opposed by the shadow Attorney-General, Senator Murphy, and went to a tied vote, to be defeated only by the Speaker's casting vote. An alternative policy was adopted of having the Attorney-General report annually to Parliament on the functions of ASIO and to appoint an administrative tribunal to establish regulations by which ASIO and other security organizations should be governed.

When the new Whitlam government took office in December 1972, it found that there were other reform measures of a higher priority than ASIO and its accountability. Within a few months, however, events relating to the Fascist-leaning Ustasha movement in Australia, heightened it. An unofficial war had been conducted over the previous decade between a small group of Yugoslav migrants supporting the wartime Nazi-collaborating Ustasha and other Yugoslav migrants plus the Yugoslav government. Consular offices of the Yugoslav government were bombed and Yugoslavs attacked, but ASIO and the Commonwealth police seemed unable to detect the offenders. Matters came to a head in March 1973 when the Yugoslav Prime Minister, Mr D. Bijedic, was to visit Australia and the police informed the Attorney-General, Senator Murphy, that they were not able to guarantee the visitor's security.[18] Senator Murphy believed that ASIO was withholding material on the Ustasha from him and he flew to the Melbourne headquarters to view it. He was accompanied by Commonwealth police briefed to enter the ASIO headquarters with him and to prevent such material being whisked away. The planned visit became known to the press and by the time the Attorney-General arrived at the headquarters he was greeted by a bevy of journalists and TV cameras, there to cover what was coined the 'Murphy raid'.

The terrorism ceased soon after, and the NSW police conducted raids on various houses in that state, where arms and explosives were seized. ASIO resented being visited by its ministerial head. A former Director-General, with an undertone of hyperbole, was to write that the visit 'sent shock waves round Australia and the western world ... and caused grave concern at home and abroad'.[19] The opposition believed that it had witnessed a violation of ASIO secrets and the CIA likewise expressed concern at the visit.

Since 1971 Whitlam had believed that the 'ASIO problem' could be solved by appointing a Royal Commission under Justice R.M. Hope of the NSW Supreme Court, and in mid-1974 Whitlam invited him to investigate not only ASIO but the other intelligence bodies, ASIS, the Joint Intelligence Organization (JIO) and the Defence Signals Directorate (DSD). Delays meant that Hope did not start sitting until March 1975. Meanwhile Whitlam reverted to the ALP's initial policy of having a judge as Director-General of ASIO and appointed Justice Edward Woodward to the position for seven years. Whitlam could ordinarily have expected to have received Hope's report and to legislate for the changes for ASIO's accountability, but he was dismissed in November 1975 and it was Malcolm Fraser, the new Prime Minister, whose government amended the ASIO Act.

The Hope Royal Commission presented three reports on its work to the government, but none of these was released. A summary of the third report was published in April 1977 under the title *Abridged Findings and Recommendations*. The government decided in May 1977 to implement immediately two of Hope's recommendations affecting the whole intelligence community and thereby ASIO's accountability, particularly at the administrative level. Thus, the budget of the intelligence community was to be scrutinized by officials outside the community in order to ensure that duplication was avoided, and an Intelligence and Security Committee of key senior ministers was established. It was serviced by a committee composed of intelligence heads (ASIO, DSD, ASIS) and others. This cumbersome device, comprising busy ministers and senior officers, never worked effectively and was to be disbanded in November 1980.[20]

Prime Minister Fraser made a statement to Parliament on 25 October 1977 outlining in general terms the government's response to the Hope report and, in May 1979, the ensuing legislation for the changes in ASIO was debated in Parliament. These changes were so extensive that an entirely new Bill was drafted to replace the 1956 Act, which had mainly served to give permanent tenure to the staff and to make ASIO's possible disbandment by a Labor government that much more difficult.[21]

These new measures expanded the powers of ASIO considerably. Its rights to open mail, tap telephones and seize and copy material under warrant of the minister were now provided for legally with warrants extending to six months' duration. Temporary warrants could be issued by the Director-General for up to 48 hours. Information could be given to state police forces and other state government departments and, with ministerial approval, to security services of other nations. The functions of the organization were now clearly defined and the scope and depth of ASIO's work more apparent. It already had the power to 'obtain, correlate and evaluate intelligence relevant to security', but with the term 'security' now more broadly defined, it included other and wider concepts such as espionage, sabotage, subversion, active measures of foreign intervention (that is, clandestine action by a foreign power) and terrorism. It was to become a more secretive body – divulging the names of ASIO officers was to be punishable by a year's imprisonment or a $1,000 fine. The actions of groups like CAPP were now to be criminal offences.

Relationships between the minister and the Director-General were formalized. The previous Act did not identify to whom the Director-General was responsible and this second Act made him 'subject to the general directions of the Minister', meaning the Attorney-General. However, he remained independent of the Minister in three specific areas: in deciding whether information should be collected on an individual; whether any particular information should be passed to other agencies; and the nature of the information to be passed to any other Commonwealth authority.

The single and very significant departure from the government's practice of following Hope's recommendations both to expand and formalize the powers of ASIO was the provision for the establishment of a Security Appeals Tribunal (SAT). This was the first attempt in the history of ASIO to make it accountable within a common law framework. It was also, as the government pointed out at the time, the first attempt in a common law country to provide a comprehensive statutory framework regulating the making of security assessments of individuals and providing a right of appeal to an independent judicial tribunal. It provided that if an officer in the Australian Public Service or any migrant was given, in intelligence parlance, 'a prejudicial security assessment', they could appeal to the SAT, composed of three people, one to be a judge. The SAT would call for ASIO to state its case, in camera; the appellant would state his or her case, also in camera; and it would then be for the SAT to announce its decision, which would be final and overrule any prior assessment. It had the potential to be a flexible and useful system for forcing ASIO to be totally accountable for security assessments. In 1983 it was to give a ruling which was to provide a significant challenge for much of the ideology upon which ASIO believed it was founded.[22]

Those Labor members of Parliament who had anticipated being able to make significant contributions to the revised ASIO Act now had to do so from the powerless position of the opposition benches. Many of the Labor Party's senior members who were to be ministers in the Hawke government, such as Bill Hayden, then leader, Lionel Bowen, deputy leader, Dr Neil Blewett, Barry Jones and Tom Uren, participated in the debate and offered support conditional on the government accepting nine amendments making ASIO more accountable. These were that a periodical judicial audit into ASIO be conducted; that the minister be fully informed on matters of the administration of ASIO; that the Leader of the Opposition be regularly briefed on ASIO actions; that the Auditor-General conduct regular audits on ASIO's accounts; that the definition of 'security' be narrowed to prevent mis-application; that the periods of time for which warrants could remain active be reduced; that SAT hear appeals against retrospective security assessments; that all people having adverse security assessments be notified; and that penalties for divulging names of ASIO officers be applied only when security was seriously prejudiced.

The government left the defence of its measures in the hands of its back-bench members, indicating that it was not going to take Labor's amendments seriously. The government did accept two small suggestions of Labor – that the Leader of the Opposition consult regularly with the Director-General and that he receive copies of the secret annual reports of ASIO. The government members adopted the argument of all previous non-Labor governments that ASIO was an important fourth arm of defence, that Labor's amendments would 'effectively emasculate' ASIO and that Australia's enemies could only benefit from open discussion of ASIO's activities. The suggestion of a judicial audit was opposed because of the implication that some judges who might be selected by a Labor government could not be trusted. 'I can think of a couple of judges', said Kevin Cairns, an MHR from Queensland, 'whose names would only have to be dropped for the security organisation to be in shambles within a week'.[23]

The opposition's arguments in favour of its amendments indicated that it had a clear understanding of how a security service ought to function in an open society and of the ways in which the Act ought to be modified for ASIO to be made more accountable. The strongest argument was put by Dr Blewett, formerly a political scientist from Flinders University in Adelaide. He condemned Justice Hope's cavalier treatment of Parliament, saying that on the one hand Hope opposed Parliament having any supervisory role over ASIO, such as being given financial information, being able to ask questions, or establishing a supervisory committee, but on the other hand Hope declared that ASIO had a role in supervising individual politicians. 'We need to think a little more about that relationship', warned Dr Blewett, who con-cluded with the remark that 'the judiciary, the Executive and Parlia-ment would all have to become involved in the adequate supervision of this organisation'.[24] The government was clearly opposed to the widen-ing of the accountability of ASIO to any further degree and it defeated the opposition's nine proposed amendments by a hefty 68 votes to 31. The knowledge and concern expressed by what were senior Labor members in this debate was a clear indication that their pursuit of reforms to ASIO would stand high in the priorities of a new Labor government.

The succeeding years actually witnessed a lessening of ASIO's accountability marked by a series of court judgments placing ASIO's actions beyond questioning even by the High Court. This remarkable situation arose through a series of challenges brought to the Court between 1979 and 1982 by the Church of Scientology in an effort to stop ASIO maintaining surveillance of its activities and passing on the information to such bodies as the Special Branch of the NSW police. Mr Justice Aickin refused this request, saying that the ASIO Act shielded ASIO from any review by the courts and that the ASIO officers were like a group of individuals in that they could maintain a surveillance on any people, as a private person could. The court implied that the Crown, with all its vast powers, could act in the same way as an individual. The Church of Scientology appealed to the High Court again in 1981, but Justice Wilson ordered that the claim be struck out, ruling that ASIO's actions were not justiciable. The Church then appealed to the full bench of the High Court, which gave its judgment in November 1982, but because the Court divided two-two in its judgment, Wilson's order remained. Two judges, including Justice Murphy, who supported the appeal, declared that ASIO's actions were not above judicial scrutiny. Chief Justice Gibbs, who opposed the appeal, raised the important question of whether ASIO would soon lose all effectiveness if its actions were scrutinized.

What the High Court gave with one hand, the SAT took away with another. A decision of the Security Appeals Tribunal on 1 June 1983 effectively pulled from under ASIO one of its oldest and strongest rationales for existence, that of preventing Communists working in the Australian Public Service from obtaining access to government secrets. A young man in the Department of Trade, who was both a Catholic and a Communist, had been denied a security clearance by ASIO in June 1982, but the tribunal overruled this action in a landmark decision, holding that the Communist Party was not 'revolutionary' in the sense of seeking to overthrow the State, and that members were simply seeking to advocate 'particular political and ideological views'.[25] A perception that had governed ASIO and its preceding surveillance bodies for 66 years now had to be abandoned. Some of ASIO's supporters were startled by this decision as, no doubt, were many of its staff. The planned removal of ASIO's headquarters from Melbourne to Canberra was getting closer all the time and many of its staff resigned and collected their superannuation rather than leave Melbourne. How much the tribunal's decision contributed to these resignations is hard to say.

Those members of the Labor Party wishing to make ASIO more accountable were presented with an opportunity to do so as a result of one of Justice Hope's very secret reports somehow being leaked to the press. This report examined various allegations, such as that ASIO had formed a secret alliance with the CIA, passing on information it had collected on Australians, and had also burgled the house of senior Liberal Party minister, William McMahon. On 5 May 1983 the *National Times* began publishing these and other items in the report, and the newly elected Prime Minister, Robert Hawke, informed Parliament on 12 May that Justice Hope would conduct another inquiry into the several intelligence agencies. The more important reason for holding an inquiry, however, was to dispose of the government's embarrassment over what became known as the Combe affair. David Combe, a former national secretary of the ALP, at that time was conducting his own public relations and lobbying business in which he was liaising with a Soviet diplomat, Valeri Ivanov, over a possible Soviet–Australian trading deal. ASIO had bugged Ivanov's house, suspecting him of being a KGB agent, and recorded Combe's conversations. Harvey Barnett, the Director-General of ASIO, approached the Prime Minister (not his minister, the Attorney-General) to warn that this former ALP official was establishing clandestine relationships with the diplomat and could not escape being drawn inexorably into a Soviet spying network to obtain secrets from a government in which he had many friends and contacts.

It was a flight of fancy by ASIO officers who, quite understandably given their narrow backgrounds, were incapable of drawing a distinction where Russians were concerned between an international business deal and an early case of espionage. The briefing by Barnett so persuaded Hawke that he summoned the Cabinet's National and International Security Committee (NISC), which agreed to Barnett's suggestion to have Ivanov deported (thus raising ASIO's overseas reputation as a clever spycatcher). The Cabinet subsequently agreed to ban all ministerial contact with Combe and the affair thereafter became public. Many of the senior ministers now appreciated that they had acted too hastily in response to Barnett's alarmist scenario, particularly when they recalled that they had not been permitted to read the transcripts of the ASIO bugs and telephone taps nor, more importantly, the reports on one of ASIO's informants, Laurie Matheson, who had established a highly profitable trading relationship with the Soviets, selling Australian mutton and cheese. With the matter in the open, it was too late to re-examine events and the second Hope Royal Commission moved into action.

Hope did not report on this affair until December 1983. While his report contained ambiguities, a book written by David Marr, *The Ivanov Trail*, shows that ASIO came out of the matter with its reputation badly tarnished. Barnett resigned soon after as Director-General. The Combe–Ivanov inquiry became an exercise in futility. However valiantly the ASIO barrister led the attack, supported by Hope, Combe could not be shown to have done wrong. The media highlighted Combe's innocence and the farcical nature of the event, while the ALP sharpened the proposals they had been enunciating over the years for making ASIO more accountable.

When Hope began hearing submissions about the organization of ASIO itself, the ALP presented, in February 1984, a 26-page submission prepared by a special party committee consisting of senior federal ministers, back-benchers, branch members and the national secretary. The submission reflected the party's platform and made recommendations that the NISC be permanently established with a secretariat, that a Security Commissioner be established as a combined ombudsman, auditor and inspector of all intelligence bodies, that a Joint Parliamentary Committee in National Security be established to oversee ASIO and the other bodies, that the opposition be fully briefed on security affairs, and that ASIO recruitment and training be widened and ASIO staff become part of the Australian Public Service.[26]

If the bungled handling of the Combe–Ivanov affair that forced the government to act wrongly under unnecessary pressure from ASIO and to cause damage to its relations with the Soviet Union was not enough to compel the government to place a tighter rein on intelligence bodies, the fiasco of the ASIS–Sheraton Hotel affair certainly was. ASIS – the Australian Secret Intelligence Service – had been established in May 1952 on the initiative of R.G. Casey, a senior member of the non-Labor government, whose fierce opposition to Communism in general and what he specifically saw as its advances in Asia led him to persuade Prime Minister Menzies to establish a special operations organization to function like the Secret Intelligence Service (SIS) in the UK.[27] This connection was reflected in the name it was given, and its principal role was to frustrate the fell hand of Communism wherever it was felt in Asia. ASIS was to be a mini-Australian version of the SIS and the CIA. Hidden within the Defence Department, it functioned through the various Australian embassies in Asia and was also a responsibility of the Australian Foreign Affairs Department. The existence of ASIS was never officially admitted and its funding was concealed in appropriations for other departments.

In acting as a spying body it seemed to achieve little, and in the special operations field it only attracted unwelcome publicity and the ire of the government. ASIS had a covert operations training base near Geelong, not far from Melbourne, in the State of Victoria, where agents were trained in explosives and weapons handling. In November 1983 an exercise was held in the four-star Sheraton Hotel, where masked agents pretended to rescue a fellow agent, but things went horribly wrong, resulting in the hotel staff being bailed up with automatic weapons and the Victorian police arresting the agents. The government's confusion and embarrassment over this affair – for most Australians and many government members had never heard of this clandestine body – were met by referring it also to the Hope Royal Commission already in session. The Victorian police wished to press charges for assault and unlawfully carrying automatic weapons, but the Australian government sided with ASIS and refused to release the correct names of the agents. Hope in his report administered ASIS a very mild wrist-slap.

In view of the principle of ministerial responsibility for the actions of their departments, including their secret intelligence bodies, and the fact that these bodies had grown to large and secretive proportions, it was not surprising that the Labor government should create the office of Inspector-General, which was to function as an ombudsman for complaints from people affected by such bodies and as a kind of fireman to smother the more unorthodox of their operations when they became public knowledge. Clearly the government did not wish to be forced to establish Royal Commissions every five years or so as crises of differing magnitude arose in the intelligence community. The other intelligence bodies, the Joint Intelligence Organization (JIO) and the Office of National Assessments (ONA), which compiles reports on economic and other matters not reported on by JIO, and the Defense Signals Directorate (DSD), recently expanded to collect and read data collected from the various foreign satellites floating above or near the Australian mainland, were also to be placed under the Inspector-General's purview.

Mr Justice Hope had included Labor's recommendations for greater accountability in his final report of 21 December 1984, although he had omitted the suggestion of a Joint Parliamentary Committee on ASIO. This, however, was included by the government in the subsequent amendment to the ASIO Act presented to Parliament on 22 May 1986. A second Act provided for the appointment of an Inspector-General of

Intelligence and Security, while a third made amendments to other Acts such as the Crimes Act, the Archives Act, Freedom of Information Act, Human Rights Commission Act and the Telecommunications (Interception Act), mainly to provide absolute secrecy for the operations of the Inspector-General.[28]

The opposition objected to these changes, particularly as they applied to ASIO. They declared that these amendments would please 'those who are committed to the destruction of ASIO', and that the Soviet embassy staff would read the *Hansard* reports of the debate 'with very considerable glee'. Such concern was unfounded, because ASIO's operating powers were actually expanded. The penalties for divulging ASIO information and the names not only of present but now also of past officers were increased to a fine of $5,000 or two years' jail, or both; and provision for telephone tapping was expanded to provide for the tapping of words, images, sounds or signals transmitted by light or electromagnetic emissions. ASIO was also authorized to communicate with overseas intelligence organizations in order to collect information about migrants or foreign intelligence agents. The opposition, like Justice Hope, objected to the establishment of a Parliamentary Joint Committee even though it was firmly hedged about with restrictions on what it could investigate and heavy punishments were provided for against any member of staff revealing information.[29]

With the implementation of the accountability provisions in the 1986 amending Act, ASIO in particular and the remainder of the intelligence community were brought under administrative, judicial and parliamentary oversight. It was not so much that time had caught up with these intelligence bodies to make them more responsible, it was more that over the previous decade an aware public and Parliament had moved towards making all public institutions more responsible for their decisions and actions. Innovations such as the Administrative Appeals Tribunal (AAT) and the Freedom of Information legislation (FOI) had had a significant impact on the administrations of public institutions at the Commonwealth and later the State level. On the grounds of preserving the secrecy of documents (mainly those from overseas) ASIO was able to remain aloof from these administrative developments – the continuing pressure to make it accountable having led to the development of these means of oversight, which took that into account. Table 1 shows the government departments that monitor ASIO and the other forms of administrative apparatus that oversee much of Australia's intelligence set-up.

The Security Appeals Tribunal has already been mentioned, and although it hears little more than two or three appeals per year, its composition of a judge and two laypersons with knowledge of migrant or public service affairs (according to the nature of the appeal) or society in general ensures that contemporary social and political values inform its proceedings. Membership of the tribunal can be for up to seven years, the average being from three to five, and it reports to Parliament annually. It is regarded as an important means of keeping ASIO honest.[30]

The Inspector-General of Intelligence and Security took office on 1 February 1987, and while he can investigate complaints (amounting to more than a dozen annually at this stage) he is charged with ensuring that the intelligence bodies, particularly ASIO, but also ASIS, DSD, JIO and ONA, do not interfere unnecessarily with the privacy of Australian citizens or permanent residents. He acts in response to complaints from individuals, ministers or of his own volition and he has wide powers to summon people to give evidence or produce documents and to impose punishments on those who refuse to comply or knowingly give false information. The Inspector-General may inquire into requests from ASIO staff for redress of grievances and he can also investigate whether instructions given by the Attorney-General to the Director-General are justified and, if not, to report the matter to the Prime Minister.

Unlike the Canadian Security Intelligence Review Committee (SIRC), which has a membership of five Privy Councillors, albeit part-time, and a staff of twelve highly skilled officers that can simultaneously investigate various aspects of the Canadian Security Intelligence Service (CSIS), the Australian Inspector-General, although empowered to investigate all of Australia's five intelligence bodies, faces the limitations imposed on him by having a staff of three people, and thus on his ability to initiate substantial investigation and review programmes.

Based on his very thin annual reports (three pages against SIRC's 77) the Inspector-General has devoted much of his labours in responding to complaints mainly from ASIO and some from ASIS staff. The ASIO staff were at first handicapped in taking their appeals to the Inspector-General because the Director-General of ASIO refused to show him the necessary documentation to support the appellants' claims, but that problem has been settled by discussion between him and the Director-General by which ASIO staff were granted unfiltered access to the Inspector-General. The problems faced by ASIS staff have not been revealed in the Inspector-General's reports, but because, like ASIO, they are not employed under the provisions of the Public Service Act and do not have various means of airing their grievances, including

TABLE 1

LINES OF ACCOUNTABILITY FOR ASIO AND OVERSIGHT BODIES

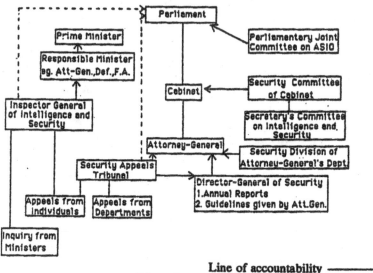

Line of accountability ————————➤
Line of responsibility to Parliament — — — — —➤

through public service trade union systems, their main recourse for settling questions in dispute would also be to the Inspector-General.[31]

On the broader question of unnecessary interference with the privacy of Australian citizens or permanent residents, the Inspector-General claims to be able to monitor DSD and ASIS in order to ensure that neither intelligence body makes an unwarranted intrusion on their privacy.[32] How such intelligence bodies can intrude and how the Inspector-General can monitor and detect such violations, if occurring, is not revealed by him to the Australian citizens about whom he rightly shows due concern. It could be that DSD frequently records satellite transmissions of overseas telephone conversations made by Australians and that the Inspector-General tries to ensure that the record is destroyed soon after being made. ASIS may monitor the totally innocent movements or actions of Australian travellers overseas and the Inspector-General seek to have this information destroyed too.

Compared with SIRC, which has been functioning for more than five years, the three-year-old office of the Inspector-General seems reluctant to share its insights and daily operations to the same extent as the Canadian institution. This probably has much to do with the nature of the appointments. The five Canadian Privy Councillors appear to be prepared to function more independently and to report on their actions and philosophies more openly than does the Inspector-General. This greater independence could be due to the Canadian officers' not being drawn from the higher levels of the public service, where the necessity to maintain confidentiality and keep secret matters of public administration is more deeply ingrained. Both Inspector-Generals have shared that type of background in Australia, and while the office continues to be filled by such people their annual reports will probably continue to amount to little more than three pages. But considering that the purpose behind the establishment of the Inspector-General's office was to intercede when an incident mishandled by the intelligence community becomes public knowledge and an embarrassment to the government, clearly his office does have a potential importance and he does serve while he only stands and waits.

The most recent body of review for ASIO is the Parliamentary Joint Committee on ASIO, formed on 31 August 1988. Its functions are limited to reviewing aspects of ASIO that are referred to it by the minister or Parliament; or the committee itself may request the minister to refer a particular matter to it for review. The secret documents obtained from overseas or communication of foreign intelligence are barred to it, however; it is prohibited from investigating intelligence collection methods or sources of information that are operationally sensitive, and the restrictions of an all-encompassing clause in the Committee's terms of reference also prevent it from reviewing any aspect of ASIO that does not affect an Australian citizen. Although opposed to the establishment of the committee, the opposition has nominated members to the seven-person body.[33]

In December 1989 the Attorney-General referred to this Joint Committee a matter which had been raised by the intelligence community (particularly ASIO) regarding the obligations of the Australian Archives Act of 1983 for all Australian government departments – including the intelligence bodies – to lodge their records with Australian Archives after 30 years. ASIO and ASIS had lodged some of their records in the archives after thorough weeding, but still wished to escape the terms of the Archives Act. The Joint Committee has called for public submissions on the question and it could be that by inquiries of this nature the committee will be able to find a public role for itself and its small secretariat.

NOTES

1. Australian Security Intelligence Organization Amendment Bill 1986, Digest of Bill, Legislative Research Service, Department of the Parliamentary Library, p.1.
2. Frank Cain, *Origins of Political Surveillance in Australia* (Sydney, 1983), Ch. 7.
3. Molotov to Kerr, British Ambassador, 14 July 1942, on establishment of diplomatic relationships with Australia. Archives of Soviet Ministry of Foreign Affairs; Alan Watt, Australian Diplomat, *Memoirs of Sir Alan Watt* (Sydney, 1972), p.130.
4. Peter Wright, *Spycatcher, The Candid Autobiography of a Senior Intelligence Officer* (New York, 1988), p.234.
5. 'Procedure for the despatch and receipt of mail in the local M.V.D. section', n.d., document F. 17, pp.5–8, 'Moscow Letters', CRS A6201, item 51, Australian Archives (hereafter AA).
6. ASIO file on I. Milner, CRS A6119 XR1, item 18, AA.
7. Frank Cain, 'Missiles and Mistrust: US Intelligence Responses to British and Australian Missile Research', *Intelligence and National Security*, Vol. 3, No. 4 (Oct. 1988), pp.11–16.
8. Report, CIA to President Truman, 27 Feb. 1948, Truman papers, Harry S. Truman Library, Independence, MO, USA.
9. Cain, 'Missiles and Mistrust', pp.16–18.
10. Menzies to Reed, 27 Feb. 1950, CRS A 1209 item 72/10048, AA; Menzies to Spry, 6 July 1950, CRS M1509, box 2/1, AA.
11. For extensive ASIO reports on the CPA see CRS A6122, item 7 and CRS A367, item C94151, AA.
12. For a history and analysis of the Petrov affair see Nicholas Whitlam and John Stubbs, *Nest of Traitors: The Petrov Affair* (Brisbane, 1974); and Robert Manne, *The Petrov Affair, Politics and Espionage* (Sydney, 1987).
13. Spry to Menzies, 13 Jan. 1956, CRS A 1209, item 72/10048, AA.
14. Notes for Second Reading Speech, ibid.
15. CPD, 31 Oct. 1956, pp.2031–26.
16. 'List of ASIO Staff Members Past and Present', CAPP Pamphlet, May Day 1980.
17. CPD, 18 Sept. 1979, p.1217.
18. Gough Whitlam, *The Whitlam Government 1972–1975* (Ringwood, 1985), pp.167–73.
19. Harvey Barnett, *Tale of the Scorpion* (Sydney, 1988), p.201.
20. CPD, 22 May 1979, p.2174; Jeffrey T. Richelson and Desmond Ball, *The Ties That Bind* (Sydney, 1985), p.64; Richard Hall, *The Secret State, Australia's Spy Industry* (Sydney, 1978), pp.159–60.
21. The 1956 Act consisted of five pages; the 1979 Act ran to 35, although 14 of these related to the new Security Appeals Tribunal.
22. See part IV of the Act, No. 113 of 1979.
23. CPD, 18 Sept. 1979, p.1210.
24. Ibid., p.1214.
25. *Federal Law Review*, No. 3, 1980, pp.102–8; Nicholas Seddon 'ASIO and Accountability', *Australian Quarterly*, Vol. 54, No. 4 (1983), pp.362–81.
26. 'Submission by Australian Labor party to the Royal Commission in Australia's Security and Intelligence Agencies', presented by R.F. McMullan, ALP National Secretary, Feb. 1984.
27. For an excellent history on ASIS and its bungles see Brian Toohey and William Pinwill, *Oyster, The Story of the Australian Security Intelligence Service* (Melbourne, 1989).
28. *Australian Intelligence and Security Organization Act*, 1986 (Commonwealth).
29. *Inspector-General of Intelligence and Security Act*, No. 101 of 1986.
30. See Part IV, ASIO Act, 1986.
31. See topic 'Complaints From Agency Staff' in *Inspector-General of Intelligence and*

Security, Annual Report 1987–88 (AGPS, Canberra 1988), pp. 1, 2.
32. 'Ministerial Director to DSD' in ibid.
33. *Extract of Annual Report of Joint Statutory Committee on ASIO 1988–89*, Department of House of Representatives.

9

The Canadian Security and Intelligence System: Fighting the Last War or the Next?

REG WHITAKER

'Is the Canadian security and intelligence system efficient and effective?' This question is an inherently difficult one for non-practitioners to answer. Scholars, journalists and other independent observers lack the kind of hands-on knowledge which can permit informed conclusions about the effectiveness of security and intelligence operations. Those who do have such information are normally unable or unwilling to talk about it in a frank, public manner.

When the public does get to learn about details of such operations it is almost always when something has gone very wrong. Hence public perceptions of effectiveness tend to be badly skewed. Occasionally bureaucrats or politicians try to redress this imbalance with publicity efforts of their own. Such efforts are usually at the expense of operational efficiency (such as well-publicized expulsions of Soviet diplomats which almost inevitably compromise hard-won counter-espionage successes) or represent irrelevant 'sting' operations.[1]

Since 1984 Canada has had the advantage of an organization unique to the wider world of security and intelligence. The Security Intelligence Review Committee (SIRC) is an independent body appointed on the advice of all parties in Parliament which has access to the operational records of the Canadian Security Intelligence Service (CSIS) and which reports publicly each year on the Service's successes and failures, to the extent that this can be done without itself compromising national security.[2] Its annual reports (four to this date) thus provide an unusual opportunity to assess relatively dispassionately the question of efficiency and effectiveness in relation to this particular agency. Despite the national security limitation, SIRC reports do offer a useful point of reference. They cannot, however, answer the question definitively, nor indeed address the broader questions which

126

go beyond the language of the CSIS Act which forms the statutory mandate, and limits, for SIRC's inquiries.

There is little point then in trying to assess the effectiveness of the Canadian security and intelligence system in any specific manner, and I shall not attempt to do so. Rather I shall attempt to answer a somewhat differently formulated question: 'Are the basic assumptions underlying the Canadian security and intelligence system appropriate to meet, efficiently and effectively, the changing requirements of the present and near future?' This question is, in principle, answerable.

This is a way of raising the prior question of 'efficient' and 'effective' *at what*? Instead of assuming that the activities of existing agencies and establishments are appropriately targeted and then trying to assess their effectiveness in achieving given goals, it may be more useful to assess the appropriateness of the goals themselves. To do this it is imperative to offer some historical perspective.

History is useful in addressing two different kinds of problems: first: *why are we continuing to do what we have been doing*?; and second: *why are we having to change the way we have been doing things*? In the case of the Canadian security and intelligence system, it is my contention that the policy-makers and practitioners have until recently failed to address the first question and are now being forced rather abruptly to face the second, more alarming, one.

For the security and intelligence world, not just in Canada but throughout the West, history effectively begins in 1945. The Second World War was, as it were, prehistory. The security and intelligence establishments, the institutional frameworks, the physical structures and facilities, the human resource investments, the international networks, the dominant paradigms, the political directives, the conventional wisdom, have all been bound up inexorably with the Cold War.

Intelligence as an activity has always been intimately related to war. In the nuclear age, war having become unacceptably costly, Cold War (bloc conflict on all fronts short of direct armed conflict) has been the medium within which security and intelligence has lived, expanded, even flourished. *Espionage* between states is war by other means – as such it is an activity peculiarly appropriate to an era of Cold War. *Subversion* – the idea of the moral and ideological integrity of states being corrupted from within by the disloyal local agents of hostile states – is also a symptomatic Cold War concept.[3]

Canada fell into an habitual pattern with the onset of the Cold War. In a dangerous bipolar world Canada not surprisingly chose sides. But choosing sides turned out to be a very long-term investment decision, with limited flexibility allowed.

On the external dimension, Canada placed its intelligence assets, such as they were at the time (not much) and what they were potentially (rather more) into fixed Cold War-driven networks. It denied itself an external intelligence gathering agency or even a centralized intelligence function, apparently preferring to buy into rights to some of the product of a process run by its allies. In the case of the Communications Security Establishment (CSE), or the Communications Branch National Research Council before it, a substantial investment in technical intelligence gathering (Techint) was sunk into the production of raw intelligence material. The latter is generally not processed in Canada but exported to the United States under the UKUSA framework to be later reimported as finished intelligence product – a paradigmatic Canadian economic pattern here extended to the world of intelligence.[4]

But the commitment goes further: Techint is like a gun, it must be aimed at a target. The UKUSA network aims at what until 1989 could be called the Soviet bloc. The network as a whole, let alone the Canadian link, represents a heavy capital-intensive emplacement that can not easily be re-aimed at new targets, any more than spy satellites can have their orbits altered to direct their imaging capacity toward new targets. In the late twentieth century, this investment may increasingly seem, to those on the outside at least, like the dead hand of the past guiding the present. Like the North Warning System with its enormous capital investment directed toward detecting a Soviet missile attack across the Arctic which never comes, the flexibility of such systems must be called into question – especially when Latin American drug-runners fly their cargoes into New Brunswick in small airplanes, undetected by high-tech warning systems.

Internally – and the main thrust of Canadian security intelligence has always been directed inward – the Cold War presented the old RCMP security service with an opportunity tailor-made to its own philosophy. Soviet espionage and Communist subversion were two sides of the same coin. Counter-espionage and counter-subversion were much the same activity. Given the perspectives of the Gouzenko affair of 1945/6 in which espionage was ideologically motivated, Communism was seen above all as the slippery slope leading to treason.

The Mounties were primarily a police force, not a specialized security intelligence agency (it was as if the Special Branch operated in Britain without MI5). To a police force, crime is the everyday tactical challenge to the practice of law and order, but revolution is the strategic challenge to the very notion of order itself. Communism embodied twin threats to public order – overthrow of both capitalist property and the state, and thus for the Mounties constituted the ultimate enemy.[5] As with the FBI in the United States, this attitude bred a highly moralistic sense of mission, which did not always mix well with good security intelligence work.[6]

The conservative ideological bias indigenous to Canadian police experience was powerfully reinforced by the Cold War, and by the international (American/British) context within which security was understood. This is reflected in the two major domestic elements of the national security state in Canada: (1) the security screening program in the public service and defence industries, and (2) the immigration security program.[7] The criteria established both by successive government directives and by the practice of the Security Service were decisively and almost exclusively anti-Communist.

These criteria remained firmly in place for decades. Yet the worst internal security crisis ever suffered in post-war Canada came in the October crisis of 1970 from an entirely different direction – an indigenous, violent (but non-Communist), separatist movement in Quebec. The evident weakness of intelligence on this threat was hardly surprising, given the forceful bias of the dominant Cold War discourse. To compound matters, the frantic and sometimes illegal attempts to catch up led to the notorious RCMP follies (illegal break-ins, mail openings, barn-burnings, falsified documents, etc.) of the later 1970s. An increasingly democratized and rights-conscious, not to say contentious and clamorous, population, along with a more investigative press, provided unprecedented resistance to invasive surveillance and countering tactics. Especially crucial was the opposition of the parliamentary separatist Parti Québécois government, elected in Quebec in 1976, to the unchecked operation of Ottawa's national security apparatus, and the partial support offered Quebec by the attorneys-general of the English Canadian provinces on grounds of protecting provincial jurisdiction.[8] Out of these controversies, of course, came the McDonald Commission, the CSIS Act and a civilianized agency, with SIRC and the Inspector General and other elements of review and oversight.

The broader international context of security and intelligence at the close of the 1980s has undergone a remarkable transformation. The collapse of the Soviet bloc in Eastern Europe in 1989–90 is clearly the most significant event in East–West relations since the origins of the Cold War in the late 1940s. In effect, the primary cause of the Cold War has been removed. There is no longer a Soviet 'bloc', and the reunification of Germany is symbolic of the eventual unification of Europe as a whole. As the Red Army retreats from its advanced position beyond its western borders, the attention of the Soviet national security apparatus is increasingly focused on trying to prevent the internal break-up of the Soviet Union itself. In these circumstances, the Soviet threat, once so menacing to Western Europe and even to North America, has shrunk to far less threatening proportions. Once a spectre haunting the West, Communism has become merely a ghost.

In the world of security and intelligence, the implications of these developments have hardly begun to be digested. The intelligence services of Eastern Europe are ceasing their careers as ancillary instruments of KGB espionage; in the case of East Germany they will soon cease their careers altogether. The Potsdam interrogation centre of the once-dreaded Stasi, the GDR secret police, took on a new life as the 'Café Stasi', a trendy punk-rock nightclub which used barbed-wire as interior decor. The legendary Markus 'Mischa' Wolf, former head of GDR intelligence, is now dedicating his considerable talents to tracking down fortunes squirrelled away in foreign bank accounts by corrupt officials of the old regime. The Czechs are reputedly thinking about opening their intelligence files to the curious gaze of the CIA.

Of course, bureaucracies grind on in accustomed routines despite political cataclysms. It has even been reported that GDR spies in West Germany have been going through their familiar motions even if they no longer have a head office to report to. Eastern European embassies in Western countries may continue for a time to offer diplomatic cover to operatives who will continue to run their networks – at least until the new democratic governments of these states get around to taking charge of personnel posted abroad. But it is patently ridiculous to imagine, as some Western intelligence officials have been suggesting, that this sort of thing can persist indefinitely. The 'Eastern bloc' is no more, and the winding up of the bureaucratic apparatus is inevitable.

No doubt the KGB continues to do as the KGB has done for generations. But the attention of the KGB, and its resources, will inevitably be turned inward as the political and territorial integrity of the USSR becomes the chief preoccupation of the Soviet state. This is symbolized by an incident in early 1990 when the armed forces had to intervene to relieve a KGB headquarters building in Armenia besieged by an angry mob. Under these crisis conditions, the global horizons of the 'world's largest intelligence service' must of necessity be drastically reduced.

There are some signs of adjustment on the part of the major players on the Western side to the new reality. The threat of international terrorism, proceeding from non-state actors, presents challenges to all great powers, East or West. A joint CIA–KGB task force on terrorism has already begun meeting. This precedent is of remarkable significance, and much more may be in the offing as the common ground shared by the old antagonists widens.

In a multipolar world in which smaller states armed with advanced, in some cases nuclear, technology and lethal non-state actors play an increasing role in threatening international order, the bipolar Cold War paradigm is not simply outmoded but is actually perverse. Its perversity lies not simply in assumptions which increasingly fly in the face of new realities. Worse is the fixed investment of technology and manpower pointed in the wrong direction. The US has launched yet another spy satellite targeted on the Soviet Union. Some $30 billion has reportedly been budgeted by the Bush administration for external intelligence in 1990/91, with half that total devoted to Eastern Europe. Despite some recognition of change, the fixation on Soviet espionage in the West continues in Western counter-intelligence circles.

In Canada, a now familiar refrain goes like this: it is not so much secrets of state but commercial high technology which the Soviets are targeting, compelling us to remain equally vigilant against Communist espionage. A secret ministerial directive on 'National Requirements for Security Intelligence'[9] is insistent about the 'protection of classified technologies' and warns of the threat of 'clandestine technology transfer'. Government and CSIS spokespersons have stressed that this concern is mainly, if not entirely, directed at Soviet intelligence. These assertions cry out for a counter-assertion. If the Soviets want and need Canadian technology, why not sell it to them and make a few bucks? Yet even if we want to do this, we are still trapped within a web of COCOM, NATO, NORAD and other obligations with a bearing on security standards and trade in strategic items which force us to lock the Soviets out, thus leaving them no choice but to steal rather than buy. This can then be pointed to as evidence of continued Soviet espionage activity justifying our continued targeting of counter-intelligence activities on the Soviet bloc: altogether, a vicious circle of bureaucratic inertia and ideological tautology. Meanwhile, new, and dangerous, threats may be given short shrift by agencies, like CSIS, reluctant to shift their long-term investments, give up assets painstakingly developed over many years, and start again.

The emergence of new threats to security, especially as embodied in international terrorism (and now even the international drug trade: the majority of Americans view drug abuse as the number one threat to national security) are imposing a paradigm shift on the world of

Western security and intelligence – not to speak of the collapsing world of Eastern security and intelligence. The enforced winding up of the counter-subversion branch of CSIS in 1987 was one clear sign that government is pressing its security and intelligence agency to move away from the old paradigm. The public is apparently less persuaded than government elites that espionage and subversion represent real threats to Canada, while at the same time people clearly identify terrorism as something to be genuinely worried about.[10] Yet the ability to respond effectively to new threats, such as imported terrorism, remains uncertain, as witness the still unsolved mystery of the Air India tragedy which took the lives of 329 people, most of them Canadian citizens.

As we move out of the old Cold War bloc system, the question not only of new definitions of threats to security, but also of new definitions of security itself, must clearly be addressed. Some creative thought has recently been going into a possible redefinition of this term to encompass global concepts of ecological survivability.[11] Even short of this, there is much to be said about redefining not only 'security' but also the term 'national'. In this regard it is worth recalling the wise words of the British Foreign Secretary who said that nations do not have friends, they have interests. Closely tied as Canada is to 'friendly' foreign agencies within the western intelligence network, we should never forget that intelligence products are designed to meet the national interests of the sponsoring state. Countries like Canada which import finished intelligence products are buying a national perspective that is always to some degree foreign. The national interests of some states may overlap with others to a greater or lesser degree, but they are never identical. In a multipolar world, national security and intelligence agencies will increasingly look to their own state's national interest. So should Canada. This may well involve employing intelligence, and counter-intelligence, against some of our friends, when the occasion demands.[12] The fixed investment in the Cold War alliance is a barrier to this.

History is sometimes a treacherous guide. The lessons learned from history are often the wrong ones. Generals, it is said, too often fight the last war. But history can also show us why the past is a different country. To be efficient and effective, the Canadian security and intelligence system needs to be a great deal more present-minded, more autonomous and oriented to Canadian national interests, less tied down by ancient alliance obligations, and more capable of flexible response to changing challenges.

NOTES

1. For an example of the latter, one need look no further than the case of the hapless Stephen Ratkai, set up by the Hungarian intelligence service to gather information on US installations in Newfoundland, and sentenced to nine years' imprisonment under the Official Secrets Act in 1989. The only information Mr Ratkai ever received was passed to him deliberately by American personnel to gain a conviction. While there may be no doubt about his guilt, the significance of this kind of counter-intelligence operation is questionable.
2. Peter Gill, 'Symbolic or Real? The Impact of the Canadian Security Intelligence Review Committee, 1984–88', *Intelligence and National Security*, Vol. 4, No. 3 (July 1989), pp.550–75.
3. For a very useful critical discussion of this concept, see Elizabeth Grace and Colin Leys, 'The concept of subversion and its implications', in C.E.S. Franks (ed.), *Dissent and the State* (Toronto, 1989), pp.62–85.
4. On Canada's role in the UKUSA network, see Jeffrey T. Richelson and Desmond Ball, *Ties that Bind: Intelligence Co-operation Between the UKUSA Countries* (Boston: Allen & Unwin, 1985) and James Littleton, *Target Nation: Canada and the Western Intelligence Network* (Toronto: Lester & Orpen Dennys, 1986).
5. Reg Whitaker, 'Left-wing Dissent and the State: Canada in the Cold War Era', in Franks, *Dissent and the State*, pp.191–210.
6. This was argued by John Sawatsky in his two investigative books on the RCMP Security Service, *Men in the Shadows: the RCMP Security Service* (Toronto: Doubleday, 1980) and *For Services Rendered: Leslie James Bennett and the RCMP Security Service* (Toronto: Doubleday, 1982). More significantly, this was also the thrust of two Royal Commissions which investigated the security process and recommended the 'civilianization' of the service: Royal Commission on Security, *Report* [Abridged] (Ottawa: Supply and Services Canada, 1969; Commission of Inquiry Concerning Certain Activities of the RCMP, *Second Report: Freedom and Security under the Law* 2 vols., and *Third Report: Certain RCMP Activities and the Question of Governmental Knowledge* (Ottawa: Supply and Services Canada, 1981).
7. Reg Whitaker, 'Origins of the Canadian Government's Internal Security System, 1946–1952', *Canadian Historical Review*, Vol. LXV, No. 2 (June 1984), pp.154–83; Whitaker, *Double Standard: the Secret History of Canadian Immigration* (Toronto: Lester & Orpen Dennys, 1987).
8. Reg Whitaker, 'Canada: the RCMP Scandals' in Andrei S. Marcovits and Mark Silverstein (eds.), *The Politics of Scandal: Power and Process in Liberal Democracies* (New York: Holmes & Meier, 1988), pp.38–61.
9. Undated. Released in censored form under the Access to Information Act.
10. Joseph F. Fletcher, 'Mass and elite attitudes about wiretapping in Canada: implications for democratic theory and practice', unpublished research paper (December 1987).
11. See, for instance, Jessica Tuchman Mathews, 'Redefining security', *Foreign Affairs*, Vol. 68, No. 2 (Spring 1989), pp.162–77; and Norman Myers, 'Environment and Security', *Foreign Policy*, 74 (Spring 1989), pp.23–41.
12. SIRC in its 1988/89 *Annual Report* (Ottawa: Supply and Services Canada, 1989) states that 'no fewer than two dozen states are known or suspected by CSIS to be engaged in activities prejudicial to national or allied interests and security, in or against Canada'. A list of this length obviously must include some non-Communist, presumably 'friendly', countries. SIRC also points to 'attempts by foreign countries – some of them widely perceived as friendly – to turn policy and events in Canada to their own purposes'. [p.23] Three 'friendly' countries believed to act, or to have acted, in the ways just described are France – one French official was expelled and banned from Canada in 1968: see Roger Faligot and Pascal Krop, *La Piscine: the*

French Secret Service From 1944 (Oxford: Basil Blackwell, 1989), pp.239–41); India – see Zuhair Kashmieri and Brian McAndrew, *Soft Target: How the Indian Intelligence Service Penetrated Canada* (Toronto: Lorimer 1989); and Israel – there is strong circumstantial evidence of Israeli involvement in sabotaging the attempted exit from Canada, with official government approval and an RCMP escort, of former Palestinian terrorist Mahmud Mohammed Issa Mohammed in 1988. There has, of course, been evidence for years of direct American activity from time to time, but as the relationship between the two countries at this level is so close it is almost impossible to sort out what might be improper or unauthorized on the Americans' part. One recent book which does deal extensively with American intelligence activity in relation to the Quebec independence movement is Jean-François Lisée, *Dans l'oeil de l'aigle: Washington face au Québec* (Montreal, 1990), pp.147–94.

PART THREE

Some Major Issues for the Future

10

Introduction

A. STUART FARSON

There are always dangers in academic crystal-gazing. The basis for the analysis may not be adequately grounded. There may be insufficient information about the present, let alone the future. And, of course, the future may change before one gets there. Justifiably, it may be argued that the organizers of the conference on which this volume of essays is based were asking for trouble when they set as their target the identification of security needs and intelligence requirements for the coming decade.

Despite the dangers of over-generalization, the product that was generated at the conference, and which is reproduced here in this volume by authors from a range of countries and disciplines, has a surprising cohesiveness. In Part One the authors cover a range of countries from different perspectives. There is a common theme throughtout – forces of continuity versus forces of change. Part Two deals primarily with the 'peaceable kingdom': Canada. The chapters focus on two aspects. First came revelations of impropriety by the Security Service of the Royal Canadian Mounted Police (RCMP) and the consequential movement towards political and judicial control to protect the rights and freedoms of Canadians. The work of the McDonald Commission which assessed the wrongdoings of the police has both epitomized this tradition and dominated discussions of security and intelligence matters in Canada since the publication of its first report more than a decade ago. More recently the pendulum has begun to swing again. This time it has moved in a direction which has encouraged debate centred on the effectiveness and efficiency of security and intelligence agencies and whether taxpayers are getting value for money. It is easy to read this shift as a reflection of more conservative thinking or changing political fortunes. But such a view gives short shrift to other equally important and perhaps more reflective considerations concerning the corporate cultures of security and

137

intelligence agencies and possible relationships between impropriety and inefficiency.

The final part of the volume deals neither with the history of security and intelligence agencies and what affects their development, covered in Part One, nor with the current shift in academic debate about them, as discussed in Part Two. Rather it raises issues relevant to the preceding material by concentrating on three themes: the nature of political change, the value of intelligence and the difficulties of counter-terrorism policy.

In the first essay Professor Franklyn Griffiths attends to the all-important question of how to interpret recent changes in Eastern Europe and what these events portend for the security and intelligence agencies of the West, particularly those of Canada. He is convinced that there is substantial evidence to indicate that the Soviet Union is on a reformist path and that Gorbachev, now committed to reform, has no other choice than to continue with it. Yet Professor Griffiths will not go so far as to say that all has changed for the better or that the Soviet threat has been eliminated. On the contrary, he argues that it is still prudent 'to maintain the USSR in adversarial posture'. Likewise, he also puts forward the proposition that even if the Soviet threat were to be eliminated altogether, states of both East and West would continue to need intelligence and counter-intelligence capacities. But in the new context intelligence organizations would have a choice. They could either risk becoming increasingly irrelevant or acquire a new range of capabilities more in character with that found in conventional police work. Such work, Griffiths argues, would inevitably focus on non-state threats – such as terrorism and the problems of global change – and would require a degree of co-operation between services that is altogether unprecedented.

Professor Griffiths' essay raises two further issues which touch on the subjects raised in the other two essays. One is the immediate need in Canada for more resources to analyse non-state threats and new challenges to national security. The other is the old question of whether the recently formed Canadian Security Intelligence Service (CSIS) on the one hand, or the RCMP on the other, would be better equipped to handle Canada's security and intelligence needs in the future.

Professor Robert Jervis's essay attempts to answer the question: 'To what extent can the variations in the success or failure to states' foreign policies be explained by the skill of their intelligence systems and the resulting acuity and accuracy of their assessments of their environments?' Logic, he argues, suggests that the policy followed would be likely to influence the outcome, and that policies in turn are themselves influenced by the beliefs of decision-makers about their environment and the state's intelligence product. Yet, when Professor Jervis looks for evidence of this, he is hard put to find substantive examples where intelligence has proven to be critical. Among his many observations as to why this should be, Professor Jervis points to the difference in the psychological make-up between policy-makers and intelligence analysts. This dissimilarity, he posits, leads to differences of opinion concerning the use to which intelligence can be put and the influence it is likely to have.

For Professor Jervis, good intelligence is facilitated by three inter-related conditions: 'the preservation of alternative analyses; the development of relevant evidence; and the full presentation of arguments that link evidence and interpretation.' He concludes that the nature of the intelligence and decision-making process in the United States makes these conditions difficult to realize.

In that Professor Jean-Paul Brodeur's chapter revisits the question of whether a police agency or a civilian security intelligence service should have primary responsibility for the counter-terrorism function it would appear to be more relevant to Canadians and to those states where the security function is split between a security service and the police than to a broad international audience. But if Griffiths' premise is correct that the security and intelligence function will in the future become more like traditional police work, it has a broader relevance. Although Professor Brodeur realizes that there is a need for coercive capacity, his conclusion is that primary responsibility for counter-terrorism should not be returned to the RCMP. Instead he puts forward the idea that CSIS should have a small unit with peace officer powers fully under the review mechanisms covering CSIS.

11

The CSIS, Gorbachev and Global Change: Canada's Internal Security and Intelligence Requirements in Transition

FRANKLYN GRIFFITHS

Lenin once described the status quo as merely a stage in the transition from the old to the new. Somebody else once depicted the East–West conflict as an exercise in competitive decadence; that is, a struggle to see which side could avoid being the first to demobilize, buckle under the stress or otherwise throw in the towel. The Soviet Union is now moving to throw in the towel. In so doing, it is adding mightily to the political–military demobilization of a Western alliance beset by threat and budget deficits alike.[1] Meanwhile, a new international agenda is beginning to claim our attention. Best articulated in the notion of sustainable development and driven most forcefully by growing recognition of the greenhouse effect, the new cause is one of global co-operation to address the consequences of an unfettered and indeed decadent industrialism,[2] including a staggeringly costly Cold War. And yet the old remains very much with us and will continue to be so.

The extraordinary difficulties encountered by the Soviet Union in making the transition to a sustainable economy and civil society are an indication of what lies ahead for humankind in finding ways to maintain itself with a modicum of freedom on this planet. The Chinese, for their part, could be stooping for a corner of the towel in a cyclical return to xenophobic politics. Be that as it may, military modernization continues in East and West alike. It promises, even after arms reduction agreements and the adoption of less menacing force postures, leaner and meaner nuclear and conventional capabilities which could look quite disturbing in an altered political context. Also, more than a few dismiss the thought of a new agenda of global co-operation as so much 'global baloney' that distracts us from the irreducible conflict of opposed social systems.[3] All the while, Gorbachev's attempts at domestic and international reform could, it seems, give way to chaos, reassertion of dictatorship and the appearance for all to see of a terminally sick man of Eurasia. But how sick would a despotic USSR seem if a downturn in the Western business cycle were at some point to yield not a recession but a depression?

In the midst of these uncertainties and more, I wish to consider the implications of Gorbachev's domestic and foreign reforms for Canada's internal security and intelligence requirements in the 1990s. My purpose is to look far forward, and therefore into the impending era of global change, as well as at the raging concerns of today. Four questions come to mind. First, to the extent that the Soviet threat to Canada is indeed abating, can we afford to be more severe in securing Canadian civil liberties against invasive activity on the part of the Canadian Security Intelligence Service (CSIS), the RCMP's National Security Investigations Directorate (NSID),[4] and the Communications Security Establishment (CSE)[5] in the 1990s? Second, are we in a position to divert a larger portion of the country's security and intelligence-gathering assets to the countering of terrorism, the drug trade and other threats, including the extraordinary challenges of global change, none of which originate primarily with foreign governments? Third, if we are to establish a secret foreign service or offensive intelligence-gathering capability,[6] should we explicitly exclude the Soviet Union and Eastern Europe as targets? Finally, have developments in the Soviet Union presented us with new opportunities in the field of security and intelligence that have yet to be acted upon? Needless to say, answers to these questions do not depend solely upon an estimation of the Soviet threat. It is, however, the Soviet factor as it relates to processes of global change that most concerns us here.

Moved principally by the need to overhaul an outdated, corrupt and inefficient economic system, the Soviet Union under Gorbachev is embarked upon a formidably complex and difficult endeavour to restructure the relationships of the state to its own society and to the outside world. Implicit in current Soviet practice is the creation of a civil society (*grazhdanstvennoe obshchestvo*);[7] a state subject to law, or *Rechtsstaat* (*pravovoe gosudarstvo*);[8] and, as articulated in the 'new thinking' (*novoe myshlenie*),[9] a foreign policy of lasting accommodation to the external environment. To the degree that these varied potentialities are fully realized, the Soviet Union will have acquired certain major characteristics of a liberal democracy. By the same token, Soviet relations with the West and with Canada in particular will have come to resemble those prevailing among the democracies today. To be sure, the prosecution of *perestroika*, *glasnost* and the like into the 1990s and beyond the millennium will meet with setbacks. Also, the institutions and practices of a reconstructed USSR will surely bear the marks of traditional Soviet and indeed Great Russian preferences.[10] Soviet democracy will nevertheless be liberalized, if only because an advanced economy cannot function properly without the encouragement of individual initiative in all its forms.

Though a future Soviet democracy will almost certainly differ from its Western counterparts in assigning greater value to the collective as distinct from the individual good, likemindedness in the conduct of domestic and foreign affairs will very largely displace conflict in Soviet relations with the Western powers and Japan. Accordingly, were today's reforms to produce not merely an increasingly democratic but a viable social order, let us say some time after the turn of the century, the Soviet Union would unquestionably have become a sustaining member of an international community which itself will have become more heavily preoccupied with the deteriorating human condition on a planet with finite carrying capacity.

A future of greater likemindedness between the Soviet Union and today's democracies is, to my mind, a desirable one. It is desirable not only in the attendant reduction of the risk of confrontation and war between major powers, but in creating preconditions for effective cooperation in addressing the challenges of global change. Whether substantially greater likemindedness among major states is indeed a real prospect depends to begin with on our reading of current Soviet developments.

ESCAPING FORWARD

Things are changing with unprecedented rapidity in Gorbachev's Soviet Union. The narrator in John le Carré's recent book (*The Russia House*) observed that *perestroika* was strictly an audio phenomenon with no visuals in sight as yet. By the end of 1989, the audio signal was coming in loud and clear; visuals of Soviet domestic life remained considerably more appalling than appealing; and the foreign policy visuals were highly appealing but ultimately dependent upon great improvement in the domestic imagery. My concern here is with current change in the Soviet Union as it bears on Canadian security intelligence requirements in the coming decade. I begin by substantiating the proposition that a future of greater likemindedness among major states is inherent in the process of *perestroika* to date.

Actions speak louder in foreign affairs, but words are also significant in the Soviet internal context. In terms of action on agreements, concessions and unilateral initiatives, Gorbachev and his colleagues

142

have made a volte-face from the expansionist priorities of previous regimes. Asymmetrical reductions for an INF agreement, substantial cuts in spending on conventional military forces, withdrawal from Afghanistan, promotion of settlements in Angola and Kampuchea, a stunning tolerance of diversity and self-determination in Eastern Europe, support for a revitalization of the United Nations, requests to join international economic institutions including the G-7 group, proposals for global and regional environmental co-operation – the lengthening list of Soviet moves is evidence of a marked accentuation of long-standing reformist tendencies in the regime's foreign behaviour. To be sure, not all has altered since Gorbachev's accession in March 1985. The Soviet Union continues to possess formidable strategic military capabilities which are being modernized. Arms transfers persist. The regime spies as before. Disinformation seems to continue. On these and other counts, bureaucratic inertia joins with prudence on the part of the West to maintain the USSR in an adversarial posture. Nevertheless, the urge to remake the world in the Soviet image has given way to a drive for lasting accommodation with the surrounding environment.

Accommodation was in some sense forced upon Moscow by the costs, opportunity costs included, of a perennial expansionism that mani-festly failed either to advance the cause of world socialism or to yield exemplary improvements in Soviet security and well-being. More important perhaps, the turn to an international policy of accommodation was abetted by evolutionary social change within the Soviet Union, and by a growing awareness that more was to be had from co-operation with others than from the endeavour to suppress opposition by amassing superior force and geopolitical position. The words of the Gorbachev leadership are especially telling in this regard.

According to Soviet new political thinking, an opposed-forces outlook on human affairs is essentially unworkable and is to be replaced by the awareness that all must join together in addressing problems common to all. The preferred Soviet frame of reference has ceased to be one of us-against-them. It is now relatively detached in its recognition that the Soviet Union is part of the larger problem, not the sole possessor of all solutions. Self-criticism and reappraisal have accordingly been authorized in the Soviet Union. They serve to subvert the expansionist state of mind.

No longer is security a condition that Moscow can obtain unilaterally and by military-technical means. Rather, it is to be had in common with others, and through collective political action that both resolves underlying sources of conflict and generates mutual reassurance. Nor are inter-national relations to be viewed as a form of international class struggle. On the contrary, the common interests of humanity take precedence over class interests in achieving social progress. Above all, joint action in addressing global problems increases greatly in importance relative to the struggle of opposed social systems. Soviet insistence on global requirements, it should be noted, is said in Moscow to originate primarily with Aleksandr Yakovlev, ex-ambassador to Canada and now Politburo member and closest adviser to the General Secretary. Though Gorbachev's USSR remains fully wedded to socialism, its contribution to global social change is to be made by force of example and in concert with others, not by striving to alter a global correlation of forces to the benefit of old-style Soviet socialism.

As with outward Soviet behaviour, the internal discourse of the regime on international relations and foreign policy has by no means reached the point where 'old' conceptions and preferences are abolished.[11] On the contrary, 'old' thinking persists under conditions of *glasnost*.[12] It will remain an active force in the Soviet Union, much as ideologically based adversarial assumptions will continue to figure in Western policy debate. It should be permitted to persist, moreover, in a polity that would aspire to greater democracy. Nevertheless, it is clear that the 'new' has the upper hand under Gorbachev. The thrust of new Soviet thinking and new foreign policy initiatives is to make the Soviet Union into something like a normal state which accepts all manner of accommodations with the surrounding order, which abstains from waging the equivalent of war against it.

I therefore submit that a future of likemindedness and productively altered conceptions of security is indeed inherent in Soviet foreign behaviour today. Gorbachev's drive to make the USSR a normal country capable of civil and even friendly relations with others who do not fully share its views deserves our wholesale, if not always our retail, approval. It should also have whatever support we can properly lend. But what might be proper in the field of security and intelligence, or any other, when the Soviet leader and his programme are so beset by adversity from within?

Gorbachev's overriding concern is economic reform.[13] Five years and more into a restructuring of Soviet economic life, little has been achieved. Reforms are half-hearted in concept and execution. Few believe that any reform entailing price increases will improve their situation. The deeply rooted impulse of the bureaucracy and party apparatus to plan from the centre continues to subvert efforts to develop a socialist market. Closures of inefficient enterprises are deferred. The prospect of greater economic inequality is contested, as is the withdrawal of grossly uneconomic price subsidies. Inflation mounts. Budget deficits remain intolerably high. Decades of life in a command economy have killed the desire of many Soviets to work. The new co-operatives do exhibit a readiness to work, but they evoke sharp controversy and are subject to counter-productive administrative restraint. Economic crime is rising sharply. Shortages of meat, soap and tea are sufficient to cause rationing. Rumours of official sabotage abound, as for example in the report that food shortages were artificially created before Khrushchev's removal and quickly ended once the leader was changed. Throughout the country, from the eastern Arctic to western Ukraine, large numbers of people in the regions and republics are demanding an end to the 'colonial' order which returns them far less wealth than they produce. In July 1989, formidably large strikes in the coal industry offered the gravest in a continuing series of indications that the Soviet economy is threatened with chaos.

The Soviet economic outlook under Gorbachev is truly bleak. Modest proposals are being discussed which, if implemented, could improve the situation somewhat. For one thing, Soviet borrowing abroad may buy time to proceed with economic reform by providing the population with a substantial volume of foreign consumer goods. For another, workers and farmers at the local level may yet respond to new incentives to produce which stem from the right to sell surplus output for hard currency. These and other stop-gap measures will, however, continue to be frustrated in the absence of a coherent economic strategy and a still more radical overhaul of the party and ministerial apparatus at all levels. Even then, mass attitudes will stand in the way of any reform that threatens to increase inequality: envy will dilute the greed required to make a market economy work.

Having seen the departure of a substantial number of conservatives from the Central Committee in April 1989, still more as a consequence of elections to the Congress of Deputies, and now the departure of yet others from the Politburo,[14] Gorbachev seemed poised to make still more far-reaching personnel changes. Insofar as economic require-ments are concerned, he stands to succeed. For, once started, the Soviet leadership has no real alternative but to carry *perestroika* forward. Indeed, as with the miners' strike and so much else in foreign as well as domestic affairs, Gorbachev reveals a remarkable ability to convert adversity and vulnerability into an ever stronger drive for domestic and international reform. Though far from universally popular even among Soviet supporters of renewal, the Soviet leader has great prerogative and to a point thrives on adversity.

It is more than a short leap from Soviet economic restructuring to Canadian security and intelligence needs. But insofar as change in Canadian requirements is dependent upon continuity of the current Soviet leadership in the face of appalling economic visuals, I suggest we assume that Gorbachev and, if not him, his priorities will be with us for a long time to come.[15] There is no alternative to *perestroika* that would avoid a Third World future for the Soviet Union. There is no alternative leader in sight. Bad economic news is surely unwelcome to Gorbachev, but it allows him to drive the reform process forward.

In fact, the entire process of change in the Soviet economy and Soviet foreign policy is one of escaping forward. As such, it is by nature fraught with uncertainty. It will take a very long time to complete. All the while, we for our part risk being immobilized by uncertainty as to what happens next in the Soviet Union and to the threat it might pose. There is a message here: do not interpret internal Soviet developments in the light of Western political experience. In evaluating the Soviet threat as it bears on possible modifications of Canadian security and intelligence policy, there is reason to expect continuity, not a reversal, in the Soviet drive toward normalcy. A broadly similar assessment emerges when current Soviet political developments are reviewed.

Gorbachev and his supporters are endeavouring to create a political system that will do real work in aggregating and resolving opposed social demands which for decades were handled by denial, repression and other administrative means. His main domestic political problem is that the system has become overloaded before it is even partially in place. Gorbachev's main foreign policy problem arising from Soviet internal political development is that change is led and governed from on high.[16] It seems thus far to have more in common with recent Iberian authoritarianism than with the precepts of democracy as understood in Northern Europe and the developed English-speaking countries. But as Salazar's Portugal and Franco's Spain made the transition to democracy, so also may Gorbachev's Soviet Union in its own way.[17]

In November 1989, however, the national question appears to threaten the very survival of the USSR and therefore the leadership of Gorbachev. Internal security forces are rushed to an ever larger number of areas in order to quell outbreaks of inter-ethnic violence. In 1988, the Soviet media report, tear gas was used more than a thousand times in maintaining public order.[18] That was a relatively good year. Meanwhile, *glasnost* brings these and many other ugly Soviet realities out into the open while also revealing progress, and a lack of it, in the creation of a law-governed state and civil society. Without doubt, the proliferation of ethnic animosity does gravely threaten a would-be

146

Soviet federalism in which republics, regions and smaller entities gain a larger capacity to determine their separate futures together. Nor do aspirations for independence and sovereignty on the part of the Baltic republics, Soviet Georgia, and conceivably one day Russia itself offer a welcome opportunity for a leader who would stoke the fires of reform.

But the national question has thus far proved to be manageable and will in my view continue to be so. Concessions, some of them possibly quite surprising if further change of the Politburo and party apparatus is accomplished, combined conceivably with increasingly direct and repressive use of the internal security forces, will provide the Soviet leader with time to make the organs of representative government and the courts into increasingly effective instruments of social reconciliation. In particular, time may be bought by the transfer of powers from the centre to those republics willing to stay in the Union. But it is democratization, centred thus far on a pre-eminent role for the Soviets at the local and regional as well as federal level, that proves to be critically important as Gorbachev leads the Soviet Union in its escape forward.

Though falling far, far short of the standards of liberal democracy, political change in 1989 was extraordinary. Of course, one party alone is allowed for now. But the CPSU already houses within itself an implicit multi-party system in the form of contrasting tendencies. These range from the conservative programme represented by Yegor Ligachev on the one hand to Boris Yeltsin's populist radicalism on the other. Gorbachev, positioned on the middle ground, employs growing public accountability to deny conservative policy preferences while averting a peremptory radicalism. As indicated by the fate of Vladimir Solovyov, the Leningrad party chief, it is becoming the rule that party leaders must be popularly elected to hold office. Elections to local and regional soviets, due to be held in 1990, shaped the composition of the party's next congress which was moved forward to October 1990. Ministerial appointments, including those suggested by Gorbachev himself, must also be approved by the new Supreme Soviet. Also, the new standing committees of the Supreme Soviet have been given the task of preparing legislation on human rights, religious freedom and any number of other matters previously dealt with in secrecy by the fused organs of party and state. Despite glaring inadequacies of the electoral process that returned the Congress of Deputies and then the Supreme Soviet of today, recent visuals of Soviet democratization point to growth in the capacity of society not only to control the state but to create conditions conducive to greater individual liberty. They denote change that begins even now to reduce the distance between the

Soviet political order and those of the liberal democracies. They point to growing social control of the state security organs in particular.

Knowing that I was to present this paper at the September 1989 conference, I sought an interview with the KGB during a visit to the Soviet Union in May 1989. Word eventually returned from the Foreign Ministry that such a meeting was 'unrealizable'. In view of what has happened in the country since May 1989, another try might produce a different response. Be that as it may, the KGB has in its fashion begun to respond to *glasnost* and to public demands for accountability.

Aside from encouraging or for that matter providing comment on its affairs in newspapers such as *Argumenty i fakty* (circulation 26 million), the KGB director, Vladimir Kryuchkov, announced in May 1989 that the organization would act to reduce the secrecy that surrounds its operations. The KGB has begun to follow through, but in a manner that continues to cite success in adversarial activity, as for example with the 'Orlov' case. It also proclaims good domestic intentions by asserting that its staff no longer includes any individuals who took part in the repression of the Stalin years. No doubt anticipating events at the Congress of Deputies, the KGB Collegium further committed itself from early May 1989 to the 'creation of a flawless mechanism of accountability to the people and supreme bodies of state authority and the [sic] active participation in the elaboration of legislative acts concerning protection of the state's constitutional foundations'.[19] At the Congress and in the presence of a vast television audience, the Soviet weightlifter Yuri Vlasov proceeded to accuse the KGB of maintaining the old order. The response of the KGB to this and other developments has been to court public support more actively.[20] More important, it may have furthered the discussion of proposals that would divorce the organization from much of its current internal security responsibilities, as with the CIA in contrast to the FBI. Vladimir Semichastnyi, one-time head of the KGB, has had some interesting things to say about mission and accountability.[21] Meanwhile and as mentioned above, the Supreme Soviet has established a standing committee on security affairs which will seek to develop procedures and rules for legislative review of KGB activities.[22] Though the Soviet national security establishment is overwhelmingly represented in its membership, the committee's operations cannot but be affected by the larger determination of the Supreme Soviet to assert its powers.

The KGB, as with all Soviet institutions, is presented with a novel situation. Thus far, it reveals little or no inclination to assimilate and act upon new political thinking about security and international relations. It has embarked upon a new public relations programme. It is possibly prepared to accept structural change and an altered mandate. Also, it has no choice but to accept a degree of legislative control by deputies who may not all be well disposed to the organization. In short, accountability has begun to set in and with it a quasi-public reconsideration of the KGB's mission. In this setting of transition, unofficial offers of Western assistance in the design of legislative review procedures are surely appropriate, as are overtures from Western intelligence services to discuss with the KGB a *perestroika* of international security operations.

AFTER THE MILLENNIUM

Now to look far ahead, say to the year 2010. If we grant that the process of *perestroika*, possibly laced with a greater measure of coercion as well as concession on the part of central authorities, finally yields a polity not wholly unlike a liberal democracy, what might become of the security and intelligence requirements of major states, Canada included?

To begin with, the reconstructed Soviet Union would continue to need intelligence and counter-intelligence capabilities. So also would the Western countries despite the abridgement of Soviet-Western differences. Persistent military–technical innovation would invite intelligence-gathering and a capacity for covert operations such as occurs today among the liberal democracies, for example in Israeli spying on the United States or French operations in New Zealand. Nor would political intelligence on the preferences and stability of governments disappear as an asset of major power statecraft. The same would surely apply to the generation of illicit influence, and to precaution against hostile groups seen to be harboured by another.

As to industrial espionage, the Soviet interest would presumably continue to be greater than that of most Western countries. But the withdrawal of the Soviet state from an unfolding market economy in the USSR would presumably be accompanied by a higher incidence of decentralized or free-enterprise economic theft analogous to what goes on among today's democracies. Indeed, the singular aptitude for crime now being displayed in the Soviet Union, and in Brighton Beach,[23] heralds a significant role for Soviet free agents in the future of international economic crime. Meanwhile, the capacity of major states to vacuum and exploit all forms of electronic communication would no doubt continue to achieve new heights.

These and other elements of continuity in security and intelligence operations could reasonably be expected in an international future characterized by thorough-going democratization of the Soviet Union. But while the necessity for intelligence activity would persist, its *quality* would be transformed. Whether the Soviet Union did most of the changing or whether something like East–West convergence began to occur, movement of the Soviet Union towards the status of a liberal democracy would join with economic and other forces at work globally to alter the international system and with it the perception of international security requirements. A bipolar international order marked by high levels of ideological conflict would have given way to a balance-of-power system in which major states were primarily occupied with non-military or civil issues and abided by the injunction not to seek the violent overthrow of another's social order. Though destabilization or electoral defeat of a foreign government could well remain within the ambit of prevailing balance-of-power activity, as might covert intervention in small-state civil wars and regional conflicts, the Soviet Union would have joined the Western countries in tacit or formal understandings to eliminate state subversion as a means in their mutual relations. An era of great adversarial causes would have ended.

Fear of communism in the West would have dissipated with the dissipation of communism itself. In the Soviet Union, perennial fear of imperialism – itself an artifact constructed to justify a world revolutionary mission – would have declined with the erosion of Soviet revolutionary objectives. Traditional national security threats being in short supply, security itself would come to have new meanings. On the one hand, I-win-you-lose thinking and fears of the worst that major powers might do to one another would have been subverted by conventional and nuclear arms control, and by economic and other arrangements serving as a whole to produce substantial political reassurance between the Soviet Union and the West; on the other, the threats that mattered would increasingly be seen to emanate not so much from other states, as from non-state sources and phenomena owing much to unsustainable man-milieu relationships on a planetary scale.

The global effects of overpopulation, profligate use of resourcs, pollution and climatic change would be upon us.[24] Though the nature and severity of local phenomena are impossible to predict, the anticipation of shared adversity would have sharpened greatly by 2010. As arable land began to 'move', forests were cut and displaced, water resources were diminished and degraded, species were threatened and lost, low-lying areas were faced with inundation or flooded, the biosphere and human health became increasingly affected by ozone depletion, and so on, we would be confronted with a rising incidence of resource-related conflict, famine, disease – possibly including new pandemics – large-scale population movements by environmental and other refugees, and with the appearance of new millennial ideologies. Meanwhile, states no doubt still constrained by debt or deficit, but determined to enhance the competitiveness and quality of life of their peoples, would be obliged to make truly wrenching choices. These choices would centre on the distribution of the costs of action both to address the causes of global change and to adapt to change.

Canada and the United States, for example, today account for some 25 per cent of the world's energy use while constituting 5 per cent of the world's population. The government of China, for its part, is determined to raise the living standard of its vast and rapidly increasingly population, and has by far the largest share of world coal reserves. How would China avoid adding substantially to the greenhouse effect in 2010? Could the Chinese way of life be expected to remain near to a state of nature in order to avoid further offence to Nature when North Americans and others, who had been responsible for the greatest share of total carbon emissions, continued to live high on the hog? And if China and other developing countries refused to accept significant emission restraints without offsetting technical aid or compensation to offset them, why would others pay the price of a debilitated attempt to address the causes of climatic change? After China, it might be added, the Soviet Union has not only the next largest coal reserves but an environmental movement determined to resist the expansion of nuclear power facilities.

Though there is an obvious military dimension to the phenomenon of global change, military power will not take major states very far in coping with the socio-economic, environmental and related dilemmas that will have risen to prominence two decades hence. In conditions of heightened interdependence, security will have acquired new meanings keyed primarily to economic competitiveness and to the regulation of transboundary processes with no single point of origin. In these conditions, pressure for the reformation of global and regional institutions, and for co-operation among major powers in particular would be compelling.

National intelligence services would thus be faced with the alternative of becoming increasingly irrelevant or acquiring a qualitatively new range of capabilities required to address a global security agenda of agricultural disruption, benign energy supply, protection of the common good, and the like. In any event, collaboration between Soviet and Western intelligence establishments would already have become extensive and intimate with regard to terrorism, international crime – including the drug trade and money-laundering, illicit private transfers of conventional arms and mass-destruction technology, large-scale refugee movements, clandestine pollution, and so on. Divorced from the high politics of the day, security and intelligence activity would share more of the characteristics of police work. Whether the CSIS or the RCMP were best equipped to cope would continue to be a Canadian issue in 2010.

Further, as continued arms competition among major powers acquired a vestigial and decadent quality, ideologically grounded conceptions of intelligence activity would also come to be viewed not only as anachronistic but as part of the problem in securing effective interstate co-operation. Arms control having led the way where military–technical conceptions of security were concerned, negotiations to constrain adversarial intelligence operations and to promote inter-agency co-operation on security matters of mutual interest would have become a commonplace of international diplomacy. Indeed, in a world of substantially greater likemindedness among major states, the creation of a global security and intelligence service might well have been raised as an actionable proposition.

Meanwhile, significant changes would also have occurred in the domestic political landscape of the major states. Soviet progression toward liberal–democratic status being a key factor in the scenario here, the political institutions of the USSR would have become increasingly responsive to the public will. As relations between state and society were restructured to benefit the latter, the Soviet national security apparatus in particular would have been made publicly accountable. Where the KGB was concerned, domestic and foreign operations alike would be subject to law and legislative review. Given Western experience in these matters, to say nothing of Soviet and Russian traditions, the state within the state would more readily be invaded than occupied by representatives of Soviet society. Nevertheless, in conditions of greater external reassurance, altered conceptions of security and surrender of adversarial ambitions, democratization and *glasnost* could serve to bring the security organs under a measure of effective public review. Along the way, the Western powers would no doubt have contributed to the process by making legislative control over the KGB an indicator of the Soviet purpose in world affairs.

As to the West, decay of adversarial relations with the Soviet Union and the emergence of a global agenda might be accompanied by a trend toward reformist and green politics. If so, reformism and East–West civil or non-military co-operation could unfold more rapidly in a restructured Europe than would be the case with the insular democracies of North America, Japan and possibly the United Kingdom. For some, heightened divergences among the Western powers over *ostpolitik* would continue to offer evidence of Soviet success in a plot to destroy NATO while the USSR completed the long march to a renewed ability to impose its will and ways. Nevertheless, greater accountability and responsiveness would be sought by Western publics and politicians where their own security and intelligence establishments were concerned. To boot, routine moves such as publicized expulsions of Soviet and East European spies would be met with mounting disbelief: rather than communicating the need for continued caution in East–West relations, such events would be discounted as bureaucratic manoeuvres to maintain budgets. Again, and in keeping with the dictum of Soviet new thinking that the real enemy is the image of the enemy, adversarial intelligence operations would come to be regarded as an impediment to effective co-operation based on new notions of security.

PROPOSITIONS

We could go on to consider alliance relations, the Japanese and Chinese role in great-power interaction, and other dimensions of an international future of global change and greater likemindedness between the Soviet Union and the West. But this inquiry has gone far enough to generate a set of propositions:

1. *Canada will need a security and intelligence service for the indefinite future.* This will be the case even in a relatively benign future of greater commonality among major powers. Canadians who applaud Phillip Knightley when he calls for dissolution of the CSIS should pause to think the implications through.[25]

2. *An adversarial perspective on security and intelligence activity that is keyed to the Soviet threat is outdated and promises to become increasingly counter-productive of security.* Those who endorse the outlook of the Mackenzie Institute should also pause to think. In East and West alike, publics and politicians should seek a reappraisal of the international security situation from their intelligence chiefs. Dollars, pounds and roubles spent will otherwise produce progressively less useful intelligence and progressively less security in an era of global change.

3. *A conception of security that attaches greater significance to co-operation in addressing non-state and global threats is more in keeping with present needs than one derived from assumptions of zero-sum*

ideological conflict. The CSIS should not wait to be prompted but take the initiative in demonstrating to Canadians that it is moving to address new security requirements as well as the old. More broadly, intelligence establishments in East and West alike will be obliged to diversify their missions and to embrace an array of police tasks if they wish to maximize public understanding and support.

4. *Greater co-operation between Soviet and Western intelligence establishments is desirable on its merits and as a means of easing the way to new understandings of security.* The CSIS should again take the initiative in seeking (a) broader collaboration with the KGB on matters of common concern, and (b) unilateral restraint in KGB adversarial operations within Canada on the grounds that it perpetuates 'enemy images' inconsistent with the needs of common security. CSIS activities in approaching the KGB should be publicized, including the fact that the CSIS does not operate within the Soviet Union.

5. *Greater openness in CSIS activity is essential in maintaining public support and demonstrating to the KGB's masters that their servants are perpetuating enemy images of the Soviet Union.* Canadians should be given an annual report detailing trends in Soviet intelligence activity in Canada. Detailed indictments should be provided to Canadians when Soviets are expelled from Canada.[26]

6. *East–West negotiations to constrain adversarial intelligence operations and promote co-operation will sooner or later be with us.* Better sooner. In matters of security intelligence, we faced in 1989 a situation analogous to that of 1959 for arms control. Some 30 years were required to realize fully that co-operation offered benefits that could not be had through self-help where the military dimension of security was concerned, and to act decisively upon it. Global change denies us the luxury of another 30 years in learning to co-operate in the security intelligence sphere. Further, if institutional and professional autonomy is to be maintained at the margin, intelligence agencies in East and West are best advised to get ahead of the curve and themselves lead in the common cause rather than rely primarily upon one another's mistakes in order to stay in business.

7. *In furthering a transition from adversarial towards common security as a basis for major-state security and intelligence operations, distinctions should be made between intelligence analysis and intelligence gathering.* We ought to begin with analysis. Exploring the ground in bilateral conversations with the KGB, the CSIS should propose to sister agencies in the West that discussions be held by NATO and Warsaw Pact intelligence analysts aimed at improving the ability to get things right by means of (a) retrospective consideration of each side's

assessments in the light of the other's understanding of its own reality at the time, and (b) discussion of the analytical capabilities required to address a common and global security agenda in the future.

8. *Democratization of the Soviet Union being a precondition for greater likemindedness between East and West, and hence a more favourable international security outlook, Westerners should consider what might be done to encourage greater public accountability of the Soviet intelligence apparatus.* The Canadian government could take the lead in seeking to make effective Soviet legislative review of KGB and GRU operations a key Western index in assessing the Soviet purpose in world affairs. Canadian parliamentarians could offer an exchange of experience with their Soviet counterparts on the design and implementation of legislative control procedures.[27] Avoiding the committee recently established by the USSR supreme Soviet to oversee military and intelligence matters, Canadian parliamentary assistance could nevertheless be lent to the work of other legislative committees in establishing standards and practices that might in due course affect the Soviet security intelligence review process.

9. *Any move to better protect Canada's democratic freedoms against invasion by the CSIS and other Canadian intelligence services should be justified on civil liberties grounds and without reference to the reduced Soviet threat.* Under Gorbachev, the Soviet threat to Canada and the Canadian way of life has abated. The USSR is preoccupied with its own problems and will remain so for many years. Throughout the world, command or barracks socialism is being proven unworkable. It provides no viable answers for the Soviet Union and, with one exception, is highly unlikely to pose a renewed and significant threat to the Canadian people and state. The exception lies in a heightened risk of inadvertent war should the Soviet Union, after all, descend into civil war and chaos. For reasons given above, I consider civil war in the Soviet Union an improbable outcome. Soviet foreign and military policies are now governed by durable reformist tendencies towards international accommodation and normalcy. All this said, the fact remains that the KGB and GRU, to say nothing of comparable East European agencies, continue to be active in Canada. The need to counter Soviet intelligence operations in Canada is unalterable in a transitional era. It will remain so for as long as Soviet activity persists.

10. *Diversion of Canadian security and intelligence assets away from counter-Soviet activity and to non-state threats such as international terrorism and problems of global change is appropriate in view of the diminished overall threat from the Soviet Union, but should be made contingent upon the development of co-operation with the KGB.*

Immediately, however, the CSIS should be provided with additional resources for the analysis of non-state threats and challenges to Canada's security. It would make little sense to set the reduced Soviet threat aside in considering possible civil-liberties restrictions on Canadian security and intelligence activity within Canada, and then to accentuate it in directing the CSIS and associated bodies to reduce their counter-Soviet effort so as to deal more effectively with non-state threats. And yet, non-state threats and global challenges to Canadian security are appreciating relative to the Soviet threat and will continue to do so. Canada should therefore maintain its ability to address Soviet activity in this country until tacit or formal arrangements are achieved with the KGB to reduce adversarial operations and start building a joint effort on behalf of global security interests. Meanwhile, the CSIS should be enabled to strive for leadership among Western agencies in analysing the security intelligence requirements of global change. At the same time, reduction of the Soviet threat obliges us to consider how much is actually spent by the Communications Security Establishment in listening to Soviet military and other communications. The CSE should be brought under parliamentary review, and ought to justify its mission and budget publicly.

11. *Canada should exclude the Soviet Union and Eastern Europe as a target area in any decision to acquire an offensive intelligence-gathering capability.* After all these years and just when the Soviet threat to Canada is in marked decline, it would be quixotic to include the USSR in a new offensive intelligence effort which in itself seems to be a dubious proposition. Should an offensive capability nevertheless be sought, the option to target or abstain from activity in the USSR, and what remains of the Soviet bloc, might be used in bargaining with the KGB on matters of mutual interest.

12. *The CSIS should move without delay to develop and gain support for a strategy of collaboration in the midst of continuing conflict with the KGB.* In adopting a mixed strategy of co-operation and resistance, we do not need to accept the KGB's image of itself as a kinder, gentler organization. Nor should we expect straightforward dealings. But East and West do share interests in security intelligence matters. The timing for initiatives in this area is right since the structure and mandate of the KGB would now seem to be under review. Aside from endeavouring to obtain increased unilateral KGB restraint in its Canadian operations, the CSIS should promote a *combined* approach to the KGB by Western agencies acting in concert. The overture should first seek greater East–West intelligence collaboration against contemporary non-state threats.[28] Second, it should aim at joint action in assessing and meeting

future security problems arising from climatic change, overpopulation, pollution and related global threats to human existence.

In sum, a transitional approach for transitional times is needed, one that begins to move intelligence agencies in East and West towards greater co-operation, and the KGB towards a posture of accommodation consistent with that of the Soviet state.

AFTERTHOUGHTS

This essay is open to attack along three main lines. First, it could be argued that by late 1989 *perestroika* had entered a crisis phase in which Gorbachev looked all too likely to be overthrown. Whoever were to come next, a conservative party leader or even a military man, the world would presumably recover some if not all of the familiar sense of insecurity. Second, it could be insisted that even were *perestroika* to struggle on, Gorbachev is not a democrat, the Soviet peoples lack the requisite political and entrepreneurial culture, and for these and other reasons a Eurasian Soviet order is unlikely to evolve into anything resembling a liberal democracy. If so, a future of greater likemindedness among major powers would in greater or lesser measure be denied, and with it the opportunity for East–West collaboration, including co-operation in the security and intelligence sphere. Third, it could be claimed that given today's rudimentary understanding of the physical processes underlying global change, a new international agenda centred on non-state threats and socio-economic issues is by no means certain to supplant established approaches to international security. Indeed, new challenges associated with global change could come to supplement, not displace, long-standing priorities in the security and intelligence field during the next two decades.

In short, it could be argued that in its essentials the situation in 2010 will be not unlike that of 1990. To expect more continuity than change in the period ahead is in my view profoundly misguided. Nevertheless, there is no denying that change could take a course different from that suggested here. The question is whether the propositions stated above for the Canadian and indeed the Western approach to matters of security and intelligence are likely to be invalidated.

To consider the minimalist view of global change first, I take it as given that we have entered upon a time of fundamental transformation in world affairs. Humankind has altered the human condition by setting in motion physical processes on a planetary scale that will transform economic and social activity, including international relations as we

157

have known them. Traditional concerns for security will be overwhelmed by the declining ability of states acting on their own or in blocs to ensure a habitable environment and decent life for their populations. Just as there is no longer an 'away' when things are thrown away, the quality of life of the nations will be eroded by transboundary processes originating 'elsewhere' even as the wisest of purely national policies are pursued. States will not get far in attempting to transfer the costs of change to others. They will be driven to qualitatively higher levels of co-operation.

Publics are already well ahead of politicians and bureaucrats in sensing the realities now bearing down upon us. Given the extraordinary rapidity with which the new consciousness of human interaction with the environment has appeared, and also the capacity of science to achieve greater precision in anticipating further change in the human condition, I see no good reason to doubt that generally accepted meanings of security will indeed be transformed in the coming two decades. Whether altered conceptions of security predominate, or serve to add new dilemmas to the old, will however depend significantly upon the internal evolution of the Soviet Union.

This analysis has linked the emergence of greater likemindedness among major powers to the abridgement of differences between the Soviet political order and those of the liberal democracies. The assumption here is that the appearance of deep-seated and enabling commonalities between the USSR and the G-7 countries will serve to put ideological conflict very largely behind us as the Soviet polity assimilates Western ways, or as a form of convergence occurs. The stunning developments in Eastern Europe and in Soviet–East European relations that have occurred in the mere months since this essay was drafted amply confirm the judgement that an abrogation of East–West ideological cleavages is inherent in Soviet political change. At the same time, it has been noted that the new Soviet order will be shaped by Soviet and Russian ways which diverge from the traditions of northern Europe and the English-speaking countries. History and tradition are manifested today in the paradox that change in the Soviet Union, including change that gives greater rights and powers to the individual, has been conceived and led from above. The characteristics of democracy in the Soviet Union are sure to be conditioned by the process that brings them into being.

Nevertheless, if *perestroika* survives the time of troubles that has now set in, the Soviet state will have been made accountable in ways not wholly dissimilar to those prevailing among the liberal democracies. Doctrine will have given way to pragmatism. Conflict between the

USSR and the G-7 countries will not disappear in these circumstances, any more than it has within the G-7 grouping. But the erosion and possibly the collapse of ideologically-based opposition will allow progressively wider joint action in meeting the demands of global change. I therefore contend that if the process of democratization now launched in the Soviet Union comes to maturity, altered conceptions of security will indeed replace, and not supplement, the political–military notions that have dominated major-state behaviour since 1945. All of which brings us back to the question of whether Gorbachev and *perestroika* will endure.

Suppose I have it wrong and Gorbachev is sooner or later broken by the forces he has unleashed in the Soviet Union. Suppose further that the regime opted for Stalinist or neo-Stalinist reaction, or for a Jaruzelski-type solution in which the military establishment played a critical role, or perhaps most likely for a Russian nationalist answer to the fundamental question of Russia's place in world history. Though each of these scenarios seems implausible in terms of the Soviet interest, the process would presumably be driven more by the dynamic of economic and political upheaval than by considered choice. As such, it could begin with the incorporation of conservative preferences into Gorbachev's programme itself.

Under the scenario of a military coup with limited and transitional objectives, we would certainly lose time – including time during which to undo born-again adversarial assumptions in the West – in making the transition to greater commonality of purpose among major states. But as the Poles eventually began to join together after the imposition of martial law in 1981, so also might the various estates of the Soviet Union. In the interim, the USSR would offer a renewed military threat to the liberal democracies in an era in which military capabilities were of diminishing value in the production of security. A transitional military regime would, however, remain committed to *détente*, and to a foreign policy of interdependence even as other elements of the new Soviet thinking were rejected or downplayed.

In such circumstances, the Western countries and Japan would continue to have actionable interests in continued co-operation with the Soviet Union on security matters old and new. All twelve of the policy propositions advanced above would remain valid. To act on these propositions, however, would be exceedingly difficult in the face of repression throughout the USSR, to say nothing of Eastern Europe. And yet the mere mention of Eastern Europe serves as a reminder of how far change has already gone, and of Poland's demonstration of the inherent limitations of the military instrument in making a moderately advanced society work. Add to this the Soviet military's interest in modernization and its longstanding acceptance of party dominance in Soviet civil–military relations, and the possibility of transitional military takeover seems remote.

Alternatively, a post-Gorbachev Soviet Union could revert to unrelieved decadence masked by triumphalist propaganda of the kind which was spouted by Romania's leader. In this the Ottoman scenario, an impoverished and highly repressive Soviet state dominated by party die-hards would make itself increasingly irrelevant in world affairs. The ideological challenge of communism would not be picked up in the West because it would not be credible. The renewed threat would be largely military and readily offset by the superior technology and productivity of the democracies. Here, too, it would be recognized that just as Stalinist foreign and military policy had been one of fulminating passivity following the real gains of war, a Romanian-style Soviet regime in the 1990s would represent a withdrawal into self-isolation following the perceived losses of reform. In these circumstances, the rest of us would look to our defences and seek out ways of doing without the USSR as best we could in dealing with global change. In terms of international opportunities lost, to say nothing of the human cost in the Soviet Union, a neo-Stalinist restoration would be a catastrophe. Needless to say, the reappearance of an antagonistic Soviet state would invalidate most of the policy prescriptions advanced in this essay.

Finally, there is Russian nationalism to be considered. In the extreme case, a regime dominated by pathological Russian nationalism in conjunction with party and military reaction would be indistinguishable from the Ottoman scenario.

A new leadership could in effect act on Solzhenitsyn's nationalist advice of 1974.[29] In so doing, it would find a way to renounce Marxism, to cut loose not only the East European peoples but the unwilling Soviet nationalities, to turn its back on Western ways, and to cultivate Russian civilization by making a new beginning through small-is-beautiful Siberian development. A theocratic Russia would renew its traditional mission of salvation on a planet that is indeed being exhausted by decadent Western ways, and is manifestly in need of an alternative to the industrial philosophy of boundless material progress. Though all too likely to be accompanied by heightened anti-Semitism and xenophobia, Russian nationalism is powerfully associated with environmentalism and appears not insensitive to problems of global change.[30] Further, to the extent that Solzhenitsyn's particular variant of Russian national thought were taken to heart, a Russia reduced to the territory of the present RSFSR would regard itself as secure from attack and thus open to dealing with others. Accordingly, a relatively benign Russian nationalism would be substantially less averse to co-operation with the G-7 countries on the full range of international security matters than would a Soviet Union governed by a decadent communism. In these circumstances a good deal of the policy prescriptions presented here would remain intact.

It should be evident that in considering alternatives to the *perestroika* of today we are actually dealing not with separable scenarios, but with intermingled conservative forces currently at work within the Soviet system. The emergence of any one of these forces to a position of pre-eminence seems quite improbable. Were the improbable to occur, in two outcomes out of three the Soviet posture would remain disposed to some degree of co-operation on international security affairs. The liberal democracies would in any event retain the ability to look after themselves in what passed for a renewed test of wills between East and West. More important, just as Russian nationalism is itself a fractured social movement, the key forces that might constitute a conservative Soviet regime are intrinsically divided and unlikely to settle on a common programme.

In short, the domestic and international situation faced by the Soviet Union serves to bias its behaviour towards reform and continued democratization through thick or thin. There is no real alternative to Gorbachev's programme. It does promise greater likemindedness among major powers and an enhanced capacity to meet the realities of global change. The going will not be easy. But we should settle on these matters and stop fretting about what comes next in the Soviet Union. We can handle what comes next. We should seize the moment and proceed forthwith to build a structure of East–West co-operation in security intelligence affairs.

NOTES

1. The ensuing malaise is evident in Francis Fukuyama, 'The End of History?' *The National Interest*, No. 16 (Summer 1989), pp.3–18, which came to my attention after this piece was drafted in July 1989 for presentation at the September 1989 Conference. It was revised and annotated in November 1989.
2. Bill McKibben provides a moving evocation of our predicament in 'Reflections: The End of Nature', *The New Yorker*, 11 Sept. 1989. The end of history, the end of nature: where Fukuyama's piece drew extraordinary attention and also derision, McKibben's message should not be set aside.

3. Thomas L. Friedman, 'U.S.–Soviet Talks Turn to New Public Dangers', *New York Times*, 5 May 1989.

4. Existence of the NSID, then cited as the National Security Intelligence Section, was first made public in July 1989. See Richard Cleroux, 'RCMP Security Team May be Rival of CSIS', *Globe and Mail*, 4 July 1989.

5. The CSE is Canada's signals intelligence establishment. Evidently it monitors Soviet communications from over the pole and in the North Pacific. See for example the comments in Seymour Hersh, *The Target Destroyed* (New York: Random House, 1986), pp.244–6. Whether and if so to what extent the CSE monitors electronic communications within Canada is not known.

6. Pressure to set up a secret foreign service would seem to be coming from Canada's allies. The Security Intelligence Review Committee (SIRC), for one, does not go along, but does recommend the occasional dispatch of CSIS agents abroad. See SIRC, *Assessing the CSIS Act: Proposals for the Special Committee of the House of Commons 1989* (Ottawa: Supply and Services, 1989), pp.18–19, released in late Sept. 1989. A sharp rejoinder to this proposal is offered by John Starnes, 'There Are Pitfalls for Canada in Spying Abroad', *Ottawa Citizen*, 31 Oct. 1989. The Solicitor General appears on balance to favour the allocation of additional resources to the task of intelligence analysis as distinct from collection. 'Accountability and Effectiveness: National Requirements for Security Intelligence in the 1990s. Notes for a Speech by the Honourable Pierre Blais, Solicitor General of Canada, to the Canadian Association for Security and Intelligence Studies conference, Ottawa, September 19, 1989', *News Release*, Solicitor General of Canada.

7. An excellent commentary is available in S. Frederick Starr, 'Soviet Union: A Civil Society', *Foreign Policy* (Spring 1988), pp.26–41. See also the searching discussion in Gail W. Lapidus, 'State and Society: Towards the Emergence of Civil Society in the Soviet Union', in Seweryn Bialer (ed.), *Politics, Society and Nationality: Inside Gorbachev's Russia* (Boulder: Westview, 1989), pp.121–47.

8. See, for example, G.N. Manov, 'Sotsialisticheskoe pravavoe gosudarstvo: Problemy i perspektivy' [The Socialist *Rechtsstaat*: Problems and Prospects], *Sovetstskoe gosudarstvo i pravo*, 6 (June 1989), pp.3–10, and A.B. Vengerov, 'Sotsialisticheskoii pluralizm v kontseptisii pravovogo gosudarstva' [Socialist Pluralism in the Conception of the *Rechtsstaat*], ibid., pp.11–19.

9. For early discussion of Soviet new thinking on international affairs, see Franklyn Griffiths, 'Current Soviet Military Doctrine', in Murray Feshbach (ed.), *National Security Issues of the USSR*. Workshop 6–7 Nov. 1986 NATO HQ Brussels (Dordrecht: Martinus Nijhoff, 1987), pp.241–58, and Tsuyoshi Hasegawa, *Gorbachev's 'New Thinking' in Soviet Foreign–Security Policy* (Washington, DC: National Council for Soviet and East European Research, Feb. 1988).

10. Joseph Conrad's *Under Western Eyes* (London: Penguin, 1980) provides a cautionary reminder of the police practice of the Russian autocracy. First published in 1911, it was more widely read in Russia than the West after 1916.

11. Signs of the old are for example to be seen in E. Primakov, V. Martynov, and G. Diligenskii, 'Nekotorye problemy novogo myshleniya' [Some Problems of the New Thinking], *Mirovaya ekonomika i mezhdunarodnye otnosheniya*, 6 (June 1989), pp.5–18. Primakov was promoted to the Politburo on 20 Sept. 1989 from being director of the USSR Academy of Sciences' Institute of the World Economy and International Relations (IMEMO). The previous IMEMO director was Aleksandr Yakovlev. The article cited is noteworthy for its inconclusive attempt to reconcile new thinking with Marxism–Leninism.

12. New thinking and the conciliatory foreign policy which it informs are themselves not without ambiguity. As noted at the outset of this chapter, in reducing the threat it poses to the liberal democracies, the Soviet Union deprives the Western alliance of an essential precondition for military strength and political unity. Those in Moscow who in greater or lesser measure remain wedded to a view of contemporary affairs as a struggle between socialism and capitalism cannot but note that a Soviet foreign

policy oriented to new thinking yields advances that were denied to Moscow in decades of two-camp struggle. In my judgement these advances are at most side benefits and not of the essence for Gorbachev and those who share his views. The dominant aim of Soviet reformism under Gorbachev is to abandon a futile competition for global power and primacy through strength in favour of Westernizing internal reforms and international co-operation.

13. For a general review, see Vladimir V. Popov, *Perestroika: An Insider's View* (Toronto: C.D. Howe Institute, Occasional Paper 7, July 1989).

14. Yet another in a continuing sequence of Politburo changes was announced on 20 Sept. 1989. See Bill Keller, 'Gorbachev Ousts Politburo Hardliners', *New York Times*, 21 Sept. 1989. More interesting than Primakov's elevation (note 16) was the promotion to full voting membership of Vladimir Kryuchkov, chairman of the KGB. A client of Yuro Andropov, Kryuchkov was a secretary in the Soviet embassy in Budapest in 1956, when Andropov was ambassador there. He entered the KGB in 1967, when it was led by Andropov, and was in charge of KGB foreign operations before becoming chairman in 1988. Andropov having been a covert reformist who was able to make at most a false start at reform in 1982–84, Kryuchkov in my view is likely to be an active supporter of reform and not an adversary of Gorbachev.

15. Consensus is emerging on this point. See for example Valéry Giscard d'Estaing, Yasuhiro Nakasone and Henry A. Kissinger, *East–West Relations; A Task Force Report to the Trilateral Commission* (New York: Trilateral Commission, Triangle Papers 36, 1989).

16. Some in the Soviet Union urge dictatorial powers upon Gorbachev so as to ensure the progress of economic reform and democratization. See Bill Keller, 'Gorbachev's Caldron Boils Onwards', *New York Times*, 11 Sept. 1989, and Adranik Miganyan, in 'Nuzhna "zheleznaya ruka"?' [Is the 'Iron Hand' Needed?], *Literaturnaya gazeta*, 16 Aug. 1989.

17. As Migranyan put it, 'Nowhere, in no country ever has there been a direct transition from a totalitarian regime to democracy. There has always been a mandatory intermediate period.' In my view the Soviet system had already made the transition from totalitarianism to authoritarianism long before Gorbachev. For the view that 'liberalization is what an authoritarian system's leaders concede to prevent democratization', see William Pfaff, 'Democracy: Communism's Rebels Are Dreaming', *International Herald Tribune*, 26 May 1989.

18. Jeff Sallot, 'Soviet Troops Counter Protests', *Globe and Mail*, 5 July 1989. See also 'Fighting Breaks out in Moldavia after Kremlin Warns Baltic States', ibid., 11 Nov. 1989.

19. 'KGB Considers State of Glasnost Within Its Ranks', Tass, 5 May 1989.

20. Esther B. Fein, 'Soviet Congress Grills K.G.B. Chief', *New York Times*, 15 July 1989, and Bill Keller, 'Moscow Proudly Presents Its Kindly K.G.B.', ibid., 14 Sept. 1989. The KGB also reports a reduction in its counter-intelligence effort within the Soviet armed forces. 'Soviet Close Spy Units', *Globe and Mail*, 5 Oct. 1989. The reference here is to *Pravitelstvennyi vestnik*, 4 Oct. 1989. Reductions in anti-dissident operations and border protection are also reported. See 'KGB Plans to Remove Barbed Wire', *Toronto Star*, 21 Oct. 1989, and 'KGB Abolishes Anti-Dissent Unit', ibid., 27 Oct. 1989.

21. See the interview in *Ogonyok*, No. 24 (10–17 June 1989), pp.24–26.

22. For detail, see Michael R. Gordon, 'Afghan War Hero Part of Soviet Effort for Legislative Oversight of Military', *New York Times*, 14 Aug. 1989.

23. Ralph Blumenthal, 'Soviet Emigre Mob Outgrows Brooklyn', ibid., 4 June 1989.

24. Jessica Tuchman Mathews, 'Redefining Security', *Foreign Affairs*, 68, No. 2 (Spring 1989), pp.162–7, and Franklyn Griffiths and Oran Young, 'Sustainable Development and the Arctic: Impressions of the Co-chairs', Working Group on Arctic International Relations (Hanover, NH: Dartmouth College, 1989). See also Peter Passell, 'Cure for Greenhouse Effect: The Costs Will Be Staggering', *New York Times*, 19 Nov. 1989.

25. To be specific, a measured and carefully regulated capability for surreptitious entry, wiretapping, and mail-opening by the CSIS and other units of the Canadian security intelligence establishment will remain a national requirement. Canadians who support wiretapping, for example, are a minority in all regions. Joseph F. Fletcher, 'Mass and Elite Attitudes about Wiretapping in Canada: Implications for Democratic Theory and Politics', *Public Opinion Quarterly*, 53 (1989), pp.225–45.
26. Tentative signs of a new openness, not dissimilar to that now displayed by the KGB, may be seen in Blais, 'Accountability and Effectiveness', David Vinneau, 'Canada's Spy Chief Speaks Out', *Toronto Star*, 18 Sept. 1989, and 'CSIS Turns to Ads in Newspapers', *Globe and Mail*, 2 Oct. 1989.
27. An instrument for the exchange of parliamentary experience now exists and should be employed. See 'Frankness Dominated Talks in Moscow, Canadians Say', *Toronto Star*, 3 Sept. 1989, which refers to a visit to the USSR by the speakers of the Commons and Senate following the formation of a Canada–USSR parliamentary association.
28. Other straws in the wind: '... but you're talking about anti-international terror. Yes it did, and also in the anti-narcotics efforts. So there's more we can do. We didn't discuss it specifically, but I'm thinking about certain kinds of intelligence interchange that can prove to be beneficial.' 'Transcript of Bush's News Conference After the Malta Talks', *New York Times*, 4 Dec. 1989. Canada and the USSR have now signed a memorandum of understanding on combined action to combat drug trafficking. 'Soviets, Canada Agree to Create Safer World', *Toronto Star*, 22 Nov. 1989. The law-enforcement agencies involved have yet to be identified.
29. Alexander Solzhenitsyn, *Letter to the Soviet Leaders* (New York: Harper and Row, 1974).
30. See Franklyn Griffiths, 'The Arctic in the Russian Identity', forthcoming in the Working Papers series, Centre for Russian and East European Studies, University of Toronto.

12

Strategic Intelligence and Effective Policy

ROBERT JERVIS

The domain and even definition of intelligence is not unambiguous. Here I shall mostly discuss the function of discerning other states' intentions and capabilities and the associated organizations charged with this responsibility.[1] Of course intelligence has other functions and meanings as well – it tries to ascertain and foil adversaries' attempts to learn secrets, seeks to influence the assessments others are making of the state, and engages in 'covert actions'. The latter activities attract most public attention, in part because they are so dramatic, in part because of their implications for democracy and responsible government. But I will leave them aside.

The most obvious and general question can be posed as: 'To what extent can the variations in the success or failure of states' foreign policies be explained by the skill of their intelligence systems and the resulting acuity and accuracy of their assessments of their environments?' Although evidence is sharply limited, the answer, I think, entails something of a puzzle, if not a paradox. On the one hand, logic would suggest that what befalls a state is strongly influenced by the policies the state follows. These policies should be sensitive to the decision-makers' beliefs about the international environment, particularly concerning others' intentions and capabilities; these beliefs should be strongly influenced by the state's intelligence. On the other hand, impressionistic evidence suggests that we are hard put to find these connections. It is far from clear that states that thrive have better intelligence organizations and analysts than those that do not. I am not convinced that history would be much different if intelligence had been saying different things to decision-makers at crucial junctures.

INTELLIGENCE AS HERO AND AS VILLAIN

One common model, at least in the popular mind, is intelligence as hero. A few stolen secrets or a series of satellite photographs provides the information allowing us to foil the enemy's plans. Although always present in literary form, this model received major impetus by the revelations of the role of Ultra, which would have been dismissed as incredible had the story been a fictional one. Of course, the exact contribution of Ultra is difficult to determine, but I think that few would deny that it was extremely important. But the circumstances were unusually – and perhaps uniquely – propitious. Not only was this a great technological feat of which the adversary remained blissfully unaware, but it allowed the Allies to tap an extremely large stream of the most secret information that revealed a great deal about the adversaries' capabilities, long-term plans and immediate military intentions. The value of the information accumulated as the Allies were able to utilize individual scraps, each of little value, to develop a coherent picture. Furthermore, this information could be synergistically combined with other sources of intelligence and deceptive operations like the Double Cross system. But these feats are not likely to be replicated.

The opposite model is that of intelligence as villain. Here the argument is that most of the state's policy failures can be attributed to failures of intelligence. Taking intelligence in its broadest sense, this is the common claim about British policy in the 1930s: if only Chamberlain and his colleagues had recognized Hitler for what he was, they could have devised a much better policy and avoided the Second World War. But without denying either that appeasement was based in part on faulty assessments or that alternative policies could have produced better results, we should not go too far. First, to a significant degree, appeasement was rooted in analysis, not of German intentions, but of British weakness. British statesmen believed that the costs of war – and even of rearmament – were so high that it made sense to err on the side of underestimating the threat. Indeed, the knowledge that Britain could not afford to fight another World War without sacrificing much of its strength and post-war position may have significantly and irrationally contributed to the perception that a war was not necessary. Second, it is not likely that a better policy would have avoided war entirely, although it could have led to fighting it under more favorable conditions.

To take another example, in the 1970s, many American hawks

blamed intelligence, in both its broad and narrow sense, for the perceived failures of policy toward the Soviet Union. But, leaving aside the accuracy of these assessments, there were so many factors impinging on American policy that it is not clear that what the United States did was highly sensitive to what it believed about the Soviet Union. To take the most obvious case, would the US have built more missiles had it correctly estimated the scope of the Soviet program? Those who most strongly criticize intelligence desired this outcome, but this does not mean it would have come about.

A final example of intelligence as villain is the failure of American – and other states' – intelligence to understand that the Shah's regime was in serious danger in 1978. Fingers have been pointed in many directions – for example, at the informal rules restricting American information-gathering in Iran; at the influence of the Shah's strong personality on Western observers; at the flawed reporting from the American Embassy; at the backbiting in Washington; at general American world-views that underestimate the influence of religion. But all these accounts assume that the US could and would have done something efficacious on the basis of a better understanding of the situation. This implies that decision-makers could have been convinced that, contrary to their preconceptions, the Shah was vulnerable; that the American policy-making procedures were agile and creative enough to devise and implement good policies; that it was within American power significantly and beneficially to influence events within Iran. Although counterfactual judgements must remain suspect, I am skeptical that these obstacles could have been overcome. To take merely the last one, I think it underestimates the power of the revolution to believe that any of the proposals advanced by key players such as Brzezinski, Sullivan and Ball could have had the intended results.

A CAUTIONARY TALE

Given the above, this is not to say that good information does not help produce good intelligence and that good intelligence does not help produce good policy. But the connections are highly mediated. All statesmen would like to have a spy in the enemy's cabinet, and the Allied use of Ultra shows that secret sources can be put to good uses. But at least as significant is the fact that in many modern periods, states seem to have derived less benefit from their extensive spy networks and interception and decoding of the other side's communications. I suspect that if one had gone to any state's top decision-maker and asked him whether an adversary could make enormous gains if it had good intelligence of this kind, the reply would be strongly affirmative. The decision-maker would be likely to say that with such access, it would take little skill for an adversary to be able to exploit the state thoroughly. In fact, in a number of instances an adversary *has* had excellent intelligence, and while the effects may not have been trivial, they were hardly of the magnitude foreseen by such a decision-maker. States have been able to follow quite effective foreign policies while suffering a degree of penetration that their leaders would have found almost unthinkable.

Perhaps the most interesting recent case of this kind is presented by the Soviet spies in Britain and the United States in the late 1940s and early 1950s. Philby and his colleagues were responsible for the deaths of many Allied agents and contributed to the failure of variouscovert operations, but what I think is surprising is how little Stalin was able to take advantage of what presumably was the steady flow of high-grade information about top-level political thinking and plans. It is an interesting experience to scan documents which were given ominous classifications in the belief that for the Russians to read them would gravely damage Western security and to realize that Soviet spies either sat in the meetings being reported or read the resulting papers. Of course, it is possible that Soviet policy would have been even less effective without this information; it is also possible that war might have resulted had Stalin not realized that the West was driven primarily by fear rather than unbridled expansionism. But, at least at first glance, what seems most striking is how little difference this excellent intelligence seems to have made.[2]

INTELLIGENCE, GOVERNMENTS AND POLICY

While bad intelligence can sometimes ruin a policy that would otherwise succeed, only to some extent can good analyses compensate for weaknesses at other stages of the policy-making process. The state's goals and animating values are beyond the purview of intelligence. If these are foolish, anachronistic or vainglorious, even the best sources of information about what others are likely to do will have limited effect. Although it is logically possible for the performance of intelligence to be vastly better or worse than that of the government and society as a whole, this is not likely to be the case. Intelligence – both the organization and the general intellectual apparatus – is very likely to share most of the characteristics of the nation in which it is embedded.[3] It would be surprising, after all, if intelligence in a totalitarian system were freely to develop challenging information[4] or if – to take a quite different sort of case – the resurgence in the power of the American Congress over foreign policy were not to be accompanied by a greater congressional interest in and use of intelligence.[5]

If we could measure the success of the state's policy and the utility and validity of its intelligence, we would probably find some correlation. It is particularly noteworthy that many policy disasters have occurred when intelligence was not consulted. When statesmen rely solely on their own beliefs about the environment they may steer the ship of state straight toward a reef, as Kennedy did in the Bay of Pigs and Khrushchev did 18 months later when he placed missiles in Cuba. But we should not be too quick to assume that this correlation always reflects direct causation. It seems more likely that many of the same factors that are responsible for the virtues or defects of the policy also explain the strength or weakness of intelligence: for example, the adequacy of the state's resources for the tasks at hand, the general level of skill in the society and government, the extent to which the government as a whole is free from disabling internal divisions and messianic impulses.

When we look at states that have got themselves into disastrous situations, particularly by accumulating excessive enemies and seeking excessive goals, we can see that part of the problem is a wildly distorted assessment of the dangers and opportunities in the environment.[6] To attribute the error to intelligence, however, would be misleading in the implication that these assessments were very much independent of the destructive urges that impelled the state on its foolish course. Could one have expected that even an excellent intelligence system in Nazi Germany would have insistently warned Hitler against declaring war on the United States or attacking the Soviet Union? To take a less extreme case, could intelligence in Wilhelmine Germany have told the Kaiser, his generals and the uneasy domestic coalition that supported the regime that Germany in fact was not being encircled by enemies, that their own policy was largely responsible for Britain's enmity or that Germany could secure its vital interests without bullying its neighbors? It should be noted that in this case intelligence, and the wider German society, cannot be considered to be guilty of 'wishful thinking' in the normal sense: they saw the environment as much more threatening than it was. They believed that others were closing in on them, that their power position was deteriorating and that time was working against them. In fact, it is almost certain that the reverse was the case and that they could have dominated Europe if there had been no war. But this optimistic – if correct – view of the world was inhibited by the general

169

intellectual and political atmosphere that characterized Wilhelmine Germany.

WHY INTELLIGENCE RARELY INFLUENCES GENERAL FOREIGN POLICY

Only rarely will intelligence challenge the basic premises and corner-stones of the state's foreign policy. Thus British intelligence in the 1930s generally did not argue that Hitler could not be appeased;[7] American intelligence during the Second World War was not in the forefront of those who worried about the Soviet Union; during the Cold War, intelligence rarely argued that Soviet capabilities were much lower than others believed, that many Soviet moves were impelled by insecurity and fear of the United States, and that small losses would not be likely to produce domino effects. Similarly, during the Vietnam War, although intelligence by and large remained skeptically objective about the American ability to win the war, it rarely questioned the predictions of the dire consequences of defeat or withdrawal. As the last two examples show, even in retrospect it is not easy to determine which view was correct. But the point here is not that intelligence was wrong – although my own judgement is that it was – but that it did not challenge the basic assessments that were held by the top decision-makers.

We cannot expect it to do so. In many cases, the underlying assumptions are so fundamental and widely shared within the society that they will permeate intelligence as well as decision-making circles. Even when they do not, the charged political atmosphere will make it difficult for intelligence to confront the issue head-on. For example, could the CIA have carried out a thorough analysis of the likelihood that 'domino effects' would follow a Viet Cong/North Vietnamese victory? If the analysis had pointed to a negative answer, would the CIA's standing in the govern-ment have been undiminished and the careers of the relevant officers unaffected?

A third limitation on the influence of intelligence is that it has no unique ability to deal with the broad questions of others' intentions or the likely consequences of foreign events. The sorts of information to which it has privileged access are rarely helpful here. Much of what is most important is generally known (for example, the situation the other state is in, the general characteristics of its history and society, its professed goals). Some information resides in the adversary's inner-most government circles or even the minds of a few decision-makers, which intelligence can rarely penetrate. Other information is simply unknowable (for example, how other states will react to situations as they develop, which the other's decision-makers themselves may not know). To the extent then that the general assessments of the adversary stem from the external environment at all, they are driven by general beliefs about international politics, publicly available information about the other side, and the sorts of analyses of the other's values and options that decision-makers can carry out without much assistance from intelligence analysts or organizations.

The Cuban missile crisis provides a striking example of intelligence providing crucial political analysis that directly guided decision-making. This was Llewelyn Thompson telling President Kennedy that his understanding of the Soviet Union led him to believe that Khrushchev would not insist on a public American promise to withdraw the missiles from Turkey in return for his retreating from Cuba.[8] Interestingly enough, Kennedy and his colleagues resisted this analysis even though it was exactly what they wanted to hear. But, in the end, they were persuaded that the situation was not as gloomy as they had thought. Cases like this seem to be rare, however.

Thus it is not really surprising that there are few if any cases in which intelligence has initiated debate on the major issues which fall within its purview. Instead, either dissidents outside the government or the policy-making process itself are more likely to generate the debates. The *Pentagon Papers* do not reveal the intelligence community deeply probing the question of whether dominos would fall if South Vietnam did; that was left to non-governmental critics. In 1950, intelligence did not take the lead in analysing the trends in world events, especially the Soviet nuclear explosion; that was left to NSC-68. Although the team A–team B episode in 1976 could be cited as a case in which the CIA took the initiative in examining the central issue of Soviet strength and intentions, this would be a superficial reading of what happened. The exercise was a product of external pressures and the subsequent stages of the investigation can best be explained by politics as well. It did not represent a serious intellectual engagement with the issues.

Even when the policy does not deal with countries about which decision-makers have deeply ingrained beliefs, it will be difficult for intelligence to persuade its masters that its basic political judgements are incorrect. This will be especially true after the policy has been set in motion and both intellectual and political costs have attached to altering it. Thus the intelligence community had little impact when it warned that most of the assumptions underpinning the American policy of intervention in Lebanon in 1982 were shaky.[9] With unusual unanimity, intelligence warned that Syria was not likely to withdraw, that the factional feuds within Lebanon were numerous, complex and hard to influence, and that even a small American presence risked antagonizing many of those America would have to work with. One reason why policy-makers paid little attention was that they thought their own general knowledge of the situation provided an adequate basis for their decisions. As one senior State Department official put it, 'A policy maker usually has some expertise of his or her own, after all. I use the intelligence community as a resource for factual information, but I don't need it for opinions. I have my own.'[10] We may be tempted to dismiss this as pure arrogance, but we should not forget that many of those who reach top positions are acute observers of politics (foreign as well as domestic) and have some justification for their self-confidence.

Only rarely will intelligence find particular bits of information that are so powerful and unambiguous that they can alter deeply held beliefs; only somewhat more frequently will the discipline and tools of intelligence permit an analytical breakthrough. It is not surprising therefore that the record of intelligence in detecting surprise attacks is spotty at best. This vital subject has spawned an enormous literature[11] and here all I want to do is stress that when analysts and decision-makers alike do not expect an attack (or do not expect it when and where it is actually coming), it will be hard for them to abandon the established wisdom and draw the correct inference. Not only will the information available usually be ambiguous, but it must be filtered through powerful pre-existing beliefs which will not be easily altered by even a significant amount of discrepant information. This is not because – or at least is not only because – people are unreasonable or have vested interests in their expectations. Usually, these views are sensible even if they turn out to be incorrect; in most cases there are good reasons to believe that the other will act as predicted. The Americans did not think it made any sense for Japan to attack them in 1941 because countries do not start wars they cannot win.

If the difficulty in obtaining good information about how the other sees the world is one major obstacle to assessment, so, ironically, can be good information about the likely outcomes of various moves an adversary might make. There are a number of cases in which states have been misled because, knowing that certain moves by an adversary would lead to disaster, intelligence analysts concluded that they would never be made. Pearl Harbor provides one example. Less well known is that a similar thinking process was in part responsible for the American failure to understand its adversary's preparations for the Tet offensive in 1968.[12] American intelligence was quite good: it knew that a North Vietnamese/Viet Cong general offensive would not spark a general uprising in South Vietnam but would lead to a crushing military defeat for the adversary. All this proved correct. The next step in the reasoning, however, was crucial and flawed. The analysts assumed that the North Vietnamese intelligence was at least as good as their own; in that case the adversary would foresee the consequences of an attack and so would not launch it. In fact, the North misread the situation in the South and did expect an uprising.[13]

The belief that the other side's intelligence must be providing a fairly good picture of what the state is doing is common, often incorrect, and has led to many international misunderstandings. It is possible, for example, that Khrushchev believed that the United States must have detected the movement of missiles to Cuba before the famous meeting between Kennedy and Gromyko. Kennedy's failure to raise the subject then would have been taken as indicating acquiescence. It is almost certain that the Russians did not believe the truth about the Cuban brigade imbroglio 17 years later. It must have strained their imagination to think that the US had just discovered the configuration of the Soviet forces on the island; much more plausible was the inference that the US was looking for an issue which could justify a more anti-Soviet position and sabotage the non-aligned summit conference that was opening in Havana. Similarly, during much of the Cold War many Americans could not believe that Soviet officials were so ignorant of American domestic politics as to really believe that big business and the President could control Congress and public opinion.

INTELLIGENCE AND POLICY-MAKERS: DIFFERENCES IN PERSPECTIVES

The strength of their pre-existing beliefs and the tendency to rely on their own judgements are not the only reasons why decision-makers resist discrepant views from the intelligence community. In many instances, the community paints a complex picture filled with obstacles to effective American policy. Only rarely do the analysts unambiguously point toward a course of action; by effect if not intent, often they will point toward caution if not indecision. Richard Neustadt, whose studies argued that the President should receive streams of conflicting information and advice, reports that in the early 1960s he was told by Dean Acheson: 'I know your theory. You think Presidents should be warned. You are wrong. Presidents should be given confidence'.[14] In principle, intelligence can yield confidence. But in practice it more often casts doubt on any particular course of action by indicating the ambiguities and weaknesses in the prevailing information, if not the possible alternative interpretations of it.

In part, this difference in perspective may stem from differences in the modal personality types of analysts and decision-makers. The latter would not seek these positions unless they had impulses toward decisiveness. Without denying that many of them have frequent bouts of self-doubt, someone who is predisposed to want to mull over all sides of an issue will not be likely to seek a job where he often has to come down on one side or the other. Similarly, many analysts chose intelligence because they enjoy the intellectual exercise of critically examining information without having the burden of reaching a final decision.

The implication of much intelligence is that there are severe limits to the state's influence; decision-makers want to know what they can do to influence the situation. These two perspectives are not logically contradictory, but they do pull in opposite directions. Decision-makers generally focus on the instruments at their command and on a small number of powerful actors. They are likely to remember cases in which their actions or those of their country made a big difference. Intelligence officials seek to understand the local situation in all its complexity and the implication of their analysis is often 'don't do something, just stand there'. Only when a decision-maker wants to 'let the dust settle' (often for domestic reasons) will his perspective be in harmony with that of the analysts.[15]

When the intelligence community and policy-makers develop very different views, the gulf between them may grow steadily wider, with each losing whatever respect for the other that it had. Douglas Porch has traced this process in France in the 1930s. The intelligence service felt sure that Hitler could only be dissuaded by force; it scorned the mainstream of French society and politics as decadent and defeatist, and did not realize the extent to which the French leadership felt driven by the need for British support. 'Annoyed that their message was not striking home, intelligence officers raised the tone of their reports, exaggerated the numbers of German soldiers, tanks and aircraft, engaged in actions designed to attract the attentions of their superiors. However, the more shrill the warnings the more they were ignored by the very people who should have been listening. In the final analysis, then, the intelligence service by its excess zeal contributed in no small measure to its failure to be taken seriously.'[16] Even in less extreme cases, decisions-makers who feel that intelligence is not being helpful will provide the analysts with less information about the problems they are concerned with and fewer reports from the field. When it is frozen out, not only is there likely to be a decline in its quality, but also in the morale of the intelligence community, and there may be a tendency to gloat if the policy fails.

MIRROR IMAGING AND LACK OF EMPATHY

Perhaps the two most important kinds of intelligence errors are the opposite failings of mirror-imaging and lack of empathy. In the former, states expect others to share their characteristics and behave like them; in the latter, states are unable to put themselves in the other's shoes and instead assume that the other's behavior is driven by unusual – and frequently malign – internal characteristics. To a significant degree, British intelligence in the 1930s was characterized by mirror-imaging. This was true on several levels. Although Chamberlain and his colleagues were not as naive as many of the early histories claimed, they vastly underestimated the differences between them and Hitler. When military intelligence tried to infer how Germany might use air power, it similarly mirror-imaged in the assumption that the Luftwaffe's thinking was like that of the RAF and the Germans would concentrate their attacks on British and French cities. As a result, Britain overestimated the threat that German air power posed to their civilians and underestimated its utility in supporting German ground forces. When they examined the structure of the German Air Force in more detail, they continued to use their own experience as a template and thus misjudged the pace and shape of the air build-up.

Although quantitative data are lacking, I suspect that too little rather than too much empathy is the more common error. Intelligence analysts – and, still more, statesmen – usually do not see others, especially adversaries, as like themselves. Furthermore, they underestimate the extent to which the other's behavior is to be explained by the situation the other faces and correspondingly give too much weight to the importance of the other's characteristic goals and beliefs. The latter pattern of inference leads them to expect the other's behavior to be quite consistent, since they foresee the playing out of the other's external drives rather than changing responses to changing circumstances. What can be particularly troublesome, especially in adversary relationships, is that the state's officials are likely to be slow to see the extent to which the other's behavior is a response to what their state is doing.

Empathy requires entering into the other's perceived world, and this is rarely easy. Often it occurs by accident, when the observer and the other side share some of the same beliefs. Thus perhaps

175

the main reason why John McCone was alone within the Kennedy administration in anticipating that the Soviets would put missiles into Cuba in the fall of 1962 was that he was one of the few who shared Khrushchev's belief that the US gained significant benefit from the degree of nuclear superiority that it had. It was therefore natural for him to see that Khrushchev would feel impelled to even the balance as quickly as possible. This was not just a matter of McCone's having a 'hard line' orientation toward the USSR – others who shared his general political predispositions but did not feel that the US was able to coerce the USSR because of the state of the nuclear balance did not predict the Soviet move.[17]

Intelligence suffers under four handicaps in trying to develop empathy with others, especially adversaries. The fourth will be discussed at some length because it raises broader issues. First, to empathize with the other is often to argue that its malign behavior is not attributable to evil characteristics and instead is largely a product of the situation in which the other finds itself. This message is likely to be unpopular, especially when the state's own actions are seen as part of the other's environment. When states do not intend to menace the other's legitimate interests, they often fail to see that the other could in fact feel menaced by them. Indeed, for an analyst or decision-maker to recognize this fear could be to cast doubt on his benign image of his own state. Second, because intelligence officials are not decision-makers, they may not understand the pressures on those who have to act in the name of their states. Freed from the disposition and need to take final responsibility for policy, analysts may not be best suited to grasping how people in those positions will behave.

Third, if the adversary is under great pressures, it may engage in pathological distortions of its environment in order to see that the chosen course of action has a good likelihood of success. It is particularly difficult for outsiders to enter into these fantasies. Thus the Japanese leaders before Pearl Harbor believed that their strategy could succeed because the United States would be willing to wage – and lose – a limited war. The Japanese did not arrive at this conclusion through careful and disinterested analysis and it would have been particularly difficult for American analysts to understand this perspective.[18]

Fourth, when, as is true for the US, intelligence is prohibited from dealing with its own state's policy, it will be particularly difficult for it to analyse the other side if the other's behavior is being strongly influenced by what the state is doing. Foreign policy is often highly interactive – states are reacting to each other and a large part of the explanation for one state's policy lies in what others are doing. But the

American intelligence community is not allowed to discuss American policy and indeed is not supposed to know more about it than is available in the newspapers. This is understandable. Intelligence and policy-making need to be separated in order to protect both communities. Policy-makers do not want their own intelligence services looking over their shoulders. Furthermore, were intelligence to do so, the political pressures on it would be even greater than they are now. But intelligence pays a high price in being cut off from valuable information and in being inhibited from developing a full picture of the other side's behavior.

Information is denied to the intelligence community not only when it focuses on American policy, but also when it would reveal American positions in much detail. Records of negotiations between the US and its adversaries are likely to fall into the latter category. Careful analysis of them could yield important insights not only into those negotiations, but also into the way the other side thinks, what its priorities are, how it formulates policy and how it views the US. But these records also reveal a great deal about American policy, and therefore are not for the eyes of intelligence analysts.

The greatest problem, though, is not with lack of access to specific documents, but with intelligence's ignorance of much of American policy and, even when informed, with the political and psychological barriers to considering it. On the face of it, it would seem foolish to try to analyse Soviet foreign policy without extensive consideration of the real and perceived American policy toward the Soviet Union that is a crucial part of the latter's environment. Similarly, how can one understand and predict Nicaraguan behavior without knowing and considering what the US is doing? A person in 1978 trying to predict whether the Shah's regime would survive presumably would have had to include an analysis of what the Shah and the opposition believed the US would be likely to do. But it is difficult for intelligence to do this. Indeed, the censorship becomes almost subconscious; analysts no longer notice American policy or privately develop a full picture that includes it before presenting a 'sanitized' version for the consumers.

Unfortunately, there is probably a trade-off between the independence and integrity of intelligence on the one hand and its influence on the other. The latter requires close and continuing contact with policy-makers. To serve them, intelligence officials need to know what problems they are working on, what kinds of information and analyses they need, how they are thinking about problems and what sorts of discussions they will have with other policy-makers. This knowledge is not gained easily; it cannot come from occasional briefings and

177

meetings. But the intensive and extensive interactions that would provide it also threaten the autonomy of intelligence analysts and organizations. Close contact increases the dangers of both seduction and rape. The latter has received most attention in popular accounts. Intelligence officials may learn all too well not only what policy-makers want to know about, but exactly what answers they want. Of course, this knowledge may not require prolonged discussions. When Secretary of Defense Laird publicly said that the Soviets were going for a first strike capability, 'There is no question about that', it was hard for intelligence to disagree fully, even in private.[19] But pressure is easier to exert when intelligence officials are in the room. These circumstances also radically increase the danger of seduction: that is, of analysts and intelligence organizations finding the lure of power so great that they want above all to please the decision-makers. Even if they do not fall into this trap, they may become so preoccupied with policy options that they begin to duplicate the thinking and functions of their policy-making colleagues rather than retaining their focus on understanding and analysing the other side.

CONDITIONS FOR GOOD INTELLIGENCE

Good intelligence is built on the presentation of alternative analyses, the development of the relevant evidence and the full presentation of the arguments that link evidence and interpretations. It appears that the informal norms and incentives within the American intelligence community do not support this kind of analysis.[20] Indeed, they form what Charles Perrow has called in another context 'an error-inducing system'.[21] That is, interlocking habits of the community decrease the likelihood of careful and penetrating analyses. In the political area, reporting often displaces analysis: rather than analysing developments and presenting alternative explanations and competing predictions, all too often the analyst is expected to summarize the recent reports from the field. This method is likely to produce good results when the reports are accurate and informative but is not likely to correct or go much beyond them. In part, the explanation is that while policy-makers feel they need facts, they have faith in their own ability to interpret events.[22] As a result, analysts are socialized into norms that discourage 'speculation'. This is reinforced by the tendency for most intelligence reports on current events to be quite short. Even though many issues are too complex to be treated in an article no longer than that one might find in the day's newspaper, decision-makers are extremely busy, few of them like to read, and those that do face enormous stacks of reports.

There might be more thorough consideration of alternative explanations and predictions if the intelligence community were a real community – that is, if analysts were encouraged to comment on each other's views. Sometimes, of course, this occurs. But all too often, the system falls into one of two traps. First, an issue may become so polarized, if not politicized, that the arguments take on a ritualistic character, mirroring those in the outside political environment. Positions are staked out and views are rebutted, but there is little real interchange or enlightenment. Second, when the issue is not immediately important or controversial, views are likely to be ignored. No one is sufficiently interested or motivated to probe deeply, to bring implicit assumptions to the surface, and to force people to develop their positions and supporting evidence with care.

KEEPING POLICY-MAKERS SOMEWHAT HONEST

After all this pessimism, it may be foolish to try to redress the balance, but in closing I do want to suggest that a well-functioning intelligence system can at least marginally improve the quality of political analysis and debate within the government and country at large. Over the entrance to the CIA headquarters are the words 'Seek the Truth and it Shall Make Ye Free.' Many cynical responses can be imagined, but before we endorse them we should remember that no other organization in the foreign policy-making process could even aspire to this standard. All the rest are deeply involved in setting and justifying policy; all of them have powerful vested interests that supplement, if not displace, the national interest. Without arguing that all the other agencies scorn the truth, they often will be tempted to regard it instrumentally. Evidence, explanations of others' behavior, and arguments are often used, not to shed light on issues, but as tools of persuasion, if not as weapons with which to beat adversaries within the government over the head.

On most controversial issues, the level of policy-making argument is very high if judged in terms of skill and ingenuity, but unfortunately low if judged by standards of reasoning and evidence. At its best, intelligence can point out to all domestic combatants the weaknesses and flaws in the arguments and information that are being relied upon. Intelligence may not be able to find the truth; still less may it be able to persuade others that it has found it. But keeping the players honest, not permitting disreputable arguments to thrive, pointing out where positions are internally contradictory or rest on tortured readings of the evidence would not be minor feats. While this would not save a country from all folly, it would provide more assistance then we get from most instruments of policy.

NOTES

1. Like most other scholars, I shall ignore non-governmental intelligence. This is unfortunate; multinational corporations have interests and agents throughout the globe. Even before the popularity of 'risk assessment' they surely tried to be well informed. As far as I can tell, we know almost nothing about the extent or adequacy of such efforts. It would be fascinating, for example, to learn what the oil companies were thinking about the Shah's future throughout 1978.
2. For similar views, see John Lewis Gaddis, 'Intelligence, Espionage, and Cold War Origins', *Diplomatic History*, Vol. 13 (Spring 1989), pp.209–12 and Harry Gelber, 'The Hunt for Spies: Another Inside Story', *Intelligence and National Security*, Vol. 4, No. 2 (April 1989), pp.399–400.
3. See the case-studies in Ernest May (ed.), *Knowing One's Enemies* (Princeton: Princeton University Press, 1984).
4. Thus in pre-war Japan the cabinet Planning Board was reorganized and its personnel replaced when it reported that the government's plan to meet its resource requirements by military expansion was not feasible. (See Michael Barnhart, *Japan Prepares for Total War* (Ithaca: Cornell University Press, 1987), pp.170–1.)
5. See Robert Gates, 'The CIA and Foreign Policy', *Foreign Affairs*, Vol. 66 (Winter 1987/1988), pp.215–30.
6. The best discussion is Jack Snyder, *Myths of Empire: Domestic Politics and Strategic Ideology* (Ithaca: Cornell University Press, forthcoming).
7. See Wesley K. Wark, *The Ultimate Enemy: British Intelligence and Nazi Germany, 1933–1939* (Ithaca: Cornell University Press, 1985), which concentrates on military intelligence.
8. McGeorge Bundy (transcriber) and James Blight (ed.), 'October 27, 1962: Transcripts of the Meeting of the ExComm', *International Security*, Vol. 12 (Winter 1987/88), pp.59–62.
9. My discussion is based on David Kennedy and Leslie Brunetta, 'Lebanon and the Intelligence Community', (Harvard University: Kennedy School of Government Case Program, 1988).
10. Quoted in Kennedy and Brunetta, 'Lebanon and the Intelligence Community', p.10.
11. The latest best treatments are Ephraim Kam, *Surprise Attack* (Cambridge, MA: Harvard University Press, 1988); and Richard Betts, *Surprise Attack* (Washington, DC: Brookings Institution, 1982). Two points that are peripheral to my discussion should be briefly noted: first, deception may play a large role here, and, second, cases in which intelligence draws the correct inference may lead to self-denying prophecies as the state's response leads the attacker to alter his plans. In this case, intelligence may be falsely blamed for 'crying wolf'.
12. James Wirtz, *Intelligence Failure in War: The American Military and Tet Offensive* (Ithaca: Cornell University Press, forthcoming).
13. Wirtz shows that the common belief that North Vietnam anticipated that even a military unsuccessful offensive would undermine American public support for the war is incorrect. But it is not trivial that intelligence is prohibited from discussing American policy: see below.
14. Quoted in John Steinbruner, *The Cybernetic Theory of Decision* (Princeton: Princeton University Press, 1974), p.332. Psychologists have found that people tend to be excessively confident of their judgements. I discuss the evidence for and

implications of this phenomenon in *Foreign Policy Decision-Making* (in preparation).

15. Many of us, having chosen academic careers, will find ourselves in greater sympathy with the intelligence officials than with decision-makers. The latter often seem to overestimate their nation's if not their own power. They may seem almost like hyperactive adolescents who pay little attention to the restraints and complexities in the environment, but their penchant for action may be highly functional. If they paid full heed to all of the warnings intelligence provides, they might be paralysed. By not seeing all of the obstacles in their path until they are embarked on a course of action, they may commit themselves to finding the resources and ingenuity to carry out the policy with at least some success. This is why Albert Hirschman refers to limited knowledge, if not ignorance, as the 'hiding hand': Albert Hirschman, *Development Projects Observed* (Washington, DC: Brookings Institution, 1976).
16. Douglas Porch, 'French Intelligence and the Fall of France, 1939–40', *Intelligence and National Security*, Vol. 4, No. 1 (January 1989), p.37.
17. McGeorge Bundy, *Danger and Survival* (New York: Random House, 1988), p.420.
18. For a different view of this case, see Scott Sagan, 'The Origins of the Pacific War', *Journal of Interdisciplinary History*, Vol. 18 (Spring 1988), pp.914–17.
19. All in all, the intelligence community did not do too badly in these trying circumstances. See Kiersten Lundberg, 'The SS-9 Controversy: Intelligence as a Political Football', Kennedy School of Government, 1989.
20. For a fuller presentation of this argument, see Robert Jervis, 'What's Wrong with the Intelligence Process?' *International Journal of Intelligence and Counterintelligence*, Vol. 1 (Spring 1986), pp.33–8.
21. Charles Perrow, *Normal Accidents* (New York: Basic Books, 1984).
22. Much of the description of what happened 30 years ago still holds: Roger Hilsman, *Strategic Intelligence and National Decisions* (Glencoe, IL: Free Press, 1956).

13

Countering Terrorism in Canada

JEAN-PAUL BRODEUR

This study is divided into three parts. First, it reviews some of the main features of terrorism with a view to assessing whether it is going through a major evolution. Second, taking the broader perspective, it addresses the problem of co-ordinating the action of all those who play a part in countering terrorism. Third, it discusses the roles played by the Canadian Security Intelligence Service (CSIS) and police forces in counter-terrorism and offers comments on the question of determining who should have primary responsibility for this task within Canada's security intelligence system.

FEATURES OF TERRORISM

The literature on terrorism suggests that agreement on what the terms implies is likely to be problematic. Schmid lists no fewer than 109 different definitions of terrorism.[1] It is probably unwise to seek the essential nature of a phenomenon which has varied so much over time and space. Furthermore, 'terrorism' is a term of condemnation and its application is ruled as much by indignation as by semantics. Hence, it is more useful to give a descriptive account of the main features and variants of terrorism than to reach for an elusive definition.

Terrorism as Reflexive Violence

By giving prominence to the significance of the target, Schmid's account stresses the fact that terrorism is *purposeful* action. It is purposeful action in a deeper sense than just being premeditated and planned: terrorists want to have their purposes known and resort to several means to publicize the rationale for their action (communiqués, symbolic victims, symbolic deeds, and so on).

Although fundamental, this point is easily forgotten. There is a natural tendency to confuse horror with terror and to forget Jenkins' dictum that all crimes that may terrify are not thereby terrorism.[2] For example, the *Report of the Senate Special Committee on Terrorism and*

Public Safety classifies genocide among terrorist acts perpetrated by the state.[3] Genocide does inspire unspeakable horror. However, the purpose of genocide (and of most assassinations) is to annihilate, not terrorize. Hence, far from advertising their deeds to generate terror, states perpetrating genocide have always tried to shroud them in secrecy and have kept denying their intentions. (One of the German code-names for the holocaust was *Nacht und Nebel*, that is 'Night and Fog'; needless to say, all those who saw through the fog were gripped by terror, but they were prevented from disseminating what they knew.)

Terrorism does not hide its face. On the contrary, it must exhibit it in order to have its effect. Events occurring in Quebec in 1989 exemplify the point. Following controversial legislation on linguistic rights, an organization devoted to the defence of the English-speaking community took a firm public stand against the newly enacted law (Bill 178). On 30 December 1988, offices occupied by this organization, Alliance Québec, were devasted by a fire. This crime of arson had all the earmarks of a terrorist act. Yet, the act's significance remained wholly ambiguous and was not interpreted by the public as an act of terrorism. It was never seriously claimed by any group, nor was its purpose ever communicated by its perpetrator(s). The fire at Alliance Québec is a cipher to which we were not given any key.

It should not be surprising that Schmid's characterization emphasizes terrorism as purposeful action. Not only was this point made by several authors such as Thornton and Jenkins, but Schmid had already in a previous book proposed viewing terrorists' violence as a method of communication.[4] Purposeful action and communication can both be characterized as attempts to convey meaning.

In linguistic communication theory there is one classical account of the act of meaning something. According to Grice, 'Paul meant something by X' is equivalent to 'Paul intended the utterance of X to produce some effect in an audience by means of the recognition of this intention'.[5] Grice's point is that if we look at the sky and find a meaningful pattern of smoke, without being able to establish a relationship between it and an intelligent being wanting to communicate with us, we will not interpret this pattern of smoke as a significant message. On the contrary, if we see a connection between that pattern and, say, a small aircraft sky-writing, it will immediately be seen as meaningful language. Grice's analysis can be extended to all attempts to communicate, whether through language or through some other medium.

In studying the impact of violent acts on society, a distinction can be made between what is labelled as expressive violence – for example, vandalism – and what we shall call reflexive violence; that is, violence as communication. Some violence may be said to be expressive even if it does not manifest any explicit intention to convey something to an audience (for example, broken windows may be an unconscious expression of frustration). Lacking in most instances the purpose to communicate, expressive violence rarely goes beyond physical aggression and signifies little, except such feelings as anger or frustration.

By contrast, terrorist organizations go through an elaborate process to make their intentions fully perceptible. Victims are chosen for their symbolic meaning. Press relations are a matter of great concern and terrorist organizations go to considerable lengths to make sure that their communiqués are acknowledged as authentic. To sum up, terrorism, as reflexive violence, is a mixture of physical force and informational content, with the latter being as important as the former. Indeed, such terrorist acts as the utterance of threats consist wholly of the use of language, whereas naked violence which does not admit of interpretation may be terrifying but is not perceived as terrorism.

There has been a significant evolution in the use of reflexive violence. This evolution is perceptible in tragedies such as the downing of an Air-India aircraft in June 1985 and the bombing of a Pan Am Boeing 747 over Lockerbie in December 1988. These acts of terrorism differ in numerous ways from those perpetrated by such groups as the Italian Red Brigades or the German Baader-Meinhof gang. These groups devoted considerable effort to explaining the meaning of their acts. By contrast, the groups responsible for the attacks against Air-India and Pan Am seem to operate on two levels of communication. The message of terror communicated to the general public was conveyed through the choice of symbolic targets and through the very large number of victims (329 and 270 respectively). However, the perpetrators of these acts remained generally silent on who their group was and on the specific meaning of their act. The identity of the terrorist groups and the precise meaning of their action remain cryptic and that part of the message seems to be intended for professionals on the opposing side (for instance, intelligence experts speculated that the Pan Am attack was retaliation for the downing of an Iranian commercial aircraft by the USS *Vincennes*). In such cases, terrorism remains communication but its messages are intended for different kinds of receivers.

If this analysis is correct, it has obvious implications for counter-terrorism. Assuming that the remedy ought to match the main aspects of the disease, the gathering and analysis of intelligence must play a part which is at least equivalent to the enforcement of the law, narrowly understood as legal coercion. This involves a recognition that counter-terrorism implies recourse to a wider range of tactics than policing operations.[6]

The Response to Terrorism

A second point that needs to be made is closely related to the previous one. In common law jurisdictions, such as the United Kingdom and Canada, government authorities insist that terrorism be treated as a crime like any other criminal act, regardless of its motivation. This places counter-terrorism squarely within the criminal justice system.

This position reflects an indeology which refuses to grant acts of terrorism any legitimacy. For instance, the Senate Special Committee on Terrorism and the Public Safety (SSCT) declares in its report that:

> for such terrorists, the grievances or causes they espouse are but excuses for their violent, criminal behaviour. Resolving or addressing these grievances will do little to satisfy or neutralize such terrorists for they will be reluctant to forswear terrorism if it means giving up the power and prestige terrorism brings.[7]

Although such a position is morally justifiable, it is highly misleading if it purports to be an accurate description of the actual response to terrorism.

Terrorism aims at several targets and mobilizes many audiences. One of its main targets is the institution having the power to grant its political demands. This institution is government. The political focus of terrorism was quite explicitly recognized by the SSCT. It recommended that responsibility for co-ordinating the federal government's responses to specific terrorist threats and incidents be transferred from the Department of the Solicitor General to the Privy Council Office (PCO). This recommendation was made for two reasons:

> First, the communication and command structure should be as direct, simple and linear as possible. Second, the highest political level (the Prime Minister and senior Cabinet Ministers) has to be fully and continuously informed and participate in major decisions.[8]

It seems inconsistent to claim that terrorists are criminals whose thirst for power and prestige should not be satisfied and then to recommend, when incidents occur or threaten to occur, that they should have a direct pipeline to the highest political level. This inconsistency can be mitigated if a distinction is drawn between two kinds of responses to terrorist incidents. One type of response concerns the management of an actual or apprehended crisis. This response may prevent the crisis from happening, or if this cannot be prevented, allow the crisis to be managed until its final resolution. A second kind of response occurs *after* the resolution of a crisis when its authors are being neutralized or in flight. This response usually falls within the scope of the criminal justice system.

It is of paramount importance to realize that there are few criminal acts which elicit both kinds of response and that terrorism is one of them. Being conscious of this fact implies a recognition of the distinctively political character of terrorism. This recognition in no way entails an upgrading of the moral status of terrorism. Ethically, terrorism is abhorrent, whatever its political overtones may be. However, the recognition that terrorism is political, either in its motivation or its goals (or in both), can only facilitate the development of an efficient strategy against it. Efficient strategies must be based on facts rather than moral postures.

COUNTER-TERRORISM: CO-ORDINATING THE WHOLE NETWORK

A wide variety of measures can be taken against terrorism. Some of these – pre-empting a terrorist attempt or, failing that, arresting the authors of such an attempt – are police operations. Other measures, such as outlawing the importation, publication and distribution of 'Mayhem Manuals', which teach readers to make different kinds of weapons, are of a different nature and are not policing operations (although the police may provide assistance).

The Whole Network

An impressive number of agencies play a part in the struggle against terrorism. Four sectors of what may be loosely defined as an anti-terrorist network may be identified.

1. Although there is little research on this aspect of private security, the *private sector* is heavily involved in the protection of persons – executives and businessmen – against terrorist attempts. Most big agencies such as Pinkerton offer a variety of protection programs. Pinkerton, to cite one example, is linked with data-banks in 83 countries.

2. *Foreign Agents*: This is a domain about which little is known and what is publicly discussed is liable to generate misunderstandings. Kashmeri and McAndrew make an overwhelming case to the effect

that agents from the Indian intelligence service are active in Canada.[9] Unfortunately, their discussion of the role played by agents of the Government of India in the Air India tragedy is much too speculative. Needless to say, India is not the only country to have agents deployed to protect its diplomats or visiting officials from terrorist attacks. It is not unreasonable to infer that countries such as Turkey, whose diplomats have been victims of terrorist violence, have increased their protection abroad.

3. *Canadian Agencies*: Acknowledging the importance of the private sector and of agents from other countries should not keep us from admitting that the most active role in counter-terrorism within Canada is played by Canadian government agencies.

4. *Informants*: This is a category which is problematic. Not only is the number of informants impossible to assess, but very little is known about their activities. They deserve to be specifically mentioned for two reasons. On the one hand, infiltration is the most powerful instrument against terrorist organizations. On the other, it is an instrument which has considerable potential for abuse. A disproportionate number of cases of police wrongdoing have involved paid informants.

There has been a call in Canada for better co-ordination of those involved in counter-terrorism. This call is fully justified. However, the objective of achieving better co-ordination can only be partially realized. First, it is unlikely that the four sectors mentioned above will be truly co-ordinated in the near future. The distance separating the private from the public and the national from the international is not only wide, it is difficult to change. As for the world of informants, it is surrounded by a wall of secrecy which has now been made into a legal fortress by recent rulings of the Supreme Court of Canada.[10]

Canadian Agencies

A number of recent and reliable descriptions of the Canadian intelligence and security community exist.[11] Broadly speaking, the different parties involved fall into four categories:

1. *Ministries and Special Committees*: the leading ministry is that of the Solicitor-General. Others involved are the Department of Foreign Affairs, the Department of National Defence, Employment and Immigration Canada, Transport Canada, Revenue Canada, Customs and Excise and the Department of Justice. According to the Security Intelligence Review Committee (SIRC, 1987), in addition to the Prime Minister, the Deputy Prime Minister and most heads of the ministries

mentioned above, the President of the Treasury Board, the Minister for International Trade and the Minister of Finance are permanent members of the Cabinet Committee on Security and Intelligence (CCSI). Among special offices and commissions, the PCO and the Atomic Energy Control Board (AECB) must also be mentioned. In sum, at least seven ministries and twelve members of the Cabinet develop policy on security and intelligence and, by implication, on counter-terrorism.

2. *Intelligence Services*: CSIS is not the only agency collecting security intelligence. The departments of External Affairs and National Defence both have their own intelligence-gathering units. The Communications Security Establishment (CSE), formally part of the Department of National Defence, collects signals intelligence (Sigint) and operates within the framework of the 1947 UKUSA Agreement, to which the US, the UK, Australia and New Zealand are also party.[12] Until 1988 the Royal Canadian Mounted Police (RCMP) collected security intelligence through the National Crime Intelligence Sections (NCIS) and the National Security Enforcement Units (NSEU). More recently the National Security Investigations Directorate (NSID) was established to provide the RCMP with the capacity to investigate security offences, especially those involving terrorism. Finally, some Canadian police forces, such as the Quebec provincial police (Sûreté du Québec), have a security intelligence unit.

3. *Law Enforcement Organizations*: even though the RCMP has primary responsibility for enforcing the law with respect to security-related offences, all Canadian police forces are entitled to exercise jurisdiction in this field of operation. In addition, organizations that police Canadian harbours, bridges and airports may play a vital part, as was recently shown by the hijacking of a bus that finally ended its journey on Parliament Hill, where no one expected it to appear. Finally, there is the RCMP's Special Emergency Response Team (SERT), which is a quasi-military unit trained for intervention in crisis situations created by terrorist action.

4. *Policy-making Bodies and Co-ordinating Mechanisms*: the structure in place for policy- and decision-making and for co-ordination at the federal level is fairly complex. It can be depicted as a pyramid topped by the CCSI. Beneath this ministerial level is the Interdepartmental Committee on Security and Intelligence (ICSI) whose membership is comprised of the most senior public servants (deputy ministers). Under ICSI are several committees and their sub-committees. The most

important of these are the Security Advisory Committee (SAC), which is fed by the Counter-terrorism Committee, and the Intelligence Advisory Committee (IAC), which is fed by several sub-committees and deals with matters of foreign inteligence. Among the different instruments for co-ordination are such special committees as the Special Threat Assessment Group (STAG) and the Interdepartmental Terrorist Alert System (ITAS). In addition to committees, certain individuals are vested with crucial responsibilities for establishing and maintaining co-ordination. These are the Clerk of the Privy Council, the Intelligence and Security Co-ordinator and the Director of the National Security Co-ordination Centre.

Even when the intelligence and security community is summarily described, it is obvious that the need for co-ordination cannot be over-emphasized.

Issues of co-ordination

In his books on the police, Ericson (1981, 1982) has emphasized the fact that the police, as an organization, process information in such a way as to make their action appear justified.[13] This description may also be applied to the intelligence and security services. It does not imply that agencies refuse to share information outside the organization. What it really means is, first, that information (or intelligence) is considered a prize possession which is to be shared only through a hard process of negotiations. In other words, there is no free trade agreement in the world of intelligence. What it also means is that there are generally two versions of a piece of intelligence: one for internal circulation and another one for external dissemination. So, even when a deal for sharing information has been struck, key elements may be missing from the intelligence transmitted. Finally, one further problem must be mentioned. The different authors who have contributed to Robertson (1987) make it clear that there is no commonly shared definition of intelligence. The same point has been strongly emphasized by Farson.[14] This situation is unlikely to promote the exchange of intelligence.

This general reluctance to share intelligence manifests itself in two principal ways. First, information may circulate through horizontal lines running across groups and organizations which are basically similar and/or operate at the same level (for example, two police forces, two intelligence agencies operating in the field).[15] Although CSIS and the RCMP are different organizations, they both may have agents in the field investigating the same situation. CSIS was not originally granted free access to the Canadian Police Information Centre (CPIC). The situation has recently been remedied: according to the Report of the SSCT (Canada, Senate, 1989, p. 16), full on-line access to CPIC for the CSIS was scheduled to be completed by December 1989. Still, these delays illustrate the difficulty of sharing information along horizontal lines. The communication failure between the Sûreté du Québec and the RCMP during the April 1989 bus hijacking that ended on Parliament Hill is another example of faulty transmission along horizontal channels.

Information may also flow vertically, running from the field of police operations up to the government. This kind of communication means that information and intelligence are transmitted from one kind of agency – the police or CSIS – to another level, which supersedes it (for example, the judiciary, an oversight committee, different levels of government). The flow of information from the field to the higher levels of government and political decision-makers is erratic, and in crucial situations is often gravely lacking in detail. There are numerous examples illustrating this point: the following passages discuss two such cases.

The Keable report (1981) contains an interesting analysis of a 1971 document entitled *Current FLQ Groups*, which purported to provide an assessment of the terrorist threat in Quebec the year after the October crisis.[16] The document, classified as 'secret', relied extensively on the RCMP Security Service files and was used as a briefing book within government. This report asserted that the FLQ groups of 1971 were 'much more aware of security' (p. 1) and were consequently 'increasingly difficult to penetrate' (p. 1). Describing one of the two main groups, the document claimed that:

> Security is a strong feature of this group. Even the leadership is not known to all members. The group appears to have a relatively sophisticated security system, making extensive use of such techniques as *liaison members*, codes, aliases and misinformation. [The leader of the group] has instilled in his adherents a high sense of security consciousness, particularly with respect to police surveillance (p. 13).

Having established the group's sensitivity to security, *Current FLQ Groups* went on to identify Carole Deveault (wrongly spelled as Devault) as the main liaison member and thus as part of the 'sophisticated' security system used by this terrorist group. The problem with this description was that it was an exercise in misinformation. As the RCMP knew, Ms Deveault was an informant controlled by a member of the anti-terrorist squad of the Montreal municipal police. Her reports were transmitted to Ottawa. As a matter of fact, it can be shown that *Current FLQ Groups* was partly written on the basis of these reports. Hence the group was infiltrated by the very person who was presented in the document as an instrument of its 'sophisticated security system'. The group was assessed as a major threat, difficult to infiltrate, whereas the police had in reality detailed reports on its activities, on a weekly basis.[17]

Another incident involving the provision of misinformation by a police informant occurred more recently. In September 1987, charges of conspiracy to murder Punjabi Planning Minister Malkiat Singh Sidhu had to be stayed, because the evidence was legally tainted. Charges were originally brought against nine men. The Crown's case rested on wiretap evidence that had to be withdrawn. Affidavits filed by CSIS to get a warrant were partly based on faulty information provided by an unreliable person. The case proved most embarrassing. The legality of the wiretap evidence was challenged in court before the very judge who had initially granted CSIS its warrant. The judge upheld his original decision, only to discover later on that he had been deceived all along. The chief of CSIS, Ted Finn, resigned shortly after it was revealed that the affidavits submitted by CSIS contained numerous errors.

While these cases suggest grave weaknesses in the system of communicating intelligence to decision-makers, other problems also appear endemic in the Canadian structure:

- The present structure is an attempt at vertical integration, which is relatively unbalanced. As a whole, it tried to co-ordinate intelligence collected in the field with planning and decision-making within the government bureaucracy. However, the police and the different agencies that collect intelligence are represented only by the highest-ranking officers. Hence, it seems that bureaucrats are over-represented on most committees and that the distance between co-ordination mechanisms and field agents is so great that it may result in the filtering out of crucial pieces of first-hand information.
- In its present state, the structure developed to ensure co-ordination suffers from a second kind of imbalance. Efforts to achieve horizontal integration are more evident in the co-ordination of various government departments than of police forces, CSIS and other government services that are collecting security intelligence.
- Particular mention must be made of the CSE. Its full integration into the Canadian intelligence community raises special problems as the CSE operates within the 1947 UKUSA Agreement.
- Finally, the present co-ordination mechanisms appear to have been

designed to manage extended crises which are slow to unfold. It is not evident that these mechanisms could respond quickly enough to deal with a sudden crisis.

THREAT ASSESSMENT AND LAW ENFORCEMENT

Even if counter-terrorism involves many departments and agencies, it can be argued that the police forces and CSIS have a leading role to play in counter-terrorism. Actually, it seems reasonable that CSIS, which is the organization most responsible for the assessment of terrorist threats, and the law enforcement agencies share the primary responsibility for curtailing terrorism in Canada. However, even this apparently reasonable statement may have controversial implications. CSIS and the police are both accountable to the Solicitor-General and to provincial equivalents with respect to non-federal police departments. It seems to follow that it is natural for the Solicitor-General to be the leading ministry for domestic counter-terrorism. None the less, this conclusion has been consistently opposed by both Senate Committees on Terrorism and Public Safety (Canada, Senate, 1987 and 1989).

Primary responsibility in collecting security intelligence

CSIS was created in 1984, following recommendations by the McDonald Commission to the effect that the Security Service should be a civilian organization distinct from the RCMP and that the members of the new service should be limited to the collection and analysis of security intelligence. This recommendation also implied that the police – and most notably the RCMP – were to keep playing an important part in counter-terrorism, namely enforcing the law. A case can be made that the role of the RCMP in the counter-terrorism field was actually strengthened by the Security Offences Act. Section 6 states that the RCMP has the primary responsibility to perform the duties assigned to peace officers in relation to security and related offences. The 1984 reform thus effected a division of labour between a civilian intelligence service and the police forces, the former being responsible for the collection and analysis of intelligence and the latter having exclusive jurisdiction in enforcing the law.

If this perception of the 1984 reform is correct, we are justified in drawing the following two conclusions:

1. Questioning that the CSIS should have the primary responsibility in the field of counter-terrorist *intelligence* is equivalent to questioning the basis of the 1984 reform triggered by the McDonald report. The

purpose of this reform was precisely to separate the function of gathering and processing intelligence from the function of enforcing security measures (policing). The way to achieve this purpose was to create CSIS and to give it the intelligence mandate.

2. If, on top of raising the issue of primacy in the field of counter-terrorist intelligence, we actually resolve it in favour of the police, then we are implicitly saying that CSIS is not fulfilling its purpose. Therefore, we ought to get rid of it. There really is no point in limiting an agency to the performance of a single function – intelligence, of which counter-terrorist intelligence is a vital part – and then divesting this agency of the primary responsibility of performing the function for which it was initially created. To make this point metaphorically, if we create a new medical speciality – for example, radiology – and then move on to assert that the primary responsibility in radiology does not belong to radiologists but to the operating surgeons, one may wonder why this new speciality was created in the first place.

We believe these remarks are fairly obvious. It does not follow from them that CSIS should be given the primary responsibility in counter-terrorist intelligence. It does follow, however, that the attribution of this primary responsibility to the police rather than to CSIS implies a rethinking of CSIS' existence.

Primary responsibility: CSIS or the RCMP

The CSIS Act divided the task of protecting the national security of Canada[18] between the civilian intelligence service and the police forces, among which the RCMP were given the primary responsibility. While the RCMP lost their Security Service, members of the CSIS were not granted peace officer powers. In this regard, the 1984 reform followed the recommendations of the McDonald Commission.[19]

It is important to check the McDonald Commission's reasons for denying the new agency authority to enforce security measures. These are stated thus in the McDonald report cited above (p. 613):

> [1] ... it is unacceptable in Canada that the state should use a secret intelligence agency to inflict harm on Canadian citizens directly.
> [2] ... the liberty of Canadians would be best protected if measures to insure security were not enforced by the organisation with the primary responsibility for collecting information about threats to that security.

What these quotations make clear is that the rationale for splitting the responsibility of protecting Canada's security between a civilian agency and the police was based on the defence of civil rights. This division of labour was not based on a design primarily intended to maximize the efficacy of CSIS and the police by forcing them to be partners.

It is also important to establish whether the concept of a split responsibility was flawed *from an agency perspective*. The primary goal of an intelligence service or of a police force is to fulfil its mandate – the protection of Canada's security, for instance. In fulfilling its mandate, an agency is required to respect human rights. However, this requirement is equivalent to a limiting condition under which the agency must operate. Although vitally important, this condition is not in itself the reason why the agency exists. Given a choice between its mandate and the limiting conditions under which this mandate is to be exercised, an organization will have a natural tendency to give primacy to its mandate.

Generally speaking, a police force would rather act upon its own information than depend on another agency for intelligence. In the same way, if given the choice, an intelligence service would rather use its own agents in a delicate operation than those of another organization. Hence, it may be predicted that the RCMP would try to maintain a rump security service and, alternatively that CSIS would attempt to carry out measures to enforce security.[20]

The first of these scenarios – the continued involvement of the RCMP in security intelligence – is the more likely. The main reason is that since the CSIS Act does not grant the CSIS members peace officer power, to enforce security measures on its own CSIS would have to circumvent the law. By contrast, there is no legal obstacle preventing the RCMP from retaining an intelligence function. Not only is there no legal prohibition, but it can be argued that the RCMP has to keep on performing a security intelligence role:

1. The National Crime Intelligence Sections (NCIS) remained in operation within the RCMP. As was noted by the first Senate Special Committee (Canada, Senate, 1987, p.48), criminal intelligence from various police sources may provide valuable information on terrorism. The changing nature of terrorism in relation to the lack of political motivation increases the probability that criminal intelligence will be germane to counter-terrorist activities. Actually, the RCMP formed National Security Enforcement Units (NSEU) within NCIS to liaise with the CSIS to exchange information relating to security and related offences.

194

2. According to the description of the intelligence network provided by SIRC (1987, p.20), the NSEU are also responsible for calling terrorist alerts and for providing assessments of threats concerning visits of internationally protected persons and designated VIPs.

3. There is an interpretation of the CSIS mandate which preserves an important role for the RCMP in the collection of security intelligence. According to this view, the CSIS role in gathering, analysing and reporting security intelligence is strictly limited to the assessment of threats. Conducting an investigation to find evidence supporting a prosecution for a security offence falls within the jurisdiction of the RCMP. The SSCT is one of the main proponents of this interpretation of the CSIS Act. It is certainly not unreasonable. However, Section 12 of the Act explicitly mentions investigation as a duty of the service and may be taken to mean that CSIS is not limited to risk assessment. CSIS reluctance to allow its members to testify in court tends to validate the SSCT's interpretation.[21]

4. There is no clear-cut distinction between the CSIS and the RCMP that runs across all their respective duties. Hence, CSIS maintains personnel in 24 Canadian Missions in foreign countries to liaise with the intelligence agencies and the police forces. However, 'as a general rule, CSIS liaison officers and RCMP officers are not assigned to the same posts, to avoid duplication of effort' (Canada, Senate, 1987, p.49). Needless to say, it would not be necessary to take measures to avoid a duplication of effort if their duties abroad were truly different.

These factors not only meant that the continuation of the RCMP in security intelligence was highly probable, they eventually led to the creation of the National Security Investigations Directorate (NSID). This outcome is not the result of some police plot to subvert the 1984 reform. It has grown out of the ambiguity of the concept underlying this reform. With its status as an RCMP directorate and more than 130 members, the NSID is more than an embryo for the future rebirth of the RCMP Security Service. Ironically, a few days after the existence of the NSID was revealed, the Honourable Ronald G. Atkey, Chairman of SIRC, gave a lecture in which he argued that the general ideal of national security was so vague and so fraught with difficulties that it should be replaced with a clearer concept, in which the different state interests of Canada requiring protection would be spelled out with more precision.[22]

CONCLUSION

Who, then, should have the primary responsibility for collecting intelligence in the field of counter-terrorism? The difficulty in answering this question lies in the fact that any straight answer comes up against a set of facts which cannot be brushed aside.

RCMP Primacy

There is no lack of arguments supporting the position of RCMP primacy, the main ones being that criminal intelligence will be increasingly crucial for countering terrorism, and that the RCMP can also claim its legitimate primacy in collecting security intelligence to be used as evidence to support prosecutions for security and related offences.

There are very strong objections to this option. First, it is in open conflict with the direction taken by the reform of the intelligence community undertaken after the McDonald report. This reform was implemented through legislation which signified that CSIS was the primary federal agency for the collection, analysis and dissemination of intelligence relating to threats to the security of Canada (Canada, Senate, 1987, p.49). As defined by Section 2 of the CSIS Act, these threats include terrorism. Second, the reform was supported by numerous arguments, some of which identified weaknesses that affected the efficiency of the former RCMP Security Service (for example, a weak capacity for analysis). All these points could be made anew against resolving the issue of primacy in favour of the RCMP and the police. Finally, the 1984 reform was initially triggered by scandals about police wrongdoing, which are still alive in the public memory. Reasserting the primacy of the RCMP might generate a credibility gap and make the force a target for the media.

CSIS Primacy

Asserting that CSIS has the primary responsibility would seem to be the only logical option. It is the only assertion which is fully consistent with the reform initiated by the McDonald Commission, implemented by the CSIS Act, and incorporated into the activities of SIRC, the Independent Advisory Team on CSIS and CSIS itself. Furthermore, it is the only position germane to the nature of terrorism, which we have sought to describe as reflexive violence, with a message that has become increasingly cryptic for the general public. The true significance of this message and its potential implications has to be assessed by an organization with a strong capacity for analysis.

None the less there are also strong arguments against this position, which tend to show that it may be illusory. If the affirmation of the primacy of the RCMP sails against the public winds of reform, the assertion of CSIS primary responsibility seems to be at odds with an undercurrent that is gaining strength in relation to field operations. It is difficult to deny that the RCMP's foothold in security intelligence is growing firmer. Furthermore, there is no telling whether the interface between criminal and security intelligence will not significantly increase in the near future. Finally, CSIS has to overcome an image problem within the intelligence and the law enforcement community: it is the agency whose members, not being peace officers, have the least power, and whose operations, being reviewed by an oversight committee, are the most subject to external scrutiny.

Potential Developments

The present situation may be described in the following way:

1. In principle and in law, CSIS has the primary responsibility for the collection and assessment of *intelligence* in the field of counter-terrorism. In fact, however, this responsibility is shared with the police and particularly with the RCMP.

2. In principle and in law, the primary responsibility for enforcing security measures belongs to the RCMP. Moreover, this responsibility is in fact *not shared* with CSIS, whose members are not peace officers. This situation contrasts with the previous one, where the legal primacy enjoyed by CSIS over intelligence is in fact shared with the RCMP.

3. Because of the imbalance described in the previous paragraph, any increase in the RCMP's role in the field of intelligence results in bolstering the RCMP's general role in counter-terrorism and brings this police force closer to holding the primary responsibility.

From the point of view of keeping a balance of power, it might be viewed as undesirable to condone a situation where the responsibility of the RCMP in countering terrorism would generally prevail. The balance of power can be preserved by taking steps to ensure that CSIS will have the primary role, both in theory and in fact, in counter-terrorist intelligence.

There are numerous ways of achieving this goal. Two suggestions can be made, the first a rather minor one. In the same way that Section 6 of the Security Offences Act asserts unambiguously the primary responsibility of the RCMP for enforcing the law in relation to security offences, Section 12 of this Act, which defines the duties of CSIS, may be amended to state that CSIS exercises the primary role in this respect. This added precision may have appeared unnecessary in 1984. It might be timely in the present situation.

The second suggestion is more radical. The basis for the involvement of the RCMP in security intelligence is that the collection of information is a prerequisite for the performance of its duties in enforcing the law with respect to security offences. As an alternative, it might be considered to grant peace officer powers to a law enforcement unit created within CSIS. This proposal is not so bold as it might seem. First, the number of arrests related to security offences is quite small. Consequently, the law enforcement unit would not have to be large. Second, it must be stressed that this unit would be accountable to SIRC like the rest of the CSIS, whereas at present SIRC has no jurisdiction over the RCMP.

These suggestions are made in the context of the current (1990) review of the CSIS Act. It would be a serious error to believe that changing nothing in the CSIS Act would be equivalent to the preservation of the status quo. Leaving the Act in its present form is in fact a way of condoning change. In spirit, the Act assumed that CSIS would be the primary agency for the collection and processing of security intelligence. This assumption is now being increasingly challenged by the rise of NSID and other security intelligence agencies. In order to keep up with the thrust of the 1984 reform, it would seem essential at least to debate whether the entire security intelligence community should not be subject to external review.

NOTES

The author would like to thank A. Stuart Farson for his assistance in editing this chapter.

1. A.P. Schmid, *Political Terrorism: A Research Guide to Concepts, Theories, Data Bases and Literature* (Amsterdam: North-Holland, 1984). See also A.P. Schmid and A.J. Longman, *Political Terrorism: A New Guide to Actors, Authors, Concepts, Data Bases, Theories and Literature* (New Brunswick, NU: Transaction Books, 1988). In *Political Terrorism* (p.111), Schmid attempts to synthesize in one dense paragraph some of the main elements which characterise terrorism. The pivotal notion used by Schmid is that of *target*. There are four kinds of target: (a) *Target of violence*: the immediate victims of terrorist violence. They are selected at random or because of their symbolic value, on the basis of their common group of class characteristics. (b) *Target of terror*: the members of the group or class of the victims, who are put in a state of chronic fear or terror. (c) *Target of demands*: the norm violation creates an attentive audience beyond the target of terror. The first sector of this audience, which may become the main object of manipulation, is made of persons such as government authorities who are in position to grant

terrorist demands (e.g. the liberation of prisoners). (d) *Target of attention*: all other sectors of the attentive audience created by the abnormal features of the terrorist process of victimization. In addition to the concept of target, Schmid also uses the concepts of process, effect and purpose of terrorism.

2. B. Jenkins, 'International Terrorism. A New Mode of Conflict', California Seminar on Arms Control and Foreign Policy, January 1975 (Los Angeles: Crescent Publications, 1975).

3. Canada, Senate, *Terrorism. The Report of the Senate Special Committee on Terrorism and Public Safety* (Ottawa: Minister of Supply and Services, 1987), p.5. See also Canada, Senate, *Terrorism. The Report of the Second Special Committee of the Senate on Terrorism and Public Safety* (Ottawa: Minister of Supply and Services, 1989).

4. A.P. Schmid and J. de Graff, *Violence as Communications: Insurgent Terrorism and the Western News Media* (London and Beverly Hills: Sage, 1982). For further development of this idea, see R.D. Crelinsten, 'Terrorism, Counter-Terrorism and Democracy: the Assessment of National Security Threats', *Terrorism and Political Violence*, Vol. 1, No. 2 (April 1989), pp.242–69.

5. H.P. Grice, 'Meaning', *The Philosophical Review*, Vol. 66, No. X (1956), pp.377–88.

6. D.A. Charters, 'Terrorism and Political Crime: The Challenging of Policing in the Global Village', Address to Future Issues in Policing: A Working Symposium, Canadian Police College, 27 June 1989. Also, A.S. Farson, 'Old Wine, New Bottles and Fancy Labels: The Rediscovery of Organizational Culture in the Control of Intelligence', in Greg Barak (ed.), *Crime of the Capitalist State: An Introduction to State Criminality* (New York: State University of New York Press, forthcoming.

7. Canada, Senate, *Terrorism* (1987), p.11.

8. Ibid., pp.62–3.

9. Z. Kashmieri and B. McAndrew, *Soft Target* (Toronto: James Lorimer, 1989).

10. These two judgments by the Supreme Court of Canada are: The Solicitor-General of Canada and the Royal Canadian Mounted Police and Superintendent Donal Heaton and Chief Superintendent Michael Spooner v. The Royal Commission of Inquiry into the Confidentiality of Health Records in Ontario and the Canadian Civil Liberties Association (1981), 23 C.R. (3D) 226; Bisaillon v. Keable (1983) 2 D.L.R. (4th) 193 (SCC).

11. In addition to the two Senate Reports quoted in note 3, there is: Security Intelligence Review Committee (SIRC), *The Security and Intelligence Network in the Government of Canada: A Description. Expurgated Copy* (Ottawa: SIRC, 1987). Also, K.G. Robertson, 'Canadian Intelligence Policy: The Role and Future of CSIS', *The International Journal of Intelligence and Counter-Intelligence*, Vol. 3, No. 2 (1989), pp.225–48.

12. J. Bamford, *The Puzzle Palace* (Harmondsworth: Penguin, 1983), pp.391–413.

13. R.V. Ericson, *Making Crime: A Study of Detective Work* (Toronto: Butterworths, 1981). Also, R.V. Ericson, *Reproducing Order: A Study of Police Patrol Work* (Toronto: University of Toronto Press, 1982).

14. K.G. Robertson (ed.), *British and American Approaches to Intelligence* (London: Macmillan, 1987). Also, A.S. Farson, 'Schools of Thought: National Perceptions of Intelligence', *Conflict Quarterly*, Vol. 9, No. 1 (1989), pp.52–104.

15. On this, see P. Gill, 'Defining Subversion: The Canadian Experience since 1977', *Public Law* (Winter 1989), pp.617–36.

16. Québec, *Rapport de la Commission d'enquête sur des opérations policières en territoire Québécois* (Québec: Ministère des Communications, 1981).

17. See Québec, *Rapport sur les événements d'octobre 1970* (Québec: Ministère de la Justice, 1980). Pages missing from this report are supplied in its sequel: Québec, *Rapport sur les événements d'octobre 1970. Passages retenus et annexes A, B, C, D* (Québec: Ministère de la Justice, 1981). Also C. Deveault, *Toute ma vérité* (Montréal: Stanké, 1981).

18. The expression 'national security' has been used for the sake of communication. Actually the CSIS Act does not use the phrase 'national security' and identifies several 'threats to the security of Canada'. In his recent lecture at Cambridge University, Ronald Atkey, Chairman of SIRC, argued that 'national security' was so vague as to defy understanding and advocated an approach similar to that taken by the CSIS Act. Mr Atkey said: 'Rather than continue to engage in the rather sterile exercise of trying to fashion an all-encompassing definition of "national security", we should reflect on the kind of State interest that a free and democratic society may legitimately pursue in a complex world, one with interlocking concerns about matters ranging from defense to economic prosperity' (p.30).

19. Canada, *Freedom and Security under the Law*. Commission of Inquiry Concerning Certain Activities of the Royal Canadian Mounted Police. Second Report, Vol. 1 (Ottawa: Minister of Supply and Services, 1981), 614, recomm. 33 and 34.

20. It may seem that we are predicting developments that were to come, with the benefit of hindsight (it is now a matter of report that the RCMP has re-created, albeit on a much smaller scale, part of its former security service). We foresaw this evolution as early as 1985 and gave a paper at a conference organized by SIRC in 1987 in which we predicted the hybridization of national security (see my chapter in Peter Hanks and John McCamus (eds.), *National Security, Surveillance and Accountability in a Democratic Society* (Québec: Cowansville, Les Éditions Yvon Blais, 1989), pp.55–70). By hybridization we meant that security intelligence would be collected by both CSIS and RCMP. Although criticized at the time by former Solicitor-General Robert Kaplan, who chaired our conference panel, we were apparently not altogether mistaken.

21. According to an article by Paul Koring in the *Globe and Mail* on 2 Sept. 1989, 80 million dollars have already been spent on the investigation to find the perpetrators of the downing of the Air-India Boeing in 1985. The RCMP is said to be in charge of the investigation. The article does not mention CSIS.

22. R.G. Atkey, 'Reconciling Freedom of Expression and National Security', The Cambridge Lectures. Canadian Institute for Advanced Legal Studies, unpublished lecture (10 July 1989).

Notes on the Contributors

Christopher Andrew is a founding editor of *Intelligence and National Security*. He is a Fellow of Corpus Christi College, Cambridge, and Reader in Modern and Contemporary History at Cambridge University. His books include *Secret Service: The Making of the British Intelligence Community* (1985) and (with Oleg Gordievsky) *KGB: The Inside Story of its Foreign Operations from Lenin to Gorbachev* (1990).

Jean-Paul Brodeur is Director of the Centre Internationale de Criminologie Comparée at the University of Montreal.

Frank Cain is Senior Lecturer in History at the University of New South Wales. He is the author of *The Origins of Political Surveillance in Australia* (1983), and is now completing a history of the Australian Security Intelligence Organization.

John J. Dziak has served as an intelligence officer with the US Department of Defense since 1965. He is the author of *Chekisty: A History of the KGB* (1988), which won the National Intelligence Studies Center award for the best US book on intelligence. An Adjunct Professor of Government at Georgetown University, he also writes and lectures extensively on Soviet affairs.

A. Stuart Farson was Director of Research for the Special Committee of the House of Commons (Canada) on the Review of the Canadian Security Intelligence Service Act and the Security Offences Act. A former Secretary-Treasurer of the Canadian Association for Security and Intelligence Studies, he has written numerous articles on security, intelligence and policing issues.

Peter Gill is Senior Lecturer in Politics and Criminal Justice at Liverpool Polytechnic. He is co-author of *Introduction to Politics* (1988, 2nd ed.), and is currently researching into the control and oversight of domestic security in intelligence agencies.

Franklyn Griffiths is Professor of Political Science at the University of Toronto. His research interests include Soviet and East–West affairs.

Robert Jervis is Adlai E. Stevenson Professor in the Institute of War and Peace Studies at Columbia University. His latest book, *The Meaning of the Nuclear Revolution*, received the 1990 Grawemeyer Award for the best book on world order.

Loch K. Johnson is Regents Professor of Political Science at the University of Georgia and former staff director of the Subcommittee on Oversight, US House Permanent Select Committee on Intelligence. His books include *A Season of Inquiry* (1988), *America's Secret Power* (1989) and *America as a World Power* (1991).

David Stafford is Chairman of the Canadian Association for Security and Intelligence Studies, Executive Director and Director of Studies of the Canadian Institute of International Affairs, and an Adjunct Professor at the University of Toronto. He is the co-author, with J.L. Granatstein, of *Spy Wars: Espionage and Canada from Gouzenko to Glasnost* (1990).

John Starnes is a former Canadian Ambassador, chairman of the Canadian Joint Intelligence Committee and the first civilian Director-General of the Security Service of the Royal Canadian Mounted Police.

Wesley K. Wark is an Associate Professor in the Department of History at the University of Toronto. An assistant editor of *Intelligence and National Security*, he has published numerous articles on intelligence and is the author of *The Ultimate Enemy: British Intelligence and Nazi Germany* (1985).

Reg Whitaker is a Professor in the Department of Political Science at York University, Toronto. He is the author of *Double Standard: The Secret History of Canadian Immigration* (1987), *The Government Party: Organizing and Financing the Liberal Party of Canada* (1977) and *Cold War Canada: The Making of a National Security State, 1945–1957* (forthcoming, 1991).